SOCIETAS DANICA INDAGATIONIS ANTIQVITATIS ET MEDIIAEVI

CLASSICA ET MEDIAEVALIA

Danish Journal of Philology and History

EDITED BY

Tønnes Bekker-Nielsen · Marianne Pade

EDITORIAL BOARD

Jesper Carlsen · Karsten Friis-Jensen
Vincent Gabrielsen · Minna Skafte Jensen · Birger Munk Olsen

VOLUME 59

MUSEUM TUSCULANUM PRESS
UNIVERSITY OF COPENHAGEN

2008

CLASSICA ET MEDIAEVALIA · VOL. 59

Copyright © Museum Tusculanum Press 2008

Composition by Bengerd Juul Thorsen

Printed in Denmark by Special-Trykkeriet Viborg a-s

ISBN 978-87-635-2580-0

ISSN 0106-5815

Published with the support of
The Danish Research Council for the Humanities

MUSEUM TUSCULANUM PRESS

University of Copenhagen

Njalsgade 126

DK-2300 Copenhagen S

www.mtp.dk

Tel. +45 35 32 91 09

Fax +45 35 32 91 13

TABLE OF CONTENTS

CATALIN ANGHELINA
    The Golden Homer:
    The Geometry of the Iliad and the Homeric Question   5

ICHIRO TAIDA
    How to Present Line 136a of the Homeric Hymn to Aphrodite   29

MARCEL LYSGAARD LECH
    Tired of What? A Note on Aristophanes, *BIRDS* 787   37

ERIK NIS OSTENFELD
    Socrates' Argumentative Strategy   41

SEBASTIAN PERSSON
    A Note on Reading Velleius Paterculus   99

PATRICK KRAGELUND
    Roman Inscriptions from Ferrara, Mazara and Nîmes   117

SPYRIDON TZOUNAKAS
    Persius' Re-reading of Horace: The Case of Some Proper Names   123

ELIAS SVERKOS
    Bemerkungen zu zwei Epigrammen   139

CARL I. HAMMER
    'The Example of the Saints':
    Reading Eugippius' Account of Saint Severin   155

DAVID SANSONE
    Tadpoles!   187

NEIL ADKIN
   The Date of Walter of Châtillon's *Alexandreis* Once Again   201

ELÖD NEMERKENYI
   Greeks and Latins in Medieval Hungary   213

DAVID BLOCH
   Kierkegaard and the Euthyphro Dilemma   225

LIST OF AUTHORS   233

THE GOLDEN HOMER:
THE GEOMETRY OF THE ILIAD AND
THE HOMERIC QUESTION

By Catalin Anghelina

Summary: The article argues for the presence of the Golden Section within the structure of the Iliad in regards both to the number of books and the number of verses. As a consequence, the Doloneia episode seems to be original to the plan of our Iliad. It also implies that the book divisions are original to the poem.

In recent years scholars have again taken up the problem of the Homeric poems' structure and division into books. The issue of the book divisions, in particular, has been considered especially important for solving, at least partially, the Homeric Question, since a clear perspective on it could shed light about the history of the text itself.

Basically, there have been three answers to how the *Iliad* and the *Odyssey* were divided into 24 books or songs. The first goes back to a tradition that believes that the division was made by scholars in Alexandria. The second holds that Peisistratos might have had something to do with it, since we have information about a text redaction in his time. According to the third view, the natural transitions from one song to the next are evidence that the divisions might have been made by the poet himself. This last opinion relies on the fact that the book divisions seem to represent more than a mere mechanical process imposed on a preexistent text.[1]

[1] The bibliography following this paper presents some of the relevant views for this discussion: 1) for the book-division being devised by Homer himself: Goold 1977: 1-34; 1960: 272-91; Heiden 1998: 68-81; 2000: 247-59; Mazon 1942: 137-41; Kirk 1962: 301-15 (the last two proposing that the Alexandrians assigned letters to a pre-existing division!); van Sickle 1980, 9 argues for Homer being the 'first divider', but probably not into 24 books;

The fact that the number of books in the poems equals the number of letters of the Ionic alphabet makes the issue even more complicated. If this was Homer's original design, then we have to admit that the division had nothing to do with the number of letters of the Ionic alphabet, since we cannot prove in any way that there was an epichoric alphabet containing exactly 24 letters during the eighth century BC. Alternatively, if, indeed, the Homeric book divisions were set by the author himself to reflect the number of letters of the Ionic alphabet, then this must have been done at a time when some epichoric alphabet comprised exactly 24 letters; Homer himself must have belonged to that group which used the 24-letter alphabet. Nevertheless, the archaeological data seem to show that the Ionic alphabets still had at least the letter *qoppa* in their inventories as late as the mid-sixth century BC; it was only around that time that this letter was taken out of some of the alphabets.[2] In addition, if the book divisions were original, the connection between the number of letters in the Ionic alphabet and the number of the book divisions would have another serious implication: since the number of letters would be intrinsically associated with writing, it would mean that the Homeric poems were originally *written* in exactly the way we have them today, in the same alphabet.

The only way to avoid these conclusions is either to ascribe the book divi-

---

see also Whitman 1958: 283. 2) For the book-division being a result of Peisistratos' activity: Broccia 1967: 19; S. West 1967: 19; 1988: 33-48; Stanley 1993: 279-96; Jensen 1999: 5-91 (a useful history of the problem can be found here); West 2001: 18. 3) For the Alexandrians (either Zenodotos or Aristarchos) being the 'dividers', the opinions are based on two accounts from antiquity: Ps.-Plut. *Vita Hom.* 2.4 and Eust. 5.32, the latter probably echoing a tradition reflected in the former, although Eustathios mentions Zenodotos as having lived after Aristarchos. For modern works, see Lachmann 1874: 93; Wilamowitz 1884: 369; 1916: 32 (both argue for Zenodotos); more recently, Richardson 1993: 20-21; Taplin 1992: 285-93; de Jong 1996: 20-35; Olson 1995: 228-39 (especially for the *Odyssey*); Pfeiffer 1968: 116. On the other hand, Nagy 1996: 110 (arguing for a gradual textualization, which may have resulted in the book-division) and Latacz 2005 argue that the division could have been made after Peisistratos, but before the Alexandrians, as a result of rhapsodic practices.

2   The epichoric Ionic alphabets had different numbers of letters according to their origins. The Chian alphabet seems to have at least 25 letters as late as the mid-6th century, when the letter *qoppa* was still in use. According to Jeffery 1961: 325-62 the alphabets from Milet (the origin of the 'standard' Ionic alphabet) also seem to have the letter *qoppa* until the middle of the 6th century, possibly later.

sions to a later period, be it Peisistratean or Alexandrian, or to find another reason why the poet might have originally composed both the *Iliad* and the *Odyssey* in 24 books. The very fact that both poems are divided into the same number of books shows that there must be a common rationale which lies behind such division, a hidden principle we are still looking for.[3]

One of the most debated issues regarding the structure of the *Iliad* is what some scholars, beginning with Drerup and Sheppard, have called 'the movements' of the poem. This theory sees the plot of the *Iliad* as three main developments or acts, which seem likely to be the result of a conscious effort by the monumental poet to interweave the different levels of the action in order to achieve an artistic effect. To Sheppard, for example, these three parts are a literary device for guiding the audience through the plot.[4]

The assumptions about different 'threads' of action in the *Iliad* start from the obvious observation that the poem as we have it displays a strange feature: after the beginning of the poem, Achilles, the main hero of the poem, does not show up again until Book 9, the Embassy Book, and then, again, only from Book 16 on, when his actions draw the plot towards its end and reaffirm Achilles as the protagonist of the poem.

Despite the fact that even in antiquity a scholar like Aristotle could claim that the *Iliad* was superior to any other poem because of its unity, the aesthetic premises which lie behind such appraisals are for the most part unknown to us. This is to say that we have never been able to completely 'enter' the mind of the monumental poet and decipher the aesthetic code in which he composed the poems.[5]

The structure of the Homeric poems displays some striking features that

3 West 2001: 19, 'There must have been a stronger reason than that this happened to be the number of letters in the Ionic alphabet'. In general, the division is considered as a result of either rhapsodic practice or the demands of the book trade, cf. S. West 1967: 20; but cf. Birt 1882: 430-46: sometimes the Homeric poems were contained in a single, huge roll.

4 Heiden 1996 believes that Books 9 and 16 are crucial to the plot (the beginning of the 'movements') since they come after Zeus' decisions in Books 8 and 15. Also, see Drerup 1913: 364 n. 2, 428, and Sheppard 1922. For Sheppard, the segmentation was 1-10, 11-18 and 19-24. Drerup's segmentation is 1-7, 8-18, 19-24.

5 Kirk 1985b: 101, 'The canons of oral poetry' and in particular those of 'monumental oral poetry' remain 'to a large degree obscure'; Heiden 1998: 69: 'The aesthetic basis of its [the *Iliad*] segmentation, if it has one, has yet to be completely discovered'. Jensen 1999: 23, calls the Homeric poems 'enigmatic' in respect to their aesthetics; she includes the issue of the book division, which she considers to be original.

are not likely to be the product of chance. The organization of the *Odyssey* in six tetrads, the symbolic distribution of Odysseus' adventures in Books 9-12 of the *Odyssey*, the responsive pattern of Book 24 of the *Iliad* in respect to Book 1, and other similar parallel structures between other books of the *Iliad*, to mention only some major obvious structural correspondences, could not have occurred randomly, unless we want to claim that the human mind can produce aesthetic symmetry unconsciously and unaware of itself. Under these circumstances, the geometry of the Homeric poems is still open to discussion, whether it is the result of an oral process or not.[6]

This is not the place to open a discussion about aesthetics in general, although, as we shall see, the solution will eventually come down to aesthetics. The fact of the matter is that the Homeric poems display a certain structure, which still needs to be decoded.
Unfortunately, we do not have much evidence other than the text itself. Starting from that, the object of this paper is to offer a new perspective on the structure of the *Iliad*.

THE PLOT AND THE PERFORMANCE TIME

The plot of the *Iliad* generates an expectation from the beginning. It is mainly the expectation to see how Zeus' promise to Thetis is going to be fulfilled, so that Achilles could eventually get *kleos* in front of his peers. Basically, whatever turns and twists occur, the plot is driven towards the fulfilment of this expectation.

The *Iliad* is a poem about Achilles. Yet, as mentioned above, one cannot overlook the fact that Achilles is absent from more than half of the poem. After the beginning, in Book 1, where the premises of the plot are set, Achil-

---

[6] Lord 1960: 168, in a polemic with Whitman, doubted whether oral poems could display sophisticated geometrical patterns: 'It does not seem likely that the force of the artistic pattern, *qua* artistic pattern, in a traditional oral song would be great enough in itself to cause either the placing or displacing of incidents'. Hainsworth 1970: 90-98 believed that large-scale structures are the result of literary composition; cf. Russo 1992: 15. For recent synoptic works about the structure of the Homeric poems, see Schein 1997: 345-59; Tracy 1997: 360-79; Stanley 1993; older, but essential, Myres 1932 and 1952; Whitman 1958: 249-84.

les appears only in Book 9 and then, with the exception of a short moment in Book 11, at the beginning of Book 16, which marks the point from where the plot is really driven by his actions.

The beginning of Book 16 brings Achilles and Patroclus together. This is the moment which, quite unexpectedly and most unfortunately for him, makes Achilles decide to return to the battlefield. From the point of view of the audience, however, this moment has been expected since Book 8, where Zeus makes his first clear statement about the way things will evolve so that Achilles can be drawn into the battle. In Book 8, Zeus predicts for the first time that Patroclus will die. In Book 15, on the other hand, after the bulk of interminable fighting which has been going on since the beginning of Book 11, Zeus makes an even clearer prediction of the future events: the Achaeans will be driven back, so that Achilles will send his companion Patroclus into the battle where, in turn, he will be killed by Hector.[7]

Thus, there are strong reasons to see the beginning of Book 16 as an expected *tournure* of the whole plot.[8] It is the turning point which marks the transition from one state of affairs to another. It is the moment when Achilles, without knowing it, seals his own destiny: allowing his beloved friend to go out and fight will lead to the death of Patroclus, which will eventually mean the death of Achilles.

This turning point occurs during the longest day of fighting between the Trojans and the Greeks (Books 11-18). It is therefore the pivotal moment not only for the *Iliad* as a whole, but also for this day. It seems then that the poet might have had some aesthetic reasons for placing this moment at the beginning of Book 16 of the poem.

Let us go back to the three-movement theory. The schemes for the division of the *Iliad* into three movements depend on the aesthetic criteria that

---

7   8.470-76; 15.58-65.
8   Taplin 1992 sees the transition from Book 15 to Book 16 as abrupt: the more natural book division would have been at 16.123/4. However, the fact that Patroclus leaves Eurypylos on the battlefield in order to go to Achilles and ask for help in the battle (15.390-405) shows the meeting between the two as a truly expected event of the plot. For more recent studies on this crucial point of the plot, see Allan 2005: 1-16; Ledbetter 1993: 481-91. Janko 1992: 310 is clear, 'Akhilleus' fateful and largely unexpected compromise [the sending of Patroclus off to the battlefield] is in any case the linchpin holding the poem's two halves together'. Schadewaldt 1997 sees Achilles' decision to send Patroclus off to fighting as 'the turning point of events'.

the proponents of such theories use. Length, thematic similarity, or performance time are among the most important criteria used to establish such patterns. Among all these criteria, the one which gained much interest was the one that relates to the performance time. The *Iliad* was a poem intended to be sung in front of an audience, and its length prevented its being sung during a single session or even a day. Therefore, it was common sense to assume that the performance was stretched over several days, be it three or even more.

The assumption that the *Iliad* was sung in its entirety over many days is invented by modern scholars and was fed by the discovery that the Homeric poems were oral poems and, therefore, composed to be sung. Nevertheless, there is no clear indication that the *Iliad* and *Odyssey* have ever been sung in their entirety over either one or many sessions to an audience. The first information we have with regard to this issue comes from a text in Pseudo-Plato (*Hipparchus* 228b), where we read about a rhapsodic custom in Athens, at the Panathenaic festival, which forced the rhapsodes to recite from Homer in sequence, taking up from where another left off:

Ἱππάρχῳ ... ὃς ἄλλα τε πολλὰ καὶ καλὰ ἔργα σοφίας ἀπεδείξατο, καὶ τὰ Ὁμήρου ἔπη πρῶτος ἐκόμισεν εἰς τὴν γῆν ταυτηνί, καὶ ἠνάγκασε τοὺς ῥαψῳδοὺς Παναθηναίοις ἐξ ὑπολήψεως ἐφεξῆς αὐτὰ διιέναι, ὥσπερ νῦν ἔτι οἵδε ποιοῦσιν.

Hipparchus ... who, among the many and beautiful deeds of wisdom he achieved, was the first to bring the poems of Homer to this land, and compelled the rhapsodes at the Panathenaea to perform them according to cues in due order, as they still do to this day.

Diogenes Laertios attributes the same innovation to Solon: τά τε Ὁμήρου ἐξ ὑποβολῆς γέγραφε ῥαψῳδεῖσθαι οἷον ὅπου ὁ πρῶτος ἔληξεν, ἐκεῖθεν ἄρχεσθαι τὸν ἐχόμενον.[9] The phrases ἐκ ὑποβολῆς and ἐκ ὑπολήψεως are equivalent in these contexts: the first rhapsode passes on the song to an-

---

9 'Proposed a (law) that Homer's poems should be recited according to cues, so that wherever the first (rhapsodes) stopped, from there the next should start'. Diog. Laert. 1.57 (*Solon*); cf. Isoc. *Paneg.* 159; Lyc. *Leoc.* 102; Plut. *Per.* 13.6; this custom was formally called the 'Panathenaic Rule' by Davison 1955: 1-21; cf. Janko 1992: 29-38.

other, who takes it up and continues the song.[10]

These passages, however, do not say that in the Panathenaic contests the Homeric poems were necessarily sung *from their beginning*. In fact, it seems that the object of the contest was not the Homeric poems *per se*, but the way the rhapsodes were proving that they were knowledgeable in them. A passage in Plato's *Ion* offers a good example of this: Socrates challenges Ion to sing the passage where Nestor advises Antilochos at the Funeral Games.[11] Ion takes the challenge up and starts the recitation exactly at 23.335, *in medias res*, proving himself in this way to be an outstanding rhapsode, who has the ability to begin singing the Homeric poems from any place he is asked.[12]

However, the information found in the *scholium* to Pindar's *Nem.* 2.1 seems to be at odds with this interpretation. After the scholiast talks about the fact that, before the poems were put together, the rhapsodes were used for singing only disparate episodes, he states that αὖθις δὲ ἑκατέρας τῆς ποιήσεως εἰσενεχθείσης τοὺς ἀγωνίστας οἷον ἀκουμένους πρὸς ἄλληλα τὰ μέρη καὶ τὴν σύμπασαν ποίησιν ἐπιόντας, ῥαψῳδοὺς προσαγορευθῆναι (thus, after the two poems had been introduced (to Attica), because the contestants stitched the parts one to another and went through the whole poetry, they were called rhapsodes). This is the only place where someone uses the word σύμπασαν, which means 'altogether', as an indication of what and how the rhapsodes sang. Nevertheless, while it is true that the passage states clearly that the rhapsodes went (ἐπιόντας) over the whole work of Homer, that is the *Iliad* and *Odyssey*, it does not say whether this took place in one session or in many; it may simply mean that the rhapsodes covered the entire text, which could otherwise also mean that there were no parts lacking between the μέρη in their recitation, that is, no skipped verses, or maybe that the Panathenaic Rule applied to the Homeric poems as whole given text.[13]

We may never be able to find out what really went on at the Panathenaic

---

10 Jensen 1980: 146.

11 *Ion* 537 a 5-7.

12 Nagy 2002, 23 calls the rhapsode a '*Virtuoso* with phenomenal powers in relay mnemonics'; his conclusion is that 'What the rhapsode can do is to start *anywhere* in the *Iliad* and *Odyssey* and, once started, to keep going'.

13 Nagy 2002, 15 believes that 'It is facile to assume that the Panathenaic Rule became a reality only when the performing rhapsodes had a written script that they could memorize'. This could be what σύμπασαν refers to.

festivals. But let us assume that the entire *Iliad* and *Odyssey* were recited over many consecutive sessions at the Panathenaic festivals, from their beginning.[14] Some legitimate questions arise. How many days were necessary for a complete recitation?[15] How many rhapsodes were involved in the contest? Which of the epics was recited first? When were the sessions adjourned, if they lasted several days? Were they interrupted at one particular, identical point? Given that the audience knew the poems very well, what was the use of breaking the story at one point or another? And, since this was a contest that had to be judged by several judges, what happened with the judges during the long sessions? Did the same judges remain seated during the many hours and sessions until *all* the rhapsodes were through with their recitations?[16]

Despite the fact that there is no information which could answer all these questions, scholars launched the hypothesis of the three-day-recitation session, based on the 'three-movement' or 'three-division' theory.[17] Thus, the fact that the *Iliad* and the *Odyssey* are too long to be recited in a one-day session would mean that there would be 'breaking' points in the poem, where presumably the bard could interrupt his song, postponing it until the next day. But even so, the recitation of *both* poems in their entirety at the Panathenaic festival seems improbable. The Panathenaic festival lasted four days; therefore, if the *Iliad* alone had taken three days, there would have been insufficient time left for the *Odyssey*, not to mention other rituals and processions.[18]

---

14 The episode of Demodocus and that of Phemios in the Odyssey suggest that oral performances in Homer's time were rather short. However, large-scale oral epic is attested in Africa. Thus, for Greece, we cannot say with certainty that lengthy epic of this type never occurred; cf. Jensen 1980: 34-36.

15 The performing of tragedies at the City Dionysia is the closest example we have about such recitations. During these festivals, three tetralogies (three tragedies and a satyr play) were performed during three days. Even so, the length of both the *Iliad* and the *Odyssey* would have exceeded the length of these recitations. See Jensen 1980: 46; Csapo and Slater 1995: 107. Notopoulos 1964 calculated that the *Iliad* could have been recited in 26.9 hours and the *Odyssey* in 20.7 hours.

16 It seems completely unnatural for different judges to have rated different rhapsodes. More likely there were the same judges who assessed the performances of all the rhapsodes.

17 The three-movement theory, which was proposed by Sheppard, has no relation to the numbers of days of performance; it pertains only to the literary structure.

18 The fact that the Panathenaic festival lasted four days is attested in *sch. rec.* Eur. *Hec.* 469,

Another hypothesis is that it was Homer himself who structured the poems in this way so that they could be sung over many days. This does not seem plausible.[19] There is no indication that recitation sessions of this sort ever existed. In fact, the Pindaric *scholium* states clearly that there was a time when the poets recited in contest only parts of the poems, and not their entirety: ὅτι κατὰ μέρος πρότερον τῆς ποιήσεως διαδεδομένης τῶν ἀγωνιστῶν ἕκαστος ὅ τι βούλοιτο μέρος ᾖδε...[20]

But perhaps there were reasons other than performance and recitations which led Homer to compose the *Iliad* so that Achilles could show up only at certain moments in the poem. What could these reasons be?[21]

The theory that follows does not take into account the question of whether the structure of the *Iliad* has any connection with the number of days in which the poem was performed. Consequently, it will address the issue only from a hypothetical aesthetic standpoint.

THE GOLDEN SECTION

The whole structure of the *Iliad* is dominated by the central day of fighting, which lasts from the beginning of Book 11 to the end of Book 18, that is to say eight books. This was clearly stated by Schadewaldt, for whom this central unit of the structure of the Iliad represented also a unit of performance.[22] It has also been long recognized that the central books of the *Iliad*,

---

1.336 Dind.; *sch. Aristid.* 98.31 f. Dind.; cf. Parke 1977: 35. For a skeptical opinion about the performing of the Homeric poems at the Panathenaic festival, see Burkert 1987: 43-62.

19 This is the conclusion reached by Heiden 1996: 5-22, esp. 22.
20 *Scholium* to Pind. *Nem.* 2.1 (*FGH* 568 F5). This passage, if true, casts serious doubts on the assumption that Homer himself set breaking points in the poems for recitation purpose.
21 The *Odyssey* seems to display a different pattern; Tracy 1997 argues for a structure in groups of four books; S. West 1967: 19 believes that the book division was imposed on the *Odyssey* 'to make it correspond to the *Iliad*'.
22 Schadewaldt 1975: 24 argues that the narrative-time of the Iliad and the performance-time could coincide in some points of the plot. Thus, Books 11 and 19 would represent natural breaks in the poem, since they begin with the sunrise.

books 11 to 15, represent a big retardation, 'eine grosse Retardation',[23] from what seems to be the culmination of the plot. Books 11 to 15 offer an interminable series of lengthy battles, whose purpose is to postpone dramatically Achilles' intervention in the fighting. Why would Homer have postponed the climax of the *Iliad* for so long?

The reason is structural and lies at the beginning of Book 16. This point is decisive for the whole plot of the *Iliad* and also fulfills the expectations for the whole central day of battle. A closer look at the position of this point within the structure of the poem suggests that its location is not accidental.

Van Thiel's edition of the *Iliad* (1996) counts 15,673 verses.[24] The book division between books 15 and 16 divides the poem into two parts, *AB* and *BC*, where *AB* has 9680 verses and *BC* 5993. The ratios *AC* : *AB* and *AB* : *BC* are extremely close (1.619 vs. 1.615), showing that point *B* divides the whole poem into what the mathematicians call 'the extreme and mean ratio'. This number is also known as the Golden Ratio, Golden Section or Golden Number and, as we shall see, is one of extreme importance in the history of mathematics. In the case of the extant text of the *Iliad*, the ratio approximates the Golden Number to the third decimal, which is quite remarkable.

Once this observation has been made, it is necessary to assess its relevance for the Homeric Question. Another issue regards the origin and importance of this proportion in the ancient world. Euclid is the first to mention it, calling it 'the extreme and mean ratio'. This is because of the property of the segments generated by the section point: the ratio between the larger of them and the smaller equals the ratio between the whole initial segment and the larger one that results from the section:

ἄκρον καὶ μέσον λόγον εὐθεῖα τετμῆσθαι λέγεται, ὅταν ᾖ ὡς ἡ ὅλη πρὸς τὸ μεῖζον τμῆμα, οὕτως τὸ μεῖζον πρὸς τὸ ἔλαττον.

---

23 Cf. van Thiel 1982: 33; Allen 1924: 194-95 talked about the 'heavy books' of the *Iliad*. The earliest discussions about retardation can be found in Rothe 1910; Finsler, 1914; Drerup 1921; Scott 1921; Schadewaldt 1938 calls this the 'Prinzip des Aufschubs'. For the concept of retardation, see Reichel 1990, 125-51.

24 Allen's OCT edition (1931) counts 15,693 verses = 9,694 + 5,999. Van Thiel takes out the verses which are weakly attested in the manuscripts: 1.265, 2.206, 5.901, 8.548 and 550-2, 9.458-61, 10.191, 11.543, 14.269, 16.614-5, 18.604, 19.177, 20.312, 21.480. The ratios for Allen's edition are similar: 1.618 and 1.615. See below for the issue of the 'exact' number of verses.

A segment is said to be divided in extreme and mean ratio when the whole segment is to the larger one what the larger one is to the smaller one. [25]

Euclid does not add any special epithets to this proportion, which he presents in a chapter dedicated to other proportions in general. The nickname of 'golden' is a modern invention, and there is no certainty about its origin. Some scholars have placed its origins in the fourteenth and fifteenth centuries.[26] The Italian mathematician Luca Pacioli, one of the encyclopedic minds of the Renaissance and a contemporary of Leonardo, wrote a three-volume treatise about this ratio and called it 'the divine proportion'.[27] The reason why such an epithet was added to the original name of 'extreme and mean ratio' is the almost mystical belief that many geometrical shapes, either natural or built up by man, have this ratio incorporated in their structure. For example, the Egyptian pyramids, the Athenian Parthenon, or Renaissance paintings have all been thought to display the 'Golden Ratio' within their structure. Nevertheless, however convincing the arguments of the proponents of the existence of the Golden Ratio in art and nature might be, dissenting opinions have raised their voice against such generalizations. There is no clear answer to the question whether the above-mentioned objects bear within them the mark of this ratio.[28]

It is not surprising that the Golden Ratio cannot be easily demonstrated to exist in particular works. One of the reasons for this is the nature of the number itself. The Golden Ratio is an irrational number, which means that it cannot be expressed as a fraction.[29] This also means that, in our example, the two segments *AB* and *BC* have no common denominator with which

---

25 Euc. *Elem.* 6.3.
26 Cf. Lasserre 1964: 76 and Boyer 1968: 55; on the contrary, Livio 2002: 6-7 attributes the name to Ohm 1825-26; cf. Sarton 1951: 47. Seminal books on the Golden Section are Zeising 1884; Ghyka 1931; Fischler 1987.
27 Luca Pacioli, *Divina Proportione* (Venice 1509).
28 See Livio 2002: 269-77 for bibliography, esp. Gillings 1972: 238. For the Parthenon, see Zeising 1884; Borissavlievitch 1958: 16-27 questions this claim. Duckworth 1960: 184-220 discusses the use of the Golden Section in Vergil. Serious doubts about all these views were raised by Markowski 1992: 2-19.
29 The rational numbers can be expressed by definition as fractions of integers.

one can build these segments.[30] The segments are said to be incommensurable. On the other hand, an irrational number is one that never ends or repeats itself. The Golden Ratio would be, in this respect, 1.6180339887…

Let us sum up the discussion thus far. First, the beginning of Book 16 of the *Iliad* has been seen as the turning point of the plot. Second, it appeared that the ratio in which the whole poem is divided by this point is an extremely good approximation of the Golden Ratio, which is an irrational number. This fact, however, may be a pure coincidence. Is it so?

The system of the number of books can provide us with an answer. The book division between Books 15 and 16 divides the whole poem into two parts, of which one is 15 books long and the other only 9. The ratio 24/15 is a good approximation of the Golden Section number, 1.6, whereas the other proportion, 15/9 approximates the Golden Section as well, 1.66. As for the central day of fighting, the same division divides it into two parts, of which one is 5 books long and the other 3. Not only is the ratio 8/5 a good approximation of the Golden Section, but its value is the same as 24/15, i.e., 1.6. The same is true of the ratio 5/3, which equals 15/9, the ratio we calculated for the whole poem. In other words, with regard to the number of books, the division at the beginning of Book 16 divides both the whole number of the poem's books and the number of books of the central day of fighting (11 to 18) into the same ratio, which approximates the Golden Section to the second decimal. This shows that the poet's initial plan concerned the approximation of the Golden Number by using the number of books rather than the number of verses.

The surprises revealed by the application of the Golden Section do not stop here. As we saw above, after Book 1 it is only in Book 9 of the *Iliad* that Achilles manifests his presence. The placement of this book within the whole plot is, again, not random.[31] Book 9 is the mirror image of Book 16

---

30 I.e., one cannot find k so that $km = AB$ and $kn = BC$, where m and n are natural numbers. In this case $AB : BC$ would be a rational number, m/n.

31 The best discussion is Whitman 1958: 'The ninth and the sixteenth books of the *Iliad* are so obviously linked to each other as focal points of the main narrative that it is unnecessary to point out how the latter completes and in a way reverses the other' (279); 'Both IX and XVI are approximately of tripartite construction' (280); 'The patterned regularity of the nine opening books and the nine closing ones…' (283); cf. also Myres 1932, 285: 'The Embassy, then, is the central incident of any version of the *Iliad* that had come to include Book IX…'

within the whole poem in respect to the division of the Golden Section.[32] This means that, proportionally, the first nine books of the *Iliad* are the whole poem what Books 16-24 are. It is as if the creator of the *Iliad* considered the placement of books by also counting from the end of the poem: the juncture at 9/10 is situated at the same distance from the beginning of the poem as is the juncture at 15/16 from the end. The Golden Section ratios work similarly. In other words, the juncture at 9/10 is the Golden Point on the segment 24-1 exactly the way the juncture at 15/16 is on the segment 1-24.

A graph showing the ordering of books in the *Iliad* is given below:

Fig. 1. *B* represents the beginning of Book 16; *EF* is the segment 11-18 (end) and *D* is the juncture 9/10: *B* is the Golden Point for *AC* and *EF*; *D* is the Golden Point for *CA*.

This theory that Homer used the Golden Section in the *Iliad* leads us to two other important questions. First, how did the poet achieve this? Second, who was Homer, and how did he have access to this mathematical knowledge?

The first question takes us into the very workshop of the Homeric composition; therefore, it is hard to answer exactly. Nevertheless, however speculative they might be, some assumptions can be made. The first regards the reason why there are 24 books. The shorter segments situated after the Golden Section provide us with a possible answer. Books 16-18, i.e., 3 books, and 16-24, i.e., 9 books, are the ones in which the fewest expansions seem to

---

32 The fact that the end of Book 9 marks the Golden Section shows that the consequent development of the action depends on Achilles' reaching a decision by the end of Book 9. By contrast, in Book 16 Achilles takes the fatal decision at the beginning of the book. This could be the reason why the poet placed Book 9 'in the mirror' in respect to Book 16. Otherwise he would have placed the Embassy in Book 10. Lord 1960: 194 noticed that the positions of Books 9 and 10 are possibly interchangeable within the poem.

have taken place.³³ The length of these episodes, their first division into books of an average length, gave the poet the numbers he needed for the Golden Section: the three-book length from 16 to 18 called for 5 books before that section in order to complete the longest and most important day of fighting, while the nine-book length from 16 to 24 called for exactly 15 books to fill in the space from the beginning to that section. This assumption also explains the big and almost endless 'retardation' from Books 11 through 15.

The most difficult part, however, was to fill in the gap from Book 1 to Book 11, which gave the poet the other ten needed books. We can understand now that the Doloneia was one of the necessary devices for filling in this gap and expanding the poem. The whole poem could not exist without it since it necessarily enters into the equation of the Golden Section. If we took the Doloneia out of the poem, it would be very difficult to reach a total of 24 books. Since Books 11-18 have the Golden Section at the beginning of Book 16, the changes could not be made there. The only addition could have been made in the first part, in Books 1-9. If the poet had tried to split one of these books in two in order to retain 24 books, he would not have had many choices. Except for Book 5, all books contain fewer verses, and a split would have reduced the number of their verses to fewer than 300; they would have become too short for what the poet probably considered to be a minimum for the *Iliad*. But the main problem lies somewhere else: Book 9 would have become Book 10, and would no longer have represented the symmetrical Golden Point within the poem's structure. In general, the whole reason for expanding the poem was to make the segments fit the ratios of the Golden Section. This includes the Catalogue of Ships. The expansions were mostly made in the segments 11-15 and 1-10 because the Golden Section required these segments to be the longest within the whole segment of which they were part.³⁴

We have already noticed that the poet's initial plan concerned the number

---

33 Mazon 1942: 243-48 pleads for an extension of a primitive poem, which relied on the last third of 'our' *Iliad*.

34 For how the poet possibly expanded the poem, see Goold 1977: 1-34. Stanley 1993: 264 shows that the books with the highest percentage of simile lines are 11 (12.1%), 12 (14.4%), 13 (10.7%), 15 (11.9%), 16 (13.7%), 17 (15.6%)! Thus, the books of the central day of fighting contain a greater quantity of similes than the others; Book 1 contains 0%. The expansions were produced on a larger scale before the Golden Point. Kirk 1962: 337-54 sees Diomedeia (Book 5) as the most obvious expansion.

of books. The beginning of Book 16, however, is situated at the Golden Section with respect not only to the number of books of the *Iliad*, but also to the whole number of verses of the poem. This position is too precise to be a coincidence. After dividing the poem into books, the poet might have worked towards this goal by carefully adding verses in both parts of the poem so that he could achieve the best possible approximation of the ratio.[35]

This brings us to the issue of the *numerus versuum* of the *Iliad*. The theory of the Golden Section cannot be separated from the history of the text itself. The base of our calculations is van Thiel's edition (1996), in which the *Iliad* counts 15,673 verses. But is this close to the number of verses of an 'original' *Iliad*?[36] We might never be able to answer this question with precision. The fact of the matter is that various papyri containing fragments from the *Iliad*, as well as citations in fourth-century authors like Plato, show textual variation and, apparently, verses which are neither included nor added in our Vulgate. These interpolations could occur when the scribes were negligent in following the copy they had in front of them, probably because they were writing from memory. They could mistakenly insert verses which had their place elsewhere or add passages in order to enhance the dramatic effect of an 'original' passage.[37]

Does all this affect our Golden Section theory and the ratios we have been talking about? Bolling believed that the Aristarchean edition contained about 15,600 verses, i.e., a bit fewer than our Vulgate. West, on the other hand, found about 166 interpolated verses.[38] In any case, the evidence of papyri from 300 to 150 BC and the quotations from fourth-century authors shows that variations were minor and mostly the result of casual processes

---

35 West's edition of the *Iliad* (1998) counts 15,655 verses = 9674 + 5981 (the ratios are 1.618 and 1.617). Here, the division at 15/16 is the 'best fit' for the Golden Point: the error is less than a verse! This raises the unverifiable hypothesis of an original 'best fit' for the poem.

36 By 'original' I mean the first written version of an *Iliad* that included all the episodes we see in the Alexandrian Vulgate. We cannot enter here a detailed discussion about the interpolated lines: see Bolling 1925 and 1950; S. West 1967; Apthorp 1980; M.L. West 2001. Van Thiel 1997: 33 argued that '…die Alexandriner im wesentlichen denselben Homertext hatten und voraussetzen wie wir'.

37 M.L. West 2001: 11-15.

38 Bolling 1950: 5 conjectured that the Peisistratean edition had 1,000 fewer verses. Elsewhere (1916, 1-30), he argued that the pre-Aristarchean edition could have had between 15,500 and 15,700 lines. M.L. West 2001: 14 thinks the situation in the 6th and 5th centuries was not so much different from the time of our earliest papyri.

like the scribal errors described above.[39] West gives all the examples of what he calls 'concordance interpolations', which are the most numerous.[40] If we count them, they are 59 before the Golden Point – that is, by the end of Book 15 – and 28 from Book 16 to the end. It is obvious that these numbers cannot in any way affect the position of the Golden Section within the whole poem. Moreover, a variation of, say, 100 verses, even if it had been introduced in only one part of the poem, would have given an error of 100/15,000, which is about .006, and could only have affected the Golden Number to its second decimal at most. The fact that the interpolations occurred in both parts of the poem makes this margin of error even smaller. In this way, the Golden Ratio can be said to work in respect not only to the number of books, but also to the whole number of verses in general, which is indeed amazing. But let us suppose that this precision is coincidental. Even so, the system of book divisions shows that the distribution of books within the structure of the *Iliad* is not accidental. The *Iliad* as we have it must have been conceived in 24 books from the beginning.

An additional observation regards the number of verses of each book. The average for the *Iliad* is 15,673/24 = 653 verses. The Doloneia comprises 578 verses (van Thiel's edition). Let us imagine that someone in post-Peisistratean times divided the text into 24 books. He would have surely noticed beforehand that the Doloneia – a clearly demarcated episode within the plot of the *Iliad* – had that number of verses. Then he would have had to devise a plan to achieve an average of about 650 verses for each book, which is pretty close to what the Doloneia represents.[41] In other words, the Doloneia would have almost exactly fitted this plan, despite the fact that it was inserted in the *I-liad* before this putative division. The coincidence is too big to be overlooked. Again, it cannot be easily explained, unless we see the Doloneia as part of an original plan, which included the division into 24 books.[42]

---

[39] These are papyri before Aristarchos; after him, that is, around 150 BC, these 'eccentric' papyri seem to die out; see S. West 1967: 15.

[40] These lines are the result of the practices described above. The term was introduced by Bolling 1950: 3 n. 6; cf. M.L. West 2001: 13, n. 31.

[41] The Doloneia might have been the 'norm' for dividing up the poem: cf. Goold 1960: 289.

[42] S. West 1967: 18-20 believes the books should have been longer if they had been Alexandrian. Apollonius Rhodius' books, for instance, are almost twice as long on the average. She also excludes Zenodotus as being the author of the divisions: why would Aristarchos

To sum up, if the theory considered here holds true, then the presence of the Golden Section within the *Iliad* as its main structural element cannot be a mere coincidence. The precision by which the beginning of Book 16 divides the poem in this ratio is likely to be deliberate. On the other hand, the system of book divisions, which closely follows this aesthetic principle, is also most likely to be original and devised by the poet himself.

The most important consequence, however, regards the Doloneia. If the Doloneia is part of the original plan of the *Iliad*, then either the information about its later (Peisistratean) insertion into the poem is false,[43] or the *Iliad* as we have it is a product of Peisistratus' editorial activity.[44]

The use of the Golden Number in the *Iliad* also raises the issue of the discovery of the irrational numbers. Could the people who used the Golden Number in the *Iliad* have knowledge of these? Claims have been made that their discovery is to be attributed to Theodoros of Cyrene in the middle of the fifth century BC.[45] Other scholars believe that the concept of irrationality could have been discovered in a geometrical way long before that, by means of the regular pentagon. This latter opinion places the time of this discovery to among the early Pythagoreans, if not to Pythagoras himself.[46] If so, it would be tempting to associate our *Iliad* with both the earliest Pythagoreans and the Homerids of Peisistratos' time.[47] This is, however, be-

---

have kept the divisions when he had such little respect for Zenodotos' work? Alpers 1975: 113-17 argues that Zenodotos was the divider, since some pre-Aristarchean papyri seem to have known the book division; cf. n. 1.

43 *Schol. T* on 10.1; for discussion, see Hainsworth 1993: 151-55; Davison 1955: 1, thinks this account is an 'embroidery' on the well-known Cic. *Orat.* 3.34. For Peisistratus being the first editor of Homer, cf. Cic. *De Orat.* 3.34; Paus. 7.26.13; Aelian *VH* 13.14; *Anth. Pal.* 11.142. Ps.-Pl. *Hipp.* 228b mentions Hipparchos as having brought the poems to Athens.

44 Interestingly, especially with regard to the above-mentioned possible expansions, the Attic painters seem to show knowledge about all the parts of the *Iliad*, not only about the last third, beginning with the last quarter of the sixth century; this is assumed to be the effect of Peisistratos' edition of the *Iliad*; cf. Johansen 1967: 224-30, 239; see also M.L. West 2001: 17-18.

45 See Junge 1907: 223-64; Heath 1921: 154-56; Burkert 1972 a: 454-65.

46 This pentagon's diagonals intersect at a point which divides them in the Golden Ratio; cf. Fritz 1945: 242-64.

47 This claim has been made by Tzetzes: cf. G. Kaibel 1899: 20; the theory is derided by Allen 1924: 233. In this respect, the name 'Homaros' may present an interesting case: it can be interpreted etymologically as 'the one fitting [the song] together with others'

yond any palpable proof. The fact is that the proportion may have been used long before this time without any knowledge of what an irrational number represents.

One final issue needs to be discussed: the fact that the number of books of the *Iliad* and *Odyssey* coincides with the numbers of letters of the Ionic alphabet. This was often seen as a result of the fact that someone wanted to match up these two numbers. Is this a necessary conclusion?

It would be hard for anyone to argue against the fact that there is some relation between the two. But what is the nature of this relation? If, indeed, the 24 books of the Homeric poems are the product of an aesthetic principle such as the Golden Section, then they do not and cannot originate in the number of letters of the Ionic alphabet. On the other hand, the coincidence is there and cannot be negated.[48] What is its origin?

If we do not believe in this coincidence, then the answer must be sought in the opposite direction: not only is it not the case that the number of letters of some Ionic alphabet influenced the number of books of the Homeric poems, but the opposite might have happened; the numbers of books, their numbering with letters, might have determined the number of letters of an 'Ionic' alphabet.

Unfortunately, the real answer lies in the shadows of history and, in this case, we can only speculate about the true facts. Nevertheless, a hypothesis of a standardization of an 'Ionic' alphabet under the influence of the number of books of the Homeric poems cannot be dismissed entirely.[49]

(< PIE *som- + *ar-), being morphologically similar to the word 'ὁμάκκοι' 'the ones who listen together [to Pythagoras]', which is how Pythagoras' adepts called themselves. Under this assumption, 'Homaros' may be an artificial creation (Pythagorean?), meant to imply the common effort of a group of people (the 'Homeridai') to make the poem fit the Golden Section. Among the most recent theories regarding the name 'Homaros', cf. M.L. West (1999), who makes the connection with Indic *samara-*, which means 'poetic contest'. However, thos connection is impossible because of a in 'Homaros', which does not allow comparison.

48 M.L. West 1983: 228-58 suggests that the number of *morae* of the hexameter, which is 24, together with the number of books of the Homeric poems, might have played a role in the arrangement of the Orphic Rhapsodies into 24 rhapsodies, *Hieroi Logoi* (1st century BC). It is not clear whether West believes there is a connection between the structure of the hexameter and the 24 books of the *Iliad* and *Odyssey*. In principle this is not impossible.

49 Goold 1960: 289-91 argues that Homer would have put an end to the 'variances' of the

CONCLUSIONS

This paper proposes a theory, which argues for the presence of the Golden Section within the structure of the *Iliad*. The use of the Golden Section in the *Iliad* regards both the number of verses and the system of book divisions. This could not have occurred by chance. The main consequence of this observation is that the system of book divisions is original to the poem.

A problematic aspect of this theory is the fact that the Doloneia seems also to be original to our *Iliad*. This raises the possibility that the *Iliad* as we have it is the result of Peisistratos' editorial interventions, unless the information about the insertion of the Doloneia in the *Iliad* by Peisistratos is false.

The Golden Section theory may have also some implications for the way the *Iliad* was written down. One may reasonably doubt that a poet could achieve such precision by simply dictating the poem. The Golden Section requires a well-devised plan, which includes a great care for the number of books and verses (in later times, the *Divine Comedy* may be a parallel case!). Our *Iliad*, then, may be the result of a 'literate' adaptation or composition, which could also mean the synthesis of pieces of extant poetry ('confusos antea'). The latter possibility fits better with the hypothesis of a Peisistratean recension,[50] which may indeed be more than a mere conjecture.

Ionic alphabets. Janko 1992: 37 believes that the introduction of the Ionic alphabet at Athens in 404/3 BC could have been the result of the fact that the Homeric texts were written in this script. Erbse 1994: 97 agrees with Goold.

50 The use of written episodes in editing the Homeric poems would account for the linguistic stability of the text; see Stanley 1993: 283-84. Oral traditions and written texts seem to have coexisted until the 5th century BC; cf. Haslam 1997: 79-81.

* Acknowledgement: I would like to thank Professor Minna Skafte Jensen for her invaluable help in improving this paper. I am also thankful to Professor Daniel Collins from the Ohio State University for helping me in editing the manuscript. It goes without saying that all the scientific errors in this paper are entirely my own.

BIBLIOGRAPHY

Allan, W. 'Arms and the Man: Euphorbus, Hector, and the Death of Patroklos' *CQ* 55.1 (2005) 1-16.
Allen, T.W. *Homer: The Origins and the Transmission* (Oxford 1924).
Alpers, K. Review of L.W. Daly '*Contributions to a History of Alphabetization in Antiquity and the Middle Ages*' *Gnomon* 47 (1967) 113-17
Apthorp, M.J. *The Manuscript Evidence for Interpolation in Homer* (Heidelberg 1980).
Birt, T. *Das antike Buchwesen* (Berlin 1882 (1959)).
Bolling, G.M. *The External Evidence for Interpolation in Homer* (Oxford 1925).
Bolling, G.M. *Ilias Athenensium* (Baltimore 1950).
Bolling, G.M. 'The Latest Expansions of the Iliad' *AJP* 37 (1916) 1-30.
Borissavlievitch, M. *The Golden Number and the Scientific Aesthetics of Architecture* (London 1958).
Boyer, C.B. *A History of Mathematics* (New York 1968).
Broccia, G. *La forma poetica dell'Iliade e la genesi dell'epos omerico* (Messina 1967).
Burkert, W. 'The Making of Homer in the 6th century BC', in *Papers on the Amasis Painter and his World* (Malibu 1987) 43-62.
Burkert, W. *Lore and Science in Ancient Pythagoreanism* Cambridge 1972).
Csapo, E. and Slater, W.J. *The Context of Ancient Drama* (Ann Arbor 1995).
Davison, J.A. 'Peisistratus and Homer' *TAPA* 86 (1955) 1-21.
Drerup, E. *Das fünfte Buch der Ilias* (Paderborn 1913).
Drerup, E. *Homerische Poetik* I (Würzburg 1921).
Duckworth, G. 'Mathematical Symmetry in Vergil's Aeneid' *TAPA* 91 (1960) 184-220.
Erbse, H. 'Zur Orthographie Homers' *Glotta* 72 (1994) 97.
Finsler, G. *Homer* I (Leipzig & Berlin 1914).
Fritz, K von. *The Annals of Mathematics* 2nd Ser. 46 (1945) 242-64.
Ghyka, M. *Le nombre d'or* (Paris 1931).
Gillings, R. J. *Mathematics in the Age of the Pharaohs* (Cambridge 1972).
Goold, G. P. 'Homer and the Alphabet' *TAPA* 91 (1960) 272-91.
Goold, G.P. 'The Nature of Homeric Composition' *ICS* 2 (1977) 1-34.
Hainsworth, J.B. 'Criticism of an Oral Homer' *JHS* 90 (1970) 90-98.

Hainsworth, J.B. *The Iliad: A Commentary* III (Cambridge 1993).
Haslam, M. 'Homeric Papyri and Transmission of the Text' in *A New Companion to Homer* (Leiden 1997) 55-100.
Heath, T. *A History of Greek Mathematics* I (Oxford 1921).
Heiden, B. 'The Three Movements of the Iliad' *GRBS* 37 (1996).
Heiden, B. 'The Placement of Book Divisions in the Iliad' *JHS* 118 (1998) 68-81.
Heiden, B. 'The Placement of Book Divisions in the Odyssey' *CP* 95 (2000) 247-59.
Herz-Fischler, R. *A Mathematical History of Division in Extreme and Mean Ratio* (Waterloo, Ontario 1987), reprinted as *A Mathematical History of the Golden Number* (New York 1990).
Heubeck, *A Commentary on Homer's Odyssey* III (Oxford 1992).
Janko, R. *The Iliad: A Commentary* IV (Cambridge 1992).
Jeffery, L.H. *The Local Scripts of Archaic Greece* (Oxford 1961).
Jensen, M.S. *The Homeric Question and the Oral-Formulaic Theory* (Copenhagen 1980).
Jensen, M.S. 'When and How were the Iliad and the Odyssey Divided into Songs?' *SO* 74 (1999) 5-91.
Johansen, K.F. *The Iliad in Early Greek Art* (Copenhagen 1967).
de Jong, I.J.F. 'Sunsets and Sunrises in Homer and Apollonius of Rhodes: Book-Divisions and beyond' *Dialogos* 3 (1996) 20-35.
Junge, G. 'Wann haben die Griechen das Irrationale entdeckt?' *Novae symbolae Joachimicae* (Halle 1907) 223-64.
Kaibel, G. *Comicorum Graecorum Fragmenta* I.1. (Berlin 1899).
Kirk, G.S. *The Songs of Homer* (Cambridge 1962).
Kirk, G.S. *The Iliad: A Commentary* I (Cambridge 1985a).
Kirk, G.S. *Homer and the Epic* (Cambridge 1985b).
Lachmann, K. *Betrachtungen über Homers Ilias* (Berlin 1874).
Lasserre, F. *The Birth of Mathematics in the Age of Plato* (New York 1964).
Latacz, J. 'Homer', in *Brill's Encyclopedia of the Ancient World* (Leiden 2005).
Ledbetter, G.M. 'Achilles' Self Address: Iliad 16.7-19' *AJP* 114 (1993) 481-91.
Livio, M. *The Golden Ratio* (New York 2002).
Lord, A.B. *The Singer of Tales* (Harvard 1960).
Markowski, G. 'Misconceptions about the Golden Ratio' *College Mathematics Journal* 23 (1992) 2-19.
Mazon, P. *Introduction à l'Iliade* (Paris 1942).

Myres, J. 'The Last Book of the Iliad' *JHS* 52 (1932) 264-96.
Myres J. 'The Pattern of the *Odyssey*' *JHS* 72 (1952) 1-19.
Nagy, G. *Poetry as Performance* (Cambridge 1996).
Nagy, G. *Plato's Rhapsody and Homer's Music* (Cambridge, MA 2002).
Notopoulos, J.A. 'Homer and Geometric Art' *Athena* 61 (1957) 65-93.
Notopoulos, J.A. 'Studies in Early Greek Oral Poetry' *HSCP* 68 (1964).
Ohm, M. *Die reine Elementar-Mathematik* (Berlin 1825-26).
Olson, D.S. *Blood and Iron* (Leiden 1995).
Pacioli, L. *Divina Proportione* (Venice 1509).
Parke, H.W. *Festivals of the Athenians* (London 1977).
Pfeiffer, R. *History of Classical Scholarship* (Oxford 1968).
Powell, B. *Homer and the Alphabet* (Madison 1991).
Reichel, M. 'Retardationstechniken in der Ilias' in *Der Übergang von der Mündlichkeit zur Literatur bei den Griechen*, ed. W. Kullmann & M. Reichel (Tübingen 1990) 125-51.
Richardson, N.J. *The Iliad: A Commentary* VI (Cambridge 1993).
Rothe, C. *Die Ilias als Dichtung* (Paderborn 1910).
Russo, J. 'Introduction' in J. Russo, M. Fernandez-Galiano & A.
Sarton, G. 'When did the term "golden section" or its equivalent in other languages originate' *Isis* 42 (1951) 47.
Schadewaldt, W. *Iliasstudien* (Leipzig 1938).
Schadewaldt, W. *Der Aufbau der Ilias* (Frankfurt am Main 1975).
Schadewaldt, W. 'Achilles' decision', in *Homer: German Scholarship in Translation* (Oxford 1997).
Schein, S. 'The *Iliad*: Structure and Interpretation' in *A New Companion to Homer* (Leiden 1997) 345-59.
Scott, J.A. *The Unity of Homer* (Berkeley 1921).
Sheppard, J.T. *The Pattern of the Iliad* (New York 1922).
Sickle, J van. 'The Book-Roll and Some Conventions of the Poetic Book' *Arethusa* 13 (1980) 5-39.
Stanley, K. *The Shield of Homer* (Princeton 1993).
Taplin, O. *Homeric Soundings* (Oxford 1992).
Thiel, H van. *Iliaden und Ilias*. (Basel & Stuttgart 1982).
Thiel, H van. *Homeri Ilias* (Hildesheim 1996).
Thiel, H van. 'Der Homertext in Alexandria' *ZPE* 115 (1997) 33.
Tracy, S. 'The Structures of the *Odyssey*' in *A New Companion to Homer* (Leiden 1997) 360-79.

West, M.L. *The Orphic Poems* (Oxford 1983).
West, M.L. *HomeriIlias* (Teubner 1998).
West, M.L. 'The Invention of Homer' *CQ* 49 (1999) 364-82.
West, M.L. *Studies in the Text and Transmission of the Iliad* (München 2001).
West, S. *The Ptolemaic Papyri of Homer* (Köln 1967).
West, S. 'The Transmission of the Text' in A. Heubeck, S. West, J.B. Hainsworth, *A Commentary on Homer's Odyssey* I (Oxford 1988) 33-48.
Whitman, C.H. *Homer and the Heroic Tradition* (Cambridge 1958).
Wilamowitz-Moellendorf, U. v. *Homerische Untersuchungen* (Berlin 1884).
Wilamowitz-Moellendorf, U. v. *Die Ilias und Homer* (Berlin 1916).
Zeising, A. *Der Goldene Schnitt* (Halle 1884).

HOW TO PRESENT LINE 136A OF THE HOMERIC HYMN TO APHRODITE

By Ichiro Taida

Summary: The subject of this paper is how to present line 136a of the *Homeric Hymn to Aphrodite*. I first show that the line is authentic, although recent editors almost always delete it. Then I argue that it should be printed in the main text. Finally I demonstrate that the number '137' is philologically preferable to '136a.' I conclude that if 136a is to be deleted, we must print the main text in the following way:

οὔ σφιν ἀεικελίη νυὸς ἔσσομαι ἀλλ' εἰκυῖα.   136
[εἴ τοι ἀεικελίη γυνὴ ἔσσομαι ἠὲ καὶ οὐκί]   137

I. INTRODUCTION

There are two editorial inconsistencies concerning the treatment of line 136a of the *Homeric Hymn to Aphrodite* (hereafter cited as *h.Ven.*). First, there is a difference of numeration. Some editors number it '136a,'[1] other editors '137.'[2] Secondly, when line 136a is omitted, the ways of acknowledging the deletion sometimes differ from that of other lines by the same editor. For example, Càssola deletes 136a and inserts it between the main text and apparatus criticus. However, when he deletes line 96 of the *Homeric Hymn to*

---

1 E.g., Goodwin 1893: 76, Monro 1896: 973, Allen & Sikes 1904: 210, Allen 1912: 69, Allen, Halliday & Sikes 1936: 69, Humbert 1936: 156, Càssola 1975: 264, Zanetto 2000: 288.
2 E.g., Hermann 1806: 96, Wolf 1807: 354, Gemoll 1886: 56. Also, Ruhnken 1749: 27 calls the line '137.'

Apollo, he prints it in the main text and uses square brackets ([ ]). Also, West deletes 136a and completely disregards it. However when he deletes *h.Ven.* 98, he prints it in the main text and uses braces ({ }).

These inconsistencies produce three problems which confuse readers: first, the lines which are numbered '136a-293' in some editions are called '137-294' in others. Compare the edition of Hermann, who calls the line '137', with the edition of Càssola, who calls it '136a'. It is inconvenient when readers refer to some editions, although a difference of numeration between editions is not unusual. Secondly, it is difficult for readers to determine the authenticity of 136a from the layouts and numerations. In other words, because ways of deleting are not consistent in an edition, it is hard for readers to know at a glance whether 136a is transmitted by manuscripts. Thirdly, future editors will be confused, because numerations and rules of editing in former editions, which they would follow, are not consistent.

Therefore, I will try to investigate about the authenticity of the line and establish a philologically consistent layout and numeration.

II. THE AUTHENTICITY OF THE LINE

We will begin by considering the authenticity of 136a from the point of view of transmitted manuscripts. Twenty one extant manuscripts preserving *h.Ven.* are divided into four groups, M, *f*, *x*, and *p*. These are derived from the non-extant archetype (Ω) as follows:[3]

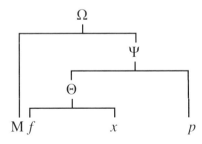

---

3 For this stemma, see Càssola 1975: 612.

At 136 and 136a these manuscripts give:

M	οὔ σφιν ἀεικελίη <u>νηὸς</u> ἔσσομαι ἀλλ' εἰκυῖα	136
	εἴ <u>τοι</u> ἀεικελίη γυνὴ <u>ἔσομαι</u> ἠὲ καὶ οὐκί	136a
f	οὔ σφιν ἀεικελίη <u>νυὸς</u> ἔσσομαι ἀλλ' εἰκυῖα	136
	εἴ <u>τι</u> ἀεικελίη γυνὴ <u>ἔσομαι</u> ἠὲ καὶ οὐκί	136a
x	οὔ σφιν ἀεικελίη <u>νυὸς</u> ἔσσομαι ἀλλ' εἰκυῖα	136
	εἴ <u>τοι</u> ἀεικελίη γυνὴ <u>ἔσσομαι</u> ἠὲ καὶ οὐκί	136a
p	οὔ σφιν ἀεικελίη γυνὴ <u>ἔσσομαι</u> ἠὲ καὶ οὐκί	136+136a

We can see from the stemma and the list of readings that Ω had:[4]

οὔ σφιν ἀεικελίη νυὸς ἔσσομαι ἀλλ' εἰκυῖα	136
εἴ τοι ἀεικελίη γυνὴ ἔσσομαι ἠὲ καὶ οὐκί	136a

Ω must have had 136a in its full form, although *p* has only the latter half of this line. The reason is that *p* committed an error in combining 136 and 136a into one line *after* Θ and *p* had been derived from Ψ.[5] Thus 136a must be an authentic line.[6]

III. WHERE MUST WE PRINT THE LINE?

Then we need to consider where to print 136a. Recent editors almost always retain only 136 and delete 136a from the main text. They include 136a in the apparatus criticus,[7] or insert it between the main text and apparatus criti-

---

4 For minor differences, we must prefer νυὸς because of its meaning, τοι judging from the stemma, and ἔσσομαι metrically.

5 Allen 1895: 267 says 'A typical instance of mechanical contamination: both lines stood in the archetype of *p*, the scribe's eye wandered from one ἀεικελίη to the other. This the commentators have recognized.' We also find the same blunder of combining two lines at *h.Ven.* 222 in manuscript A which belongs to *p*.

6 Of course, that 136a was in the archetype Ω does not necessarily mean it was in the original.

7 E.g., Allen & Sikes 1904: 210, Allen 1912: 69, Evelyn-White 1936: 414, Allen, Halliday & Sikes 1936: 69.

cus,[8] or omit it completely.[9] However, I am opposed to the ways in which the recent editors represent the deletion, for two reasons.

First, they provide a distorted account of the transmission of 136a. This may lead the reader to believe that no manuscript or only worthless ones have 136a, but it is certain that Ω and some trustworthy manuscripts have it, as mentioned above.

Secondly, the ways keep readers away from the judgment on the deletion of 136a should be left to the readers. When editors do not print line 136a in the main text, the reader who is not deeply familiar with the text and its transmission must disregard 136a or regard it as an inauthentic line. It is very likely that the reader does not judge whether the deletion of 136a is justified or not. However, the deletion is not necessarily correct. There is no conclusive proof and the deletion is an unsettled question. Some other editors conversely delete 136 and retain 136a.[10] Moreover, instead of deleting a line, other conjectures have been proposed.[11] It is not immediately understood

---

8   E.g., Gemoll 1886: 56, Càssola 1975: 264.
9   E.g., Zanetto 2000: 170, West 2003: 168.
10 E.g., Hermann 1806: 96, Wolf 1807: 354.
11 For example, Van der Ben 1986: 15-17 places 136a after 138. Humbert 1936: 156 proposes a compound form: οὔ σφιν ἀεικελίη γυνὴ ἔσσομαι, ἀλλ' ἔϊκυῖα (however, judging from his apparatus criticus, I think this form must be derived from a misreading of the manuscripts). Van der Ben's solution in which both verses are retained is noteworthy, although it is difficult to demonstrate that the shift of 136a might have happened in the manuscript trans-mission. Editors usually delete a verse, but deletion is a radical solution. They may believe that *h.Ven.* 136-136a are derived from two recensions fused together (e. g., Allen & Sikes 1904: xliii), but they do not have a certain proof. We can offer other solutions in which two verses are retained. For example, we can retain the reading of the manuscripts as follows (translation based on Evelyn-White 1936: 415):

ἀδμήτην μ' ἀγαγὼν καὶ ἀπειρήτην φιλότητος	133
πατρί τε σῷ δεῖξον καὶ μητέρι κεδν' εἰδυίῃ	134
σοῖς τε κασιγνήτοις οἵ τοι ὁμόθεν γεγάασιν,	135
—οὔ σφιν ἀεικελίη νυὸς ἔσσομαι ἀλλ' εἰκυῖα—	136
εἴ τοι ἀεικελίη γυνὴ ἔσσομαι ἠὲ καὶ οὐκί.	136a

take me now, unwedded and unproven in love,
and tell your father and careful mother
and your brothers sprung from the same stock
– I shall be no ill-liking daughter for them, but a likely –
that I shall not be an ill-liking wife for you.

which deletion or conjecture we should adopt, but it is certain that, whatever an editor adopts, he adopts the deletion or the conjecture by his own judgment which is not always completely justified. Therefore the judgment on the deletion of 136a should be left to the readers.

We must include 136a in the main text and present it with square brackets ([ ]) or braces ({ }), when we delete the line. Editorial deletion is usually presented in this way[12]. It is most appropriate for deleting 136a.

In this case, I regard an εἰ clause at 136a as the object of δεῖξον at 134 (Wolf 1807: 354 may interpret the text like this). Examples of δείκνυμι with an εἰ clause as object are found in, e.g., Th. 1.76.4 δεῖξαι ἂν μάλιστα εἴ τι μετριάζομεν, App. *Anth.* 124.2 δείξεις εἴ τι φρονεῖς καί τι περισσὸν ἔχεις. Also, I regard the εἰ clause as an alternative indirect question which means 'tell (δεῖξον) whether I shall be an ill-liking wife for you or not.' The meaning is a delicate substitute for her real meaning (i.e. 'I shall not be an ill-liking wife for you.' Van der Ben 1986: 16-17 interprets the meaning of this εἰ clause in similar way). For examples of an εἰ clause which is a substitute for the real meaning, see *Il.* 5.183 σάφα δ' οὐκ οἶδ' εἰ θεός ἐστιν and *Il.* 8.110-11 ὄφρα καὶ Ἕκτωρ εἴσεται εἰ καὶ ἐμὸν δόρυ μαίνεται ἐν παλάμῃσιν.

Of course, the reading seems strange in some points. First, 136 is a parenthetical sentence and it is introduced by asyndeton. However, there is another example of parenthetic expression which is introduced by asyndeton in lines 12-15 (see West 2003: 160). Secondly, the repetition of ἀεικελίη and ἔσσομαι is awkward. However, the poet sometimes uses similar repetitions (e. g. 76/79, 113/116, 117/121, 134/138). Lastly, at first sight, some words at 136a do not sound like epic language. ἠὲ καὶ οὐκί does not have corresponding ἤ and -ή of γυνή is strangely scanned as short by epic correction. However, we find ἠὲ καὶ οὐκί without a corresponding ἤ in Q.S. 13.561 although ἠὲ καὶ οὐκί always has ἤ in Homeric poems. Also, there is one shortened -ή of γυνή at *Od.* 11.237 among 41 examples in Homer.

On the other hand, the reversed reading 136a-136 may be possible. It is not unusual for scribes to copy in reverse order (For example, *h. Ven.* 130-31 are transposed in the manuscript D which must be a copy of *f*. Reynolds and Wilson 1968: 158 say, 'In poetry verses are often copied in the wrong order.'):

πατρί τε σῷ δεῖξον καὶ μητέρι κεδν' εἰδυίῃ	134
σοῖς τε κασιγνήτοις οἵ τοι ὁμόθεν γεγάασιν	135
εἴ τοι ἀεικελίη γυνὴ ἔσσομαι ἠὲ καὶ οὐκί·	136a
οὔ σφιν ἀεικελίη νυὸς ἔσσομαι ἀλλ' εἰκυῖα.	136

In this case too, I regard an εἰ clause at 136a as the object of δεῖξον at 134 and the εἰ clause as an alternative indirect question.

12 Square brackets and braces have commonly been used for editorial deletions (cf. West

IV. WHAT MUST WE CALL THE LINE?

Finally we consider what to call the line. As we have seen at the beginning of this paper, recent editors usually call it '136a,' but some editors called it '137.' The line is the 137th in the archetype Ω, the reliable manuscripts and the *editio princeps*.[13] Thus the number '137' is philologically authentic.

On the other hand, I think that the number '136a' is not suitable for designating the line. There are two reasons for thinking so.

First, an unfounded verse gave rise to the number '136a.' As far as I know, Goodwin 1893: 76 was the first person to give the number '136a' (in his apparatus criticus). I think Goodwin wanted to make the hymn exactly 293 lines long, consistent with previous editions, and arrange the layout of his apparatus criticus as conveniently as possible for readers. I offer here the reason for my inference. Originally *h. Ven.* has 294 lines in the reliable manuscripts, the *editio princeps* and, as we have seen above, some modern editions: e.g., Hermann 1806, Wolf 1807 and Gemoll 1886. We hereafter cite such editions as Editions A. On the other hand, in editions of Wolf 1784, Baumeister 1860 and Abel 1886, which we hereafter cite as Editions B, the hymn has only 293 lines, because they adopt the compounded verse of 136 and 136a (εἴ σφιν ἀεικελίη νυὸς ἔσσομαι, ἠὲ καὶ οὐκί.) which Ruhnken 1749: 27 had proposed. The compound verse is different from *p*'s compound verse. Ruhnken's compound verse is philologically unfounded and recent editors do not adopt it.[14] Editions B give the numbers '137-293' to the lines which Editions A called '138-294.' Although Goodwin rejects Ruhnken's verse, he calls these lines '137-293' following Editions B. The reason is probably that the numeration of Editions B were widely accepted and he wanted to retain the numbering. He retains 136, uses * to mark the following line (136a) as

---

1973: 80-81). As we will discuss later, Goodwin 1893: 76 includes 136a in the main text and marks it as deleted with the mark *. Monro 1896: 973 also includes 136 and 136a in the main text. However it is difficult to judge which line Monro deletes, because added marks are somewhat obscure.

13 Chalcondyles 1488.
14 Allen & Sikes 1904: 210 say, 'Ruhnken's attempt to construct a single verse out of the two is unsuccessful.'

deleted and prints the deleted line in the main text.[15] Thus when he comments about this line in apparatus criticus, he needs a new number to indicate the line. The number '137,' which Editions A had given to this line, was used for the following line (πέμψαι ... αἰολοπώλους,) in his edition as in Editions B. As a result Goodwin calls it '136a.' It follows from what has been said that the designation '136a' is caused by Ruhnken's unfounded verse.

Secondly, the number '136a' conveys the false impression that this line is a surplus one and deserves to be deleted. It is important to keep in mind that, as we have seen above, the deletion of 136a is an unsettled question.

Therefore we can be fairly certain that the number '137' is philologically more correct than '136a.'

V. CONCLUSION

If 136a is to be deleted, one must print the main text in the following way:[16]

    οὔ σφιν ἀεικελίη νυὸς ἔσσομαι ἀλλ' εἰκυῖα.   136
    [εἴ τοι ἀεικελίη γυνὴ ἔσσομαι ἠὲ καὶ οὐκί]   137

The lines which are called '136a-293' in most of recent editions should be numbered '137-294.' Of course, it is difficult to reject the now widely accepted numeration ('136a-293'), because we must retain established numerations as far as possible.[17] Even if a future editor may adopt the numbering ('136a-293'), line 136a should at least be printed in the main text, leaving the judgment on its deletion to the readers.

---

15 This is consistent with the way in which another deleted line is presented in Goodwin's text. See the line 139 of the *Hymn to Apollo* in his edition.
16 I translate the verses as follows:
    I shall be no ill-liking daughter for them, but a likely.   136
    [whether I shall not be an ill-liking wife for you]   137
17 See West 1973: 78.
* This paper is a revised English version of my paper in Japanese (with English summary) published as 'Aphrodite sanka ni kansuru bunkengakuteki chusyaku: 136-136a gyou wo chuushinni' in *Seiyou Kotengaku Kenkyu* [*Journal of Classical Studies*] 54 (2006), 14-26.

REFERENCES

Abel, E. *Homeri hymni, epigrammata, Batrachomyomachia* (Leipzig 1886).
Allen. T.W. 'The Text of the Homeric Hymns: II' *JHS* 15 (1895) 251-313.
Allen. T.W. *Homeri Opera* v. (Oxford 1912).
Allen, T.W.; Halliday, W.R.; Sikes, E.E. *The Homeric Hymns* 2nd ed. (Oxford 1936).
Allen, T.W.; Sikes, E.E. *The Homeric Hymns* (London 1904).
Baumeister, A. *Hymni Homerici* (Leipzig 1860).
Càssola, F. *Inni Omerici* (Milan 1975).
Chalcondyles, D. Ἡ τοῦ Ὁμήρου ποίησις ἅπασα (Florence 1488) (The *editio princeps*).
Evelyn-White, H.G. *Hesiod, The Homeric Hymns and Homerica* 2nd ed. (Cambridge, Mass. & London 1936).
Gemoll, A. *Die homerischen Hymnen* (Leipzig 1886).
Goodwin, A. *Hymni Homerici* (Oxford 1893).
Hermann, G. *Homeri Hymni et Epigrammata* (Leipzig 1806).
Humbert, J. *Homère, Hymnes* (Paris 1936).
Monro, D.B. *Homeri opera et reliquiae* (Oxford 1896).
Reynolds, L.D.; Wilson, N.G. *Scribes and Scholars: A Guide to the Transmission of Greek and Latin Literature* (London 1968).
Ruhnken, D. *Epistola critica ad Valckenarium* (Leiden 1749).
Van der Ben, N. 'Hymn to Aphrodite 36-291: Notes on the Pars Epica of the Homeric Hymn to Aphrodite' *Mnemosyne* 39 (1986) 1-41.
West, M.L. *Textual Criticism and Editorial Technique: Applicable to Greek and Latin Texts* (Stuttgart 1973).
West, M.L. *Homeric Hymns, Homeric Apocrypha, Lives of Homer* (Cambridge, MA & London 2003).
Wolf, F.A. *Homeri Odyssea cum Batrachomyomachia, hymnis, ceterisque poematibus* (Halle 1784).
Wolf. F.A. *Homeri et Homeridarum opera et reliquiae* v. (Leipzig 1807).
Zanetto, G. *Inni omerici* 2nd ed. (Milan 2000).

TIRED OF WHAT? A NOTE ON ARISTOPHANES, *BIRDS* 787

By Marcel Lysgaard Lech

Summary: In this note I try to reintroduce the anonymous reading of Ar. *Av.* 787 τοῖς χοροῖσι τῶν τρυγῳδῶν instead of the transmitted τοῖς χοροῖσι τῶν τραγῳδῶν for palaeographic, textual and historical reasons.

In this note, I shall attempt to explain why we should reconsider the anonymous reading τοῖς χοροῖσι τῶν τρυγῳδῶν in the famous passage in Aristophanes' *Birds* 787-89. The established text runs as follows:

εἶτα πεινῶν τοῖς χοροῖσι τῶν τραγῳδῶν ἤχθετο,
ἐκπτόμενος ἂν οὗτος ἠρίστησεν ἐλθὼν οἴκαδε,
κᾆτ᾽ ἂν ἐμπλησθεὶς ἐφ᾽ ἡμᾶς[1] αὖθις αὖ κατέπτατο.

This passage has for more than a century been regarded as evidence that tragedies were performed in the morning and comedies in the afternoon.[2] At issue in these verses, however, is this: of what exactly are the spectators expected to be tired of. Is it really 'tragic choruses' (τοῖς χοροῖσι τῶν τραγῳδῶν)?

The Leiden 'Scaliger' edition (1624) has an anonymous reference (*qui-*

1 N. Dunbar *Aristophanes: Birds* (Oxford 1995). Following Blaydes *Aristophanis: Aves* (Oxford 1882), N. Wilson *Aristophanis Fabulae* I (Oxford 2007) prints ὑμᾶς which I think is correct. It does not have any bearings on the argument of this note, but clearly solves the main problem regardless of the readings of *Av.* 787, that is who the man bestowed with wings would return to: 1) ἐφ᾽ ἡμᾶς, the chorus of birds or 2) ἐφ᾽ ὑμᾶς, the audience watching the play.
2 See the discussion in Dunbar 1995: 480-82 *ad loc*. She argues against the reduction of comedies, but we do not agree on this particular passage, see below.

dam) preferring the reading τοῖς χοροῖσι τῶν τρυγῳδῶν,³ which gives this passage an entirely new meaning; it has, however, never attracted the favour of editors. Nan Dunbar in her commentary writes: 'if τρυγῳδῶν is right, the passage would be a last-minute substitution, made after the order of performance for the comedies had been determined by lot and *Birds* had been assigned a late place in the list. But no change is needed.'⁴

In anticipation of the question, 'why not accept the anonymous reading τρυγῳδῶν?', Dunbar states, 'Ar. *may* have thought tragic choral parts more likely to be boring than dialogue, but since the choral element was important even in late tragedy, τοῖς χοροῖσι may simply mean a dramatic production' (my italics).⁵

That the choruses were boring stems from the scholium on this passage (which admittedly reads τραγῳδῶν) explaining τοῖς χοροῖσι τῶν τραγῳδῶν ἤχθετο with ὡς μακρῶν ὄντων τούτων, that is, because of the lenght of the choral odes. This, however, is not an adequate explanation⁶ since the choral element had had a vigorous impact through the 'New Music' in the later half of the fifth century BC – a modernization of musical practice that expanded the musical, metrical and choreographic possibilities for the performers⁷ – which Aristophanes so manifestly employs and criticizes at the same time in *Birds*.⁸ A quick look at the length of the odes in both Sophocles and Euripides, contra those of Aeschylus, also allows us to cast doubt upon the claim of the scholiast, who must have had a hard time 'reading' choral odes. Could Aristophanes really expect his audience to find tragedy or their choral odes boring? The Athenians spent enormous resources on tragic productions,⁹ so they must have found them interesting (and beneficial) in

---

3 Se Wilson 2007: app. *ad loc.* and Dunbar 1995: 482 *ad* 786-87. See also Ar. fr. 156 (*PCG*): {A.} καὶ τίνες ἂν εἶεν; {B.} πρῶτα μὲν Σαννυρίων ἀπὸ τῶν τρυγῳδῶν, ἀπὸ δὲ τῶν τραγικῶν χορῶν Μέλητος, ἀπὸ δὲ τῶν κυκλίων Κινησίας. *Vesp.* 1537: ὅστις ἀπήλλαξεν χορὸν τρυγῳδῶν. *Ach.* 886: ἦλθες ποθεινὴ μὲν τρυγῳδικοῖς χοροῖς. See O. Taplin, 'Tragedy and Trugedy' *CQ* 33 (1983), 331-33.
4 Compare Ar. *Ec.* 1158-9
5 Dunbar 1995: 481-82 *ad* 786-87.
6 Pace J. van Leeuwen *Aristophanis: Aves* (Leiden 1902), 122 note 6: 'recte schol.'
7 On this, see E. Csapo 'Later Euripidean Music' *ICS* 24-25 (1999-2000), 399-426, and 'The Politics of the New Music' in P. Murray & P. Wilson (ed.) *Music and the Muses* (Oxford 2004), 207-48.
8 See A. Barker 'Transforming the Nightingale' in Murray and Wilson (2004), 185-204.
9 E.g., Lys. 21.1 ff., Plu. *Mor.* 349a, Dem. 4.35-36.

some way; if they really were bored by them, this passage seems to be our only evidence of such a thought.[10]

To be sure, Aristophanes was keenly interested in tragedy. *Frogs* immediately springs to mind, but from *Acharnians* to *Plutus*, tragedy had a special place in the comic universe of this author,[11] not because it was boring, but because it was fascinating and (to some) provocative.[12] And while at times Aristophanes does negatively criticize some tragedians (e.g. the 'chill' Theognis at *Ach.* 11-12) we ought not to think that such judgment was true of all the tragic poets or even that the audience shared this opinion. Aristophanes normally names the bad poets who are destroying tragedy (e.g., *Pax* 803ff, Melanthius; *Thes.* 168, Philocles; *Ra.* 86, Xenocles), while tragedy itself remains pure (Ar. *Ra.* 93: λωβηταὶ τέχνης).

It is, however, common for the comedians to poke fun at the jokes (Ar. *Vesp.* 57ff.) and scenery of their rivals (Eup. fr. 62 *PCG*). In the same vein, in *Frogs* the god of theatre, Dionysus, annoyed by the comic banalities of Aristophanes' rivals utters: ὡς ἐγὼ θεώμενος, ὅταν τι τούτων τῶν σοφισμάτων ἴδω, πλεῖν ἢ 'νιαυτῷ πρεσβύτερος ἀπέρχομαι (15-17). It is interesting to notice that what makes Dionysus πλεῖν ἢ 'νιαυτῷ πρεσβύτερος are the comedies of at least one of his opponents at the festival of that year, Phrynichus,[13] the same poet against whom in 414, Aristophanes (with *Birds*) and that year's winner, Ameipsias, competed. Thus the change proposed here provides us with an example of Aristophanes making his chorus comment on the quality of the competing choruses, in a play where he puts great ef-

---

10 Plato Comicus fr. 138 (*PCG*) does not claim that the choruses are boring, quite the opposite actually, though bad compared to the good old days. Three caveats must however be noted: 1) we are not in a position to know what kind of chorus he is referring to; 2) if a tragic chorus, then it might be a critique on the choral style of the popular New Music, compare it then with Ar. fr. 81 (*PCG*), and thus possibly untrustworthy; 3) the nature of the passage (νῦν δὲ) seems to be an example of a nostalgic view, making the statement an exaggeration and thus untrustworthy.
11 M. Silk *Aristophanes and the Definition of Comedy* (Oxford 2000) 38.
12 Fascinating: e.g. *Ra.* 52-54, provocative: e.g. *Nu.* 1371-72.
13 Since the argument of this note contrasts 'the reduction of comedies'-theory, it should be entertained that the poets of the comic competition at the Lenaea 405 BC. were Aristophanes, who won, Phrynichus, second prize, Plato, third, (Ar. *Ra. Hyp.* III) and perhaps Ameipsias and Lycus, who ended up failing this year.

fort into the chorus to make it stand out musically and visually.[14]

I have tried to argue against reading the manuscripts from a historical point of view, but I also claim that the insistence of editors on reading τραγῳδῶν is premised on the traditional contrast between comedy and tragedy. Yet the relationship between comedy and tragedy is far more complex than this simple binarism implies.[15] Moreover, this is not necessarily the Aristophanic view of the competitions of the Lenaea and the Great Dionysia, as Ar. fr. 156 (n. 3) shows.[16]

The historical viewpoint can be reinforced by a paleographic survey. A scribe's unfamiliarity with the word τρυγῳδία and the easy misspelling of τρυγ- to τραγ- readily facilitate the change of τρυγῳδῶν to τραγῳδῶν. This type of corruption is found in Pl. Σ R. 394c: κωμῳδία ἐστὶ πόησις (sic) ... καθ' ἣν τῷ νικήσαντι γλεῦκος ἆθλον ἐδίδοτο, ὃ τρύγα ἐκάλουν. παρὸ καὶ ἥδε τὸ πρὶν τραγῳδία (sic. l. τρυγῳδία) κοινῶς ἐλέγετο· ὕστερον δέ, ἀπὸ τοῦ κατὰ κώμας ἄρξασθαι ταύτην πρὶν εἰς ἄστυ μετελθεῖν, κωμῳδία ὠνομάσθη.[17] Here τραγῳδία should clearly be changed to τρυγῳδία, as the editor notes. Likewise, in the ms. Vaticanus Palatinus 128,[18] τραγῳδόν is transmitted instead of τρυγῳδῶν in Ar. Vesp. 1537. I think that the same scribal error has been transmitted in our passage, and thus I see no need to keep the traditional reading of the mss. Instead I would recommend the anonymus' *lectio difficilior* τοῖς χοροῖσι τῶν τρυγῳδῶν. This will provide yet another passage where Aristophanes launches an attack on his rivals, quite in the spirit of competition of Old Attic Comedy.[19]

---

14 L.P.E Parker *The Songs of Aristophanes* (Oxford, 1997) 297, L.M. Stone *Costume in Aristophanic Comedy* (Salem, 1984) 384.

15 As e.g. in Arist. *Poet.* II 1448a 15-17. See the discussion of this issue in Silk 2000 53ff. On 55: 'Greek tragôidia and kômôidia have some contrasting features. None of these, makes tragedy and comedy... a pair of opposites.' See also O. Taplin 'Fifth-Century Tragedy and Comedy: A Synkrisis' *JHS* 163-74.

16 Indeed the much discussed καί in Ar. *Ach.* 500; τὸ γὰρ δίκαιον οἶδε καὶ τρυγῳδία, implies a similarity between the two genres, not a contrast, see Silk 2000: 39ff. Aristophanes was perhaps especially fond of tragedy (Euripidean at least), so that Cratinus fr. 342 (PCG) could tease him with his passion, see Silk 2000: 48 ff.

17 Text as G.C. Greene *Scholia Platonica* (Haverford 1938).

18 Ms. (J) in M. Macdowell *Aristophanes: Wasps* (Oxford 1971) and (Vp3) in Wilson 2007.

19 I wish to thank D. Jacobson (Berkeley), D. Bloch (Copenhagen) and J. Mejer (Copenhagen) for valuable suggestions.

SOCRATES' ARGUMENTATIVE STRATEGY

By Erik Nis Ostenfeld

Summary: The literature on Socratic argumentation has been dominated by generalisations about the strategy of a Socratic conversation (Robinson and Vlastos have led the way, in different directions) or, at the other extreme, recently by total despair of finding a unitary pattern (Polansky, Brickhouse and Smith). In this article I shall attempt to provide a more well-founded picture of Socratic argumentation than has to my mind been offered so far. This is done by a *systematic* examination of the arguments found in the so-called early dialogues. Briefly the results demonstrate that (1) the overwhelming amount of refutation is indirect (R. Robinson was right and Vlastos wrong); (2) indirect refutation is mainly used to refute definitions of moral terms, whereas direct refutation is used on other (positive) moral theses. This does not exclude indirect refutation from being used also for establishing important moral theses; (3) more than half of the indirect refutations are conducted without the support of external premises ('basic reductio'); (4) there is a reliance on *endoxa* in both direct and indirect refutation ('extended reductio'); (5) there is a methodological development from *hypothesis* in elenchus to elenchus in *hypothesis*; (6) we find four distinct patterns of elenctic argument in the texts, three indirect and one direct. Hence I present a defence of Robinson against the influential Vlastos and also a counter-argument against the recent scepticism of e.g. Brickhouse/Smith.

CONTENTS

The argument will take the following course:

I. Robinson: Socrates' argumentation and use of elenchus
II. Vlastos and his followers, and a few critics

    III. Methodological considerations
    IV. Forms of elenchus (direct and indirect refutation, and the distinction)
    V. Forms of reductio ((a) basic, (b) extended, (c) the distinction))
    VI. *Endoxa*
    VII. *Hypothesis* and *epagoge*
    VIII. Conclusions: (a) Patterns of argumentation, (b) Aim, scope and value of elenchus, (c) summing up

I. ROBINSON

Richard Robinson's ground-breaking book, *Plato's Earlier Dialectic* (Oxford 1953 (2nd ed.), corr. repr. 1966) started the modern preoccupation with what goes on in the so-called earlier dialogues.[1] Robinson examined the text with the competence of a logician and discovered the basic mechanism of the Socratic argument (the elenchus).

His great contribution was to point to the division between direct and indirect argument. He looked at *Protagoras*, *Euthyphro*, *Laches*, *Charmides*, *Lysis*, *Republic* I, *Gorgias*, *Meno* and *Euthydemus* and counted thirty-nine arguments of which most (in fact thirty-one) seemed to be indirect.[2] Moreover, he pointed out that every indirect argument is basically a destructive hypothetical syllogism (if A, then B, but not B, therefore not A), in other words, modus tollendo tollens (MTT). Finally, he divided indirect arguments into those that need extra premises and those that do not.

Where Robinson was less convincing was when he began speculating on Plato's thoughts about this distinction between direct and indirect arguments and his conception of the logic of the elenchus: according to Robin-

---

[1] I shall only discuss the first quarter of Robinson's book. The greater part of it deals with the dialectic of the middle dialogues. Let me add here that, merely for convenience of reference, I use the terms 'early' and 'middle' dialogues quite unashamedly, well aware that even this quite broad, well-established chronology has recently come under attack. This would have no consequences for my argument which only requires a handy reference to an identifiable group of dialogues. What I mean by 'early dialogues' will appear in section iv below.

[2] Robinson 1966: 24.

son, Plato regarded all elenchus as the deduction of a contradiction from the refutand alone, without any additional premise.[3]

This analysis is followed by an illuminating account of *epagoge* and its relation to syllogism, the use of 'cases' (eliminative and accumulative) and finally a section on *epagoge* and definition: there is no necessary connexion between definition and *epagoge* (in spite of Aristotle *Met.* 13.4). *Epagoge* is just one means of establishing the premises of the syllogism that refutes, e.g., definitions.

II. VLASTOS AND THE RESPONSES

G. Vlastos was the next[4] who contributed significantly to the study of the elenchus. In his 1983 article he went against Robinson's analysis and claimed that the elenchus is mostly *direct* refutation, used to establish positive moral theses.[5] In the posthumous book *Socratic Studies* this is offered as 'The Standard Elenchus': p, and further q and r (unargued for) are accepted. Then *not-p is derived from q and r*. Finally, Socrates concludes that it has been demonstrated that not-p is true, and that p is false.[6] So the elenchus is positive and constructive, understood as a search for moral truth. Vlastos says:

> The premises from which Socrates derives not-p *generally do not include p* and even when they do, there are others in the premise-set elicited from the interlocutor, not deducible from p (my emphasis).[7]

---

3 Robinson 1966: 32.
4 In 1979, G. Santas wrote an impressive book on Socrates with a ch. V on Socratic arguments. He analysed more than 17 arguments taking modern logic as his tool. But while the individual arguments are thus reconstructed and evaluated in illuminating ways we are not offered a general conclusion as to the nature and strategy of the elenchus (if such there be) and no stand on or critique of Robinson's work. This is what Vlastos (1983) offers.
5 Vlastos 1983: 38 n. 29 Cf. Vlastos 1994: 12.
6 Vlastos 1994: 11.
7 Vlastos 1994: 3.

So we may take it that p may *sometimes* be included as a premise. However, on the very same page, we read:

> What Socrates does in *any* given elenchus is to convict p of *being a member of* an inconsistent premise-set ... The question then becomes how Socrates can claim (in standard elenchus) to have proved that the refutand is false, when all he has established is its inconsistency with premises whose truth he has not tried to establish in that argument. (my emphases).

Is p now *always* a premise? Or perhaps only a kind of premise (a presupposition)? There appears here to be some unclarity about the status of p.

Moreover, Vlastos contends that in *indirect* elenchus 'the falsehood of p is demonstrated by *assuming its truth alongside that of q and r* and arguing that, since the premise-set {p, q, r} is inconsistent and the interlocutor stands by the truth of q&r, he must infer that p is false.' And then comes the surprising bit: 'So in point of logic there is *no substantial difference* from the *standard* elenchus' (my emphases).[8] Whatever is going on here, one should have thought that there is a substantial difference between deriving ¬p *from q&r* and deriving it *from p with the help of q&r*. Vlastos seems to have obliterated the distinction between direct and indirect argumentation and to have overlooked or ignored the possibility of what I shall call 'Basic Reductio' (from p alone).

Part of Vlastos' problem is that he is disinclined to see here the use of *endoxa* for reasons to which I shall return. Robert Bolton has discussed Vlastos' objections to *endoxa*.[9] There have been various other responses to Vlastos' analysis. Thus H. Benson thinks that Socrates did not believe in the premises, and that the elenchus can only reveal inconsistencies.[10] Carpenter and Polansky think there is no single and constant method.[11] Finally, and at the most extreme, Brickhouse and Smith argue that there is no such thing as the elenchus.[12]

---

8 Vlastos 1994: 12 n. 34.
9 Bolton (1993).
10 Benson 2002: 105 with references in n. 11.
11 Carpenter and Polansky 2002: 90.
12 Brickhouse and Smith 2002: 147.

I shall now undertake, on the basis of a registration of the arguments to be found in the early dialogues, to counter this rather despairing attitude with a demonstration that Vlastos must be mistaken on most of the points mentioned, that Robinson was much more right than his later critics have realized and that we do have several patterns in the texts that deserve the title 'elenchus'.

III. METHODOLOGICAL CONSIDERATIONS

The means by which to seek knowledge of definitions in the early Platonic dialogues is (typically) the elenchus (to which reductio belongs). Elenchus means *testing* (e.g., the oracle is tested, not refuted) but also and very often testing with a negative result: *refuting*. Socrates says little of the elenchus but does a lot of it. We need then an elucidation of the mechanism of this elenchus, more particularly its core: the reductio and its formal feature, the indirect proof. Let us first take a brief look at some modern conceptions of the reductio to get a clearer picture of this tool.

Reductio ad absurdum (indirect refutation)
First level (extensional) information can be got from the *Internet Encyclopaedia of Philosophy*:

> Use of this Latin terminology traces back to the Greek expression *hê eis to adunaton apagôgê*, reduction to the impossible, found repeatedly in Aristotle's *Prior Analytics*. In its most general construal, *reductio ad absurdum – reductio* for short – is a process of refutation on the grounds that absurd and patently untenable consequences would ensue from accepting the item at issue. This takes three principal forms according as that untenable consequence is:
>
> - a self-contradiction (*ad absurdum*)
> - a falsehood (*ad falsum* or even *ad impossibile*)
> - an implausibility or anomaly (*ad ridiculum* or *ad incommodum*)

The first of these is *reductio ad absurdum* in its strictest construction and the other two cases involve a rather wider and looser sense of the term. Some conditionals that instantiate this latter sort of situation are:

- If that's so, then I'm a monkey's uncle.
- If that is true, then pigs can fly.
- If he did that, then I'm the Shah of Persia.[13]

To get a deeper understanding (let it be definition (A)) of the meaning of reductio we turn to a printed modern dictionary of philosophy:

> a method of *indirect proof* in which one *deduces a contradiction from the contradictory of the proposition to be proven*. If one wishes to prove P, one supposes not-P (the contradictory of P) to be true. One deduces a contradiction from not-P, say *Q and not-Q*. Since a proposition which leads to a contradiction cannot be true, not-P is seen to be false. And since the relation between a proposition and its contradictory is such that the falsity of one requires the truth of the other, the falsity of not-P requires the truth of P.[14]

Apparently all reductio is indirect proof from a negative premise. Note too that here the contradiction deduced is a full self-contradiction, Q and –Q;[15] Also, the contradiction is deduced from the contradictory of the proposition to be proved, a method in some way similar to what we find in Euclid.[16] This view is elaborated in the next fuller definition (B):

> (1) A proposition P is proved by taking as a premiss the *negation of P* and demonstrating that, *in conjunction with previously established premisses or axioms,* a contradiction follows. Also known as *indirect proof.*

---

13   *The Internet Encyclopaedia of Philosophy* s.v. 'reductio ad absurdum' Nicholas Rescher.
14   *Dictionary of Philosophy and Religion*. W.L. Reese (ed.) (Sussex 1980) on 'reductio ad absurdum' (with my emphases).
15   Cf. *Enc.Brit.*, Macropedia vol. xi, 44 Table 5, 15. ed. 1977. It is not, as Hall says on Socrates (*Enc.Phil.* (P. Edwards (ed.) s.v. 'Dialectic'): if P implies –P, then –P is true (and P is false), though that too is a kind of reductio (cf., e.g., *Cambridge Dict.Phil.* and the *Internet Enc.Phil.* on 'reductio ad absurdum').
16   See n. 25.

(2) The negation of a proposition P is proved by taking P as a premiss and demonstrating that, in conjunction with previously established premisses or axioms, a contradiction follows.[17]

Importantly, in this account it is specified that among the premises are 'previously established premises or axioms'. We shall return to these below in the context of *endoxa*. This procedure is even more like some demonstrations in Euclid. Further, it is not clear what 'contradiction' is involved here. However, it seems that (1) would cover certain Euclidean demonstrations (using a negative premise, see below), while (2) would, as we shall see, cover Socratic reductios (dealing with and refuting positive suggestions). Reductio is then here seen as embracing both what is here called 'indirect' proof and Socratic reductio, i.e. both establishment and refutation It is noteworthy and surprising that only a species of reductio is here considered indirect proof.[18]

A third different and still wider definition (C) has it that 'reductio ad absurdum' refers to both the following argument forms:

(1) 'if A then B and not-B, therefore not-A' and 'if not-A then B and not-B, therefore A' ... known as *the method of indirect proof.* (2) inferring not-A having derived a *contradiction* from A, *and* inferring A having derived a contradiction from not-A.[19]

In (1) again only a species of reductio is viewed as indirect proof. But note that here it is different: it is not the schemata of e.g. geometrical demonstrations (proofs by contradiction) that are classified as 'indirect proof' but MTT arguments. They are different in that it is not a formal contradiction that is deduced but only one of a pair of contradictories, the other being a (previously accepted) background assumption (the minor). On the other hand, in (2) we recognize the procedures of definitions (A) and (B) above. If

---

17 *The Oxford Companion to Philosophy* Ted Honderich (ed.) (Oxford 1995) on 'reductio ad absurdum' (with my emphases).
18 Cf. *Routledge Enc.Phil.* vol. V, 808 s.v. 'reductio ad absurdum': 'when p is itself negative the rule is also called indirect proof'.
19 *The Cambridge Dictionary of Philosophy* Robert Audi (ed.) (Cambridge 1995) om 'reductio ad absurdum' (my emphases).

'deriving a contradiction' involves deriving a full and formal contradiction, Q and not-Q, then such a proof by contradiction (RAA), a species of reductio, is rather frequent in ordinary argumentation against proposed definitions (as in mathematical contexts). However, it could also be that what is meant is that, say, –P is deduced from P, or vice versa.[20] Notice that deductions are not here conceived as operating with added premises. Still, (2) answers more or less to (A) or (B) above. In (B) too, reductio is the wider term, but in (C) it embraces both MTT and refutatory and establishing arguments by contradiction. Hence (C) is the broadest definition of reductio so far.

In sum, according to (A) all *reductio* is indirect proof, while (B) and (C) agree that reductio embraces indirect proof as a part. On the other hand, the understanding of *indirect proof* in the first and the second definitions of reductio are not exactly identical but overlapping (Euclidean arguments) but are both at variance with the third (MTT). Hence we still need an adequate idea of what indirect proof means and covers, and how it relates to reductio.

(D) In a standard philosophical encyclopaedia we find it implied that all indirect proof is reductio:

> *Indirect proof* (reductio) … proves a proposition A by showing that the *denial of A together with accepted* propositions B1, B2, …, Bn leads to a contradiction. … rests on using premises that are far better established than the denial of A.[21]

This supports the Euclidean reading of the first and especially the second definition of reductio above. In (D), as in (A) and (B), indirect proof is a reductio with a *negative* premise.[22] However, in (C), MTT arguments are regarded as indirect proofs, and only such arguments. This leaves us with a vague idea of indirect proof. Add to this that reductio is either limited to indirect proof from a negative premise (A) or wider in different degrees (B) and (C).

---

20 See, e.g., *Penguin Dict.Phil.* (ed. Th. Mautner). London 1997, s.v. 'reductio ad absurdum.' Cf. n. 13 above.
21 *Enc. of Philosophy* (ed. P. Edwards), vol. 5, 66, s.v. 'indirect proof' (my emphases). Cf. the corresponding definition of 'reductio', ibid. 73.
22 Cf. also *Enc.Brit. Micropedia* vol. 8, 465, 15th ed. 1977.

This is a confusing and unsatisfactory situation still leaving the reader in the dark both as to what exactly reductio and indirect proof are and what their relation is. Apart from mere convention there seems to be no reason, for example, to deny the title of indirect proof to all cases of reductio, i.e. also to instances where the premise is positive. This too is an indirect proof of the contradictory of that same premise. Hence it is salutary to turn to Richard Robinson who in a Platonic context puts it concisely and unequivocally thus:

(1) *Every reductio is an indirect argument* (23), and
(2) *Every indirect argument is a reduction to a falsehood* (25) (and is in outline a destructive hypothetical syllogism (MTT)(24)),

the reason being that *indirect argument* covers both *refutation* (showing that the *thesis itself* leads to contradiction) and *establishment* of a thesis (showing that its *contradictory* leads to contradiction=so-called indirect proof).[23]

Hence, as for *reductio*, though we may say that reductio is *one form* of indirect argument, if we regard it solely as refutatory, we may say, as we shall say in the sequel, that it is *identical* with indirect argument, if we include the use of reductio in establishing theses.[24] It is a matter of argumentative strategy. Moreover, as we shall see, technically reductio embraces MTT and RAA. The table on the following page should clarify the scope and relations of elenchus, reductio and indirect proof.

---

[23] Robinson 1966: 23 (with my emphases): 'To *refute* a thesis *indirectly* is to *deduce a falsehood from that thesis*; in other words, to show that the thesis entails a consequence which is so repugnant to you that you would rather abandon the thesis than keep it and the consequence along with it. To *establish* a thesis *indirectly* is to *deduce a falsehood from the contradictory of that thesis*; in other words, to show that its contradictory is false because it entails an intolerable consequence. Reduction to absurdity is a case of indirect argument, for absurdity is one form of falsehood.'

[24] E.g., Arist. *An.Pr.* I, 17 37a9-12 is an example of the (attempted) *use of* reductio ad impossibile as indirect proof. (Reductio ad impossibile is a form of reductio ad absurdum.)

Elenchus (refutation)					
Indirect argument *Reductio* (with/without added premises (AP))				Direct argument	
(a) To self-contradiction (RAA, *via thesis*), cf. Zeno's arguments,[25] Ryle's 'strong reductio'[26]	(b) Ad absurdum (MTT)	(c) Ad contradictionem facti (MTT)	(d) To self-contradiction (RAA, *via contradictory of thesis* to establishment and proof), cf. Aristotle and Euclid. Ryle's 'weak reductio'[27]	(e) Refutation[28]	(f) Establishment
Formally nonsense[29]	Nonsense[30]	Empirically false[31]	Not only logical falsehoods		

[25] In the following, I restrict the modern technical label RAA to *reductio to formal inconsistency* in accordance with, e.g., Lemmon 1965 (see section VIII below for the formalization of the RAA). The RAA model bears a striking similarity to what seems to have been Zeno's method. He typically deduced inconsistent statements from the propositions he wanted to refute. E.g., if things are many, they must be both like and unlike (Plato, *Parm.* 127e). See G.E.L. Owen (1957-8'), Hussey 1997: 151-53 and Kneale & Kneale 1962: 7f. A number of Socratic MTT (Modus Tollendo Tollens) arguments may be (re)construed as RAA arguments, typically where it is demonstrated that the definiendum and definiens have logically inconsistent properties. See Section v (C) below for illustrating examples (*Chrm.* A and *Grg.* J). Regarding distribution of MTT versus RAA: App. A indicates that RAA is noticeable especially in *Euthyphro*, *Charmides*, *Laches* and *Meno*.

[26] Ryle's analysis is found in Ryle 1971: 197.

[27] Aristotle used reductio ad impossibile to validate other syllogistic figures by transposition into the first figure. Thus he denied the conclusion of, e.g., a Baroco syllogism and helped by its major deduced a contradiction of its minor and then inferred the original conclusion. Similarly, Euclid sometimes argues indirectly for a theorem by deducing from its contradictory consequences that conflict with axioms (or *endoxa*) or their consequences, e.g., the incommensurability of the diagonal (Ps.-Euc. *El.* 10.117), the infinity of prime numbers (Euc. *El.* 9.20) and the congruence of internate interior angles formed by a straight line falling on parallel lines (Euc. *El.* 1.37-

Among the types of reduction shown in the table (a-d), type (d) is only found *with,* whereas (a), (b) and (c) are found both *with* and without extra premises. So this amounts, in theory, to seven kinds of reductio. Apart from reductio we have direct refutation and of course direct proof. It remains to be seen how many we find in actual fact, what is the power of each and whether they differ in any significant way from each other.

Indirect arguments take the form of hypothetical syllogism (MTT or RAA), and are reductions to falsehood (absurdity or contradiction: of facts or, at the extreme, self-contradiction). Moreover, indirect arguments, as we shall see, are divided into those that require an *extra* premise (or more) and those that don't. *Direct* arguments do not use the thesis at all but are conducted by means of extra premises.[32]

IV. THE FORMS OF ELENCHUS
(DIRECT AND INDIRECT REFUTATION)

I now want to investigate the actual use of refutation in Plato's so-called earlier dialogues. By 'earlier dialogues' I mean *Apology, Crito, Euthyphro, Laches,*

---

40). Cf. Arist. *An.Pr.* 1.23, 41a23-37. It shows only that a theorem is true if axioms are true or that both are false. This is also called 'proof by contradiction'. But this is 'weak reductio' as opposed to 'strong reductio ad absurdum' according to Ryle. The latter is 'strong' in the sense that it deduces 'consequences which are inconsistent with each other or with the original proposition', not merely a belief inconsistent with other beliefs. It shows that the original proposition is not only false but nonsensical. It may be suggested that some Socratic arguments (e.g., *Prt.* B and *Grg.* J) could be construed similarly as indirectly aiming at positively *proving the contradictory* of an opponent's claim by showing that the latter in conjunction with an axiom (*endoxon*) leads to contradiction. Such arguments are not simply refutations but imply positive doctrines and always involve extra premises.

28 Cf. App. A with 26 direct refutations.
29 E.g., *Euphr.* B and C and *Chrm.* A, B and D (only the first is with extra premises. See App. A for identification of arguments).
30 E.g., *Lys.* B and C, *Prt.* A, and *Rep.* A are without, while *Rep.* B is with extra premises.
31 E.g., *Lys.* A, *Euphr.* C, *La.* A, and *Ap.* A are without, while *Ap.* B is with extra premises.
32 Vlastos 1994: 12 focuses on direct elenchus. He criticizes Robinson for thinking that indirect elenchus is more frequent and thinks that the logic of the two is substantially the same.

Charmides, Hippias Minor, Euthydemus, Lysis, Ion, Menexenus, Protagoras, Gorgias, Meno, Republic I and perhaps *Hippias Major* and *Alcibiades* I (of dubious autheticity). *Republic* I and *Meno* have been included as both contain useful illustrations of Socratic method. *Ion, Hippias Major, Euthydemus* and *Menexenus* have not been included in the analysis for lack of relevant or suitable material.[33]

Out of a total of 71 registered arguments (cf. Appendix A for argument identification) I have found *26 direct refutations* and *45 indirect* arguments including *34 without extra premises* (what I shall call 'Basic Reductios'). Apart from some odd occurrences in *Ap.* and *Cri.*, direct refutation is only evident in *H. Mi.*, the later part of *Prt.*, the early part of *Grg.*, and the later parts of *Rep.* I and *Alc.* I. Elsewhere, indirect refutation is preferred.[34] If one takes a developmental point of view, which is particularly controversial when dealing with the early dialogues, it seems tempting to assume that direct refutation is a comparatively late device.[35]

Basic Reductios are especially interesting as examples of arguments that derive their force entirely from their own elements and logical properties. The other indirect arguments rely partly on external material (so-called *endoxa*) the status of which needs examination. A further topic will be a clarification of what are the powers and the actual use of the different refutations. Aristotle famously claims that the elenchus does not prove anything (it is reasoning but not a scientific demonstration of truth).[36] Can this claim be

---

[33] *Menexenus* and *Euthydemus* are in different ways non-typical and *Hippias Major* is possibly non-genuine. I have however touched on *Alc.* I as it seems genuine to me. *Ion* has not been found argumentatively useful. In any case, I have not aimed at exhaustiveness.

[34] See App. A. These results should be compared with Robinson 1966 ch. 3 who counts 'roughly *thirty-nine arguments of which thirty-one seem to be indirect*. Thus about three-quarters of the arguments appear to be indirect. The fraction is greatest in *Charmides, Lysis, Euthydemus*, smallest in *Republic I* and *Protagoras*'. It should be noted that of the 39 arguments most are not identified and those that are are scattered about in his text. It will appear that I agree with Robinson in general but certainly not on details. My disagreement with Vlastos on what is 'Standard Elenchus' is manifest. Indirect refutation occurs in almost twice as many cases of the listed arguments.

[35] I assume that *Prt., Grg., H.Mi.* (dealing with sophists) and *Alc.* I are relatively late.

[36] Elenchus is reasoning (*SE* 171a2f) to the contradictory (ibid. 168a37f, 167a23f). But dialectic (using elenchi and proceeding by interrogation) does not *prove* anything (*SE* 172a13, *Top.* 105b30f), it does not get at truth and provide knowledge which is only reached in

upheld in a Socratic context? Perhaps the answer lies in a differentiation between various kinds of elenchus and not least in what counts as proof.

Let us take some simple and typical examples, first of *indirect refutation:*

Conversation with Menexenus in *Lysis* 211d-213d: What is friendly (*philon*)? the lover, the loved, or both?
(A) nothing that does not *reciprocate* love is friendly, but then you cannot be a friend of animals, wine, bodily exercises, etc. (too narrow)
(B) the *loved* is friendly no matter its attitude, but then the hated is an enemy, and then people may be loved by their enemies, and hated by their friends (too broad)
(C) the *lover* is friendly, but then the same consequences occur as above.

These three reductios are all *without help of extra premises* and of the form: P→Q, ¬Q ⊢ ¬P. The reductio is either to a clash with common experience (A) or simply logically absurd (B) and (C). The information resulting here is three negations of a definition (falsehoods). The arguments with Lysis and Menexenus that follow are similarly all indirect without help of extra premises.

The next refutation is *direct*:
Gorgias A. 458e3-461b, esp. 460a-c (direct):[37]

   1) the orator may *misuse* the art (459b3-5)   P
   2) but the orator must (also) *know about right and wrong* (460a3-4)
   3) a man who has *learnt* any craft is such as his knowledge has made him (460b4-5) *epagoge*
∴ 4) he who has learnt about justice is just (460b6-7) 3 cf. craft analogy
   5) the just man performs just actions (b8)
   6) he wishes to do them (c1-2)
∴ 7) he will never want to do injustice (c3-4) 6
∴ 8) the orator must be just (c4-5) 2,4
∴ 9) *the orator never wants to do injustice* (c5-6) 7,8   ¬P

   'epistemic reasoning' on demanding conditions (*An.Post.* 71b 17-25).
37 For a critique, see Waterfield 1994: 139 and Santas 1979: 150-55 (cf *H.Mi.* 368b, 369a on craft analogy). Robinson 1966: 29 and Vlastos 1983: 38 n. 29 both correctly consider this direct refutation.

54   ERIK OSTENFELD

This dubious argument is no reduction, as the thesis plays no role in the refutation. It is *direct* refutation of the implied injustice in misuse of the art rhetoric. The refutation depends entirely on premises extraneous to the thesis: (2) an admission by interlocutor and (3) an empirical generalization.

However, not all arguments are that easy to classify. The following two arguments are of *disputed* type:

Protagoras A. 330a3-332a1   (MTT)
  1) no parts of virtue resemble the others (330a3)   P
  2) justice exists (c1-2)
  3) justice is just (c7-d1)
  4) holiness exists (d2-5)
  5) holiness is holy (d5-e2)
 ∴ 6) holiness is not-just (i.e. unjust) (331a7-b1) 1,3,4
 ∴ 7) justice is not-holy (i.e. unholy) (331a8-b1) 1,2,5
  8) [this is not the case: absurd]
 ∴ 9) justice is more or less identical with holiness
       (333b5-6) 1,6-8 MTT   ¬P

Here, the refutandum plays a role in its own refutation. Hence it must be a case of reductio ad absurdum and an indirect argument.[38] The 'i.e.' in (6) and (7) is a Socratic 'assumption'. It could be queried whether (2)-(5) are added premises or deduced from (1), as seems likely. But this is a minor point here. The important question is to find a safe way of deciding whether an argument is direct or indirect. Let me finish with another disputed argument:

Euthyphro B. 9e-11a (RAA, AP)
  1) the pious is what is loved by all gods   P
     (dilemma: 'Is the pious loved by the gods because it is pious, or is it pious because it is loved by the gods?')
  2) we have in each case two different things: carried and carrying, led and leading, seen and seeing, and loved and loving (10a5-12)
  3) the carried is carried because it is being carried, the led is led because it is being led, the seen is seen because it is being seen (b1-6)

---

38 Cf. Taylor 1976: 110, who correctly sees it as a red. ad abs., whereas Vlastos 1994: 12 wrongly interprets it as direct.

∴ 4)   whenever something comes to be or undergoes something, it is a *thing* coming to be/being affected by something, *because of* the *process* of coming into being/affecting (c2-6) 3 *epagoge*

5)   what is loved is either a coming into being (*gignomenon*) or something affected (*paschon*) by something (c7-9)

∴ 6)   what is loved is loved *because* it is being loved [by an agent, i.e. a lover] (c10-13) 4,5 MP

now

7)   *the pious* is loved because it is [itself] pious (d6-8) but

∴ 8)   *the god-loved* is loved because it is loved by the gods (d9-10) 6

∴ 9)   [the pious and the godloved have diffent properties] 7,8

∴ 10)   the pious and what is godloved are different (d12-14) 9 cf. Leibniz' law

∴ 11)   [the pious is what is loved by all gods & the pious is not what is loved by all gods] 1, 10

∴ 12)   [the pious is not what is loved by all gods] 1,11   RAA   ¬P

Comments: The definiens is shown (in part by extra premises) to have other characteristics than the definiendum; it has another logic than the definiendum,[39] the ignoring of which leads to self-contradiction. Hence the refutation is again *indirect*. (4), an independent premise, is a generalisation from a series of examples in (2) and (3). From (4) and (5) we deduce a new case (6). Why is (7) agreed to? It seems that in the general view, divine acceptance is only an attribute, not the essence of the holy,[40] and the holy is not 'a coming into being' or 'something affected' requiring a process of such acceptance. Vlastos wrongly takes the argument to be a direct elenchus.[41]

---

39 Cf. *Charmides* (A) and *Gorgias* (J) analysed in Section v (c) below. *Chrm*. (B) and (D) and *Euphr*. (C) not dealt with here are other examples.

40 Cf. the status of *Chrm*. A2 below. Allen (1970) 41 refers to 'similar specimens of argument' in *Chrm*. 159c-160b, *Ap*. 27bc, *Euthyd*. 279c-280a, *La*. 192e-193d, *Prt*. 349e-350c. But *Ap*. 27bc (= *Ap*. C) and *Prt*. 349e-350c (= *Prt*. D) are direct in our analysis. However, he rightly sees that conditional priority of activities to properties is the issue.

41 Vlastos 1994: 12 and 1983: 39 n. 32.

The distinction between indirect and direct refutation

It has been claimed that it is in some cases difficult to judge whether a given argument is indirect or direct.[42] But a safe criterion of an indirect argument is that it is a reductio (ad absurdum or ad impossibile) of the thesis which is thus integral to the proof. *Indirect* arguments are, as Robinson noted, in the form of hypothetical syllogism (MTT or RAA), and are reductions to falsehood (absurdity or contradiction: of facts or, at the extreme, self-contradiction). Moreover, all arguments *from negative instance* or counter-example (many in the early definition dialogues) are indirect. They are basically falsification arguments that falsify the consequences of theses. *Direct* arguments, on the other hand, do not use the thesis at all but are conducted by means of external premises.[43]

So far we have considered the formal differences between indirect and direct refutation. Are the uses different? That is, does Socrates (Plato) use these two forms of refutation for different purposes? Vlastos claims not only that direct refutation is 'standard' refutation but also that it is used to prove Socrates' own moral theses.[44] Now a look at a table of conclusions of indirect and direct refutation (Appendix B)[45] is enough to correct the Vlastonian picture: *indirect refutation is 'standard'*, if quantity is a criterion (45:26), and only six of the ten theses mentioned by Vlastos[46] are in fact 'established' by direct refutation. Indirect refutation is used mainly to refute *definitions of moral terms*, whereas direct refutation focuses largely on *other moral theses* (e.g., 'listen to experts in morals', 'the deliberately criminal is the only good person', 'it is worse to do wrong', 'correction is better than licence', 'the beautiful is identical with the good').[47] Moreover, there is in fact no warrant

---

42 Robinson 1966: 23-24. He points, e.g., to disproof of a universal proposition 'all x is A' by negative instance 'this x is not A', which he classifies, rightly, as indirect, but supposes (less convincingly) could be interpreted as direct.

43 Vlastos 1994: 12 focuses on direct elenchus. He criticises Robinson for thinking that the indirect is more frequent and thinks that the logic of the two is substantially the same.

44 Vlastos 1994: 12.

45 Text in capitals signifies 'Basic Reductio'.

46 Vlastos 1994: 11-12.

47 See App. B. The refutations classified as direct are refutations even if the conclusion is not formulated in the negative. But the positive formulation helps incidentally to see that refutations can lead to constructive results.

for claiming that Socrates does not use *indirect* argument for *establishing* moral theses ('justice is holiness', 'temperance is wisdom', 'might is not right', 'life of pleasure is not attractive and not the good').

V. THE FORMS OF REDUCTIO: BASIC AND EXTENDED

Basic Reductios are especially interesting as examples of arguments that derive their force entirely from their own elements and logical properties. Other indirect arguments rely partly on external material (so-called *endoxa*) the status of which will be examined below. Let us begin with a case of Basic Reductio.

(a) Basic Reductios

Rep. A. 331e1-333e2 (MTT)
1) justice is to give what is owed (*opheilomenon*) (331e3-4)   P
2) justice is to give the appropriate (*prosekon*) (332c2)
3) medicine and cookery give appropriate to somebody/something (c5-d1)
∴ 4) justice is *benefiting friends, harming enemies (d2-9)* 2,3 analogy
5) in war (e5)
6) also in peace (332e13f)
7) useful for contracts (33a12-14)
8) for transaction of money (b10)
9) in depositing money (c7-10)
∴ 10) when the money is useless (d11-12) 9
∴ 11) *justice is useless* (e1-2) 10 (contrary to 4 with implicit *endoxon* that justice is useful)
∴ [12) justice is not benefiting friends, harming enemies] 4, 11 and *endoxon* MTT   ¬P

Comment: Although not formally a MTT[48] it can be said to be a MTT in outline. It is a case of leading a thesis to self-contradiction without added premises. Premises 5-9 are just explications of the definition and so far infer-

---

48 E.g., we miss a conditional premise.

ences of the meaning of (4). (10) is leading the way to the crucial consequent (11), which runs counter to the notion that justice is useful, a common background notion that cannot be disregarded, as an ancient Greek moral view must respect it on pain of being 'absurd'. That justice is useful is implied in (4). However, (11) is a non sequitur as it does not follow from (5) which has been 'forgotten' in the meantime. As appears from (3), the craft analogy plays a crucial role in formulating the thesis in what appears to be a hopeless way: virtue does not seem like medicine and cookery in offering a concrete product to certain groups of people.

Other examples are close at hand:

Rep. C. 334b8-334e5 (MTT)
1) friends/enemies are those that *seem* good/bad (334b8-c5)   P
   (reformulation)
∴ 2) mistakes make it possible that we should help the 'bad', harm the 'good' (c12-d1)   1
∴ 3) right to injure the innocent (d5-6)   2
4) [not right to injure the innocent, absurd, offending against moral intuition]

∴ 5) right to injure wrongdoers, help rightdoers (d9-11)   4
∴ 6) right to injure (mistaken bad) friends and help (mistaken good) enemies (d12-e5)   5
7) [not right to injure friends, contrary to original definition]
∴ 8) [justice is not benefiting those that *seem* good, etc.] 1,3,4,6,7
   MTT   ¬P

Comment: the reductio to a dilemma is here from P *without the help of added premises*.[49] It is implied by the reductio's focus on 'mistaking' that morality should involve knowledge. Notice that this MTT in two steps illustrates that some progress is made in spite of eventual failure. I have indicated that by numbering the premises continuously.

---

[49] Premise (1) is an interpretation or explanation of the initial definition.

Euthyphro C. 12d-13d (RAA)
    1. the pious is the part of justice or right (*dikaion*) concerned with care
       (*therapeia*) of the gods (12e6-8)   P
    2. care aims at good/benefit of object cared for (13b7-9) *epagoge*
    3. piety does not aim at making gods better (13c10)
∴ 4. [piety and care do not have the same properties] 2,3
∴ 5. [they are not identical] 4 Leibniz' Law
∴ 6. [piety is care & piety is not care] 1,5&I
∴ 5. piety is not care of the gods (13d3-4) 1,3,4 RAA   ¬P

Comment: this definition implies that piety makes the gods better which it obviously does not. Hence it is not care of gods. The argument if viewed as in outline a RAA is valid and sound. There are *no added* premises from outside. Premise (2), which is reached by induction, is basically an explication of the meaning of 'care' and thus need not be regarded as extraneous.

Here are two other basic reductios:

Euthyphro D. 13d-14b (MTT)
    1. piety is a service (*huperetike*) to the gods (13d8-9)   P
    2. service has a goal (13d9-e5) *epagoge*
∴ 3. piety produces many fine things (13e12) 1,2 analogy
    4. [this is not the case] (too wide)
∴ 5. [piety is not a service to the gods]   1,2,3,4 MTT   ¬P

Again, (2) is an explication of the definiens.

Apology A. 24b3-25c4 (MTT, contradiction of facts)
    1. Socrates corrupts the young (24c4, d4-5)   P
    2. all others improve them (24e-25a11) (absurd in itself and neglect of
       third possibility)
    3. the opposite is the case in all kinds of animal breeding (25a12-c1)
    4. [education is an art like animal breeding]   implicit analogy
    5. [Socrates does not corrupt the young]
       1,2,3,4 MTT   ¬P

This argument is in a certain sense valid but definitely *not* sound: one must object to (2) as absurd indeed and not a consequence of (1), but it has been admitted as such by the answerer, and is part of what Meletus means by (1). So we may explicate (2) as the conditional needed for a formal MTT: 'if Socrates corrupts the young, then he is the only one who does so' (P→Q). Moreover, (4), an unstated premise and assumption, is clearly objectionable. (4) looks like an extra premise (a background assumption), but it is not technically an extra premise in that it is part of (implied by) (3) which, qua minor premise (¬Q), is not in our context technically an extra premise.[50]

Basic Reductio (MTT or RAA) is used to *prove* 34 theses:[51] 27 of these theses are negations of a suggested definition, the remaining 7 concern particular persons (Socrates and Alcibiades) and 2 particular moral theses. If the interpretation of these arguments as Basic Reductios is correct, this list suggests that the main area of this particular form of refutation is definition, and, not surprisingly, that the information acquired in this way is negative (what x is not). However, even this modest information is not valueless, if it goes against expectations or prejudices. Thus it is interesting to be told, e.g., that 'temperance is not (self-)knowledge', or that 'piety is not service to the gods'. And importantly, what is established here about suggested definitions is not just inconsistency but truth/falsity. Based on contradiction without the help of extra premises, this is the *strongest possible proof* of a falsity one can get. In other cases, where there are only two (contradictory) possibilities, the information is of course bound to be more illuminating and helpful. E.g., the interrelations of the virtues (identity), 'Socrates does not corrupt the young', 'Alcibiades does not know about justice or usefulness', 'life of pleasure is not good'. Let us now look at an illustrating example of Extended Reductio.

---

50 The reason is that the minor premise in a MTT (a negative premise, the denial of the consequence of the conditional) is in general the background knowledge (often moral) that guards against 'absurdities', and, crucially, it is not part of the premises from which the absurdity is deduced. For practical reasons too (i.e. to facilitate the distinction between Basic Reductio and Extended Reductio) it is important to keep these premises apart from the minor premise. Note that on an RAA interpretation the minor of the corresponding MTT gets a role parallel to other premises (see, e.g., *Chrm.* A in section v (c) below).

51 See Appendix C.

(b) Extended Reductios (with extra premises)

Apology B. 25c5-26a7 (MTT, AP, contradiction of facts)
1) Socrates corrupts the young intentionally (25d6-8)   P
2) the bad harm their surroundings, the good improve them (25d1-5)
3) nobody wants to be harmed (universal desire for well-being) (25d7-10)
∴ 4) *if* Socrates corrupts others, he will likely himself be harmed, and he knows this (25e2-5) 2 UI[52]
∴ 5) [he does not want to be corrupted or harmed] 3 UI
∴ 6) either he does not corrupt, or he [at least] does not do so intentionally (25e6-26a2) 4,5 MTT   ¬P

Here (2) is an added premise (AP) from common experience from which together with the thesis (1) potential self-harm is deduced (4). Hence it is clear that the thesis must go, as the added premise is general and fundamental. (3), another extra premise, is the foundation of the minor (5) which is deduced from it.

Gorgias K. 497e-498c (MTT, AP), second argument (slightly abbreviated).
1) pleasure is identical with the good, pain with evil   P
2) the intelligent and brave are good, the fools and cowards are bad (497e4-6)
3) the intelligent can feel joy and pain (498a1-2)
4) the fools can feel joy and pain (497e6-498a1)
∴ 5) both the intelligent and the fools feel joy and pain to the same degree 3,4 (498a3-c2)
∴ 6) the good and bad feel joy and pain to the same degree (c4-5) 1,2,5
∴ 7) the good and bad are equally good and bad 1, 6 (e6-8)
8) [the good and bad are not equally good]
∴ 9) [pleasure is not identical with the good, etc.] 1,7,8 MTT   ¬P

Here (2), (3) and (4) are extra premises: (2) is a basic value statement, while (3) and (4) are common experience. The absurdity (7) is the joint result both of the extra premises and of the thesis which is what makes this a reductio. The extra premises are background knowledge that could not sensibly be

---

52 In general I use Copi's notation (Copi 1968) for logical rules (for quantification and inference). E.g., UI = universal instantiation and &I = conjunction introduction.

rejected. Hence they force us to reject the thesis as false. It should be added that this proof is clearly best reconstrued as a MTT and not a RAA. The strategy is not the frequent one that definiendum and definiens have different properties (cf., e.g., *Grg.* J and *Chrm.* A in section v (c) below). In outline we have a MTT: if (1) then (7), but not (7), hence not (1). The thesis together with the extra premises has a self-contradictory result.

The next argument reaches the same absurd conclusion in a slightly more complex way, using material partly from (K), partly new:

Gorgias L. 498d-499b (MTT, AP), 'repetition' of K
   1)   pleasure is identical with the good   P
   2)   the good are good because they have good in them, and the bad are bad because they have bad in them (498d2-4)
∴ 3)   the pleased have good in them (d4-6) 1,2 by analogy
∴ 4)   the pleased are good (d6-7) 2,3
∴ 5)   the pained have bad in them (d7-8) 1,2   by analogy
∴ 6)   the pained are bad (e1-2) 2,5
∴ 7)   the pleased are good and the pained are bad, the more so the better/worse (e2-5) 4,6 Conj.
   8)   the intelligent and brave, and fools and cowards, feel pleasure/pain equally, the latter maybe more (e5-8, cf. K5 above)
       Syllogizing (what has been agreed):
   9)   the intelligent and brave are good, fools and cowards are bad (499a1-4=K2 above)
  10)   the pleased are good, and the pained are bad (a4-5=7 above)
∴ 11)   the good and the bad feel pleasure/pain equally, the bad maybe more (a6-7) 8,9
∴ 12)   the bad are just as good as the good, maybe better 10,11 (a7-b1=K7 above)
  13)   [the bad are not just as good as the good, etc.]
∴ 14)   [pleasure is not identical with the good] 1,12,13 MTT   ¬P

The identical theses of (K) and (L) are both reduced to absurdity and the arguments are therefore clearly indirect.[53]

---

[53] Vlastos 1983: 38 n. 29 incorrectly thinks these arguments are direct.

Euthyphro A. 6e-8b (MTT, AP)
    1.   the pious is what is dear to the gods (6e11-7a1)   P
    2.   but gods are in discord about just/unjust and other values (7e1-5)
    3.   they like what seems just, fine and good, but hate what seems unjust, ugly and bad (e6-9)
∴ 4.   the same things are considered, e.g., just by some, unjust by others (7e10-8a3) 2
∴ 5.   the same things are loved and hated and are both god-loved and god-hated (8a4-6) 3,4
∴ 6.   the same things are both pious and impious (8a7-9) 1,5 absurd
    7.   [this is not the case]
∴ 8.   [pious is not what is dear to the gods] 1,6,7 MTT   ¬P

This is another clear case of added premises: (2) and (3) help to deduce an absurdity from the thesis. The added premises are founded on basic religious thought. So the definition must go. It is possible to interpret this argument as an RAA: the definiens and the definiendum have different properties; the god-loved is also god-hated, but the pious is not also not-pious, so they cannot be identical. However, the text lends itself best to the MTT interpretation offered above. It needs less filling in.

Republic B. 333e3-334b7 (MTT, AP)
    1)   cleverness in defence is combined with cleverness in attack (333e3-5)
    2)   cleverness in saving from disease combines with cleverness in inducing illness (e6-8)
    3)   cleverness in protecting army combines with 'stealing' enemy's plans (334a1-4)
∴ 4)   [cleverness is for opposites] 1,2,3 *epagoge*
∴ 5)   being clever at keeping involves being clever at stealing (a5-6) 4 UI

∴ 6)   if the just is clever at keeping money safe, he is also clever at stealing (334a7-8) 5
    7)   [but he *is* clever at keeping money] (*Rep.* A 9, above)
∴ 8)   the just is a sort of thief (a10) 6,7 MP
∴ 9)   justice is a kind of stealing (334b3-6) 8
       (contrary to implicit *endoxon* that justice is good)

64   ERIK OSTENFELD

∴ 10)   [justice is not benefiting friends, harming enemies]   *Rep*. A 4, B 9
and *endoxon* MTT

Comment: here the reductio, building on the 'result' of *Rep*. A9 (above), with the help of an (implicit) empirical generalization (4), leads to contradiction: justice, which is supposedly good (beneficial), is a kind of stealing. The contradiction is again also dependent on (assuming, not arguing for) the craft analogy in *Rep*. A1-4. *Aporia* follows (334b7f). The strategy here is to add to the already absurd conclusion of the previous argument (*Rep*. A) to generate an intolerable consequence.[54]

Extended Reductio (MTT or RAA) is used to prove eleven theses.[55] Of these nine are more or less explicit negated definitions (marked with x), while one is a concrete proposition. The percentage of *negated definitions* is thus even higher than in Basic Reductio which appeared to be used almost exclusively in refuting definition attempts. We shall see that direct refutation results in a high percentage of other conclusions.

(c) The distinction between Basic and Extended Reductio

While it will not seem to be a serious problem to decide which argument is direct and which is indirect, it can be a real problem to destinguish Basic Reductios from Extended Reductios. More specifically, to decide when an *endoxon* is 'extra' or 'added' and when it is just an *implication* of the refutandum or its derivations. In the latter case we do not have a true Extended Reductio (in our terminology). Take first a clear example of an Extended Reductio:

Protagoras B.   332a4-333b6 (indirect, MTT, AP)
   1)   [temperance and wisdom are distinct]   P
   2)   Folly (*aphrosyne*) exists (332a4)

---

54   The just is a sort of thief. Cf. the 'result' of the *H.Mi.* that the good person is a criminal. This is remarkably inconsistent with what we learn further on in the conversation with Polemarchus (in argument *Rep*. D). There the craftsman and the virtuous are said to be 'unable' to work for the opposite of their art. There seems to be an element of sophistry at play here.
55   See App. D.

3) Wisdom (*sophia*) is the contrary (a4-5)

4) right and advantageous action is temperate (a6-8)
5) people are temperate with temperance (a8-b1)
6) wrong action is not temperate but foolish (b1-3)
∴ 7) [right and wrong actions are opposites] 4,6
∴ 8) foolish behaviour is the opposite of temperate (b3-4) 4,6,7; cf. Arist. *Top.* 2
∴ 9) foolish behaviour is due to foolishness, temperate behaviour to temperance (b4-6) 5,8 UG
10) what is done with strength is done strongly, etc. (b6-c1)
∴ 11) what is done in same manner is done by same agency, and what is done in contrary manner is done by contrary agency (c1-3) 9,10 *epagoge*
12) something *kalon* exists (c3)
13) its contrary is the *aischron* (c4)
14) something *agathon* exists (c5)
15) its contrary is the *kakon* (c5-6)
16) there is high pitch (c6-7)
17) its contrary is low pitch (c7-8)
∴ 18) every contrary has one contrary only (c8-9) 12-17 *epagoge*
∴ 19) folly is contrary to temperance (e4-5) 8, 11
∴ 20) folly is contrary to both wisdom and temperance (332e5-333b4) 1,3,19 inconsistent with (18)
∴ 21) no distinction between temperance and wisdom (333b4-5) 1,20,18 MTT −P

The strategy is to show that if the distinctness of temperance and wisdom is asserted, then we end up with folly having two contraries. Arguably (4) and (6) are extra premises. However, 11 and 18 are clearly extra premises obtained by *epagoge*. (11) is referred to in *Top.* 2.9 under the term 'co-ordinates'). (18) is assumed in Aristotle, but not universally.[56] We have here a case of reductio that Aristotle would recognize. He typically assumed additional premises.[57]

---

56 Cf. Arist. *Top.* 2.7, 113a14f; 8.3, 158b27f.
57 Cf. R. Smith 1997: 119-20, also for references to Aristotle (*An.pr.* 1.44, 50a29-38, *An.post.* 1.26). See also Ross 1949: 36-37.

The contradiction arises because folly is shown, first, to be the natural opposite of wisdom, then, via right and wrong action, to be also the opposite of temperance. If we have to adhere to the principle that every contrary has one contrary only, then we would be inclined to say that folly (*aphrosyne*) must be ambiguous between e.g. 'stupidity' and 'senseless'. Socrates, however, prefers to collapse its 'two' contraries, temperance and wisdom. This raises the question why it is that (20) (or a special interpretation of it) and with it the thesis (1) must go and not that (18) must go. The answer here is simple: the thesis or the refutandum (1) is merely a postulate, while (18) is close to being a logical principle.

We may refer also to an example already cited in section v (b): *Gorgias* K 497e-498c (MTT, AP). It has clearly added premises that are extraneous to the thesis.

As final cases one may take *Euthyphro* (A) (cited in v (b)) where premises (2) and (3) cannot well be reduced to implications of 'what is dear to the gods', just as premises (4) and (5) of *Euthyphro* (B) (cited in section IV) which are even more clearly extraneous premises.

But let us now look at a few other examples with less obviously extra premises:

Protagoras A. 330a-332a1 (MTT, with added premises?) P
   1) no parts of virtue resemble the others (330a3)
   2) justice exists (c1-2)
   3) justice is just (c7-d1)
   4) holiness exists (d2-5)
   5) holiness is holy (d5-e2)
∴6) holiness is not-just (i.e. unjust) (331a7-b1) 1,3,4
∴7) justice is not-holy (i.e. unholy) (331a8-b1) 1,2,5
   8) [this is absurd]
∴9) justice is more or less identical with holiness (333b5-6) 1, 6-8
      MTT   ¬P

We have already met this argument in another context (section IV). The problem now is whether (2)-(5) are independent premises or really implied, as I shall assume, in (1) in that 'parts of virtue' implies the existence of the several virtues and their self-predication (whatever that exactly means). The next two arguments are RAA:

Gorgias J. 495d-497a (abbrev. RAA, with added premise?)
1. argument against hedonism
    1) pleasure is identical with flourishing, and pain is identical with being miserable   P
    2) flourishing is the opposite of being miserable (495e2-4)
    3) [opposites cannot be had by the same subject at the same time] (495e6-496b5) *epagoge*
    ∴4) you cannot have flourishing and being miserable together (496b5-7) 2,3
    ∴5) if something is had/lost together, it is not good/bad (flourishing/being miserable) (495c1-5) 4

but
    6) you may have pleasure and pain together (497a2-3)
    ∴7) [pleasure and flourishing do not have the same properties] 4,6
    ∴8) pleasure and flourishing are not identical (497a3-5) 7 Leibniz' Law
    ∴9) [pleasure is flourishing & pleasure is not flourishing, etc.] 1,8
    ∴10) [pleasure is not identical with flourishing, etc.] 1,9 RAA ¬P

This is a poor argument based on a superficial assumption that pleasure is not and flourishing is an opposite. (2) is presumably to be conceived of as a logical claim and itself derivable from (1) and as such not an independent proposition. (3) is strictly an unstated but argued-for premise, necessary for the argument. Being an independent (?) logical principle (illustrated by experience), it is the well-chosen back-breaker of the identity stated in the thesis.

The strategy of the argument is to show that the definiendum and the definiens have *different properties*. This could of course be done by MTT: 'if pleasure is identical with thriving, it cannot be had together with pain, but in fact it can. So pleasure is not identical with thriving'. However, this is not the easiest reading of this argument. The mechanism of this particular type of argument may be illustrated by one of many similar RAA arguments:

Charmides A. 159b-160d (abbrev. RAA, with added premises?)
    1) *sophrosyne* is quietness (159b5-6)   P
    2) *sophrosyne* is fine (c1-2)
    3) physical quietness is not fine (d4-7) *epagoge*
    4) psychical quietness is not fine either (160a8-b2) *epagoge*

∴ 5)   quietness is not fine (b3-6) 3,4 *epagoge*
∴ 6)   *sophrosyne* is not quietness (b7-9)   ¬P

The interesting premises here are the value statements (2)-(4). (2) is a basic value statement, while (3) and (4) are common experiences and 'implications' of quietness. By 'implications' (in quotes) I mean that they are not obviously independent premises, but on the other hand they (esp. perhaps (3) and (4)) are not strictly logically or conceptually implied either. *The definiendum is, once more, shown to have other properties than the definiens*. It is absurd to a Greek to accept a thesis that forces one to regard a virtue as not fine. Hence it seems tempting to regard this rather usual type of argument as a MTT: (a) if *sophrosyne* were quietness, it would not be fine, but (b) it *is* fine; hence (c) *sophrosyne* is not quietness. On this interpretation, (2) would be the minor premise (not 'extra' according to our terminology). However, (a) is not in the text, and there are arguably more unstated premises that may be brought out in an analysis that is fuller and also more accurate according to our modern standards:[58]

1)   *sophrosyne* is quietness   P
2)   *sophrosyne* is fine
3)   physical quietness is not fine
4)   psychical quietness is not fine either
∴ 5)   [quietness is not fine] 3,4 *epagoge*
∴ 6)   [*sophrosyne* and quietness do not have the same properties] 2,5
∴ 7)   [they are not identical] 6 cf. Leibniz' law of identity
∴ 8)   [*sophrosyne* is quietness & *sophrosyne* is not quietness] 1,7 & I
∴ 9)   *sophrosyne* is not quietness 1,8 RAA   ¬P

This is a modern way of formulating the reductio argument. Admittedly, the characteristic and required statement of a formal contradiction like (8) is never found in practice in Plato, as far as I am aware, although it is discussed in the *Phaedo* (100a, 101d). Socrates also leaves us to infer the rather obvious premise (6) and apparently regards the argument as ending with (7). In spite of this, the RAA model seems to reflect the present train of thought better than the MTT model would do alone, and it is probably not so modern after all: the RAA model bears a striking similarity to what seems to have been

---

58   See for instance E.J. Lemmon 1965: 26 and R. Smith 1997: 120. I am also indebted to a colleague, Dr Lars Bo Gundersen for advice here.

Zeno's method. He typically deduced inconsistent statements from the propositions he wanted to refute (cf. n. 25 above).

VI. THE STATUS OF THE PREMISES: *ENDOXA*

The framework of the elenchus is conversation (dialectic) with a partner who typically has made some claim to knowledge. The roles are divided: Socrates puts the questions and the partner has to answer seriously, giving his own personal opinion, not referring to public opinion. However, often premises of the elenchus are provided by common opinions (so-called *endoxa*) or established by various forms of induction. It is a debated question whether Socrates is committed to these (and other) premises. One would have thought that he must be, as he stresses that the conversation is a common enterprise.[59] On the other hand, there is also some emphasis on the test being of the respondent.[60] However, as we shall see, the two views on the conversation are entirely compatible.

In Xenophon's account Socrates argued διὰ τῶν μάλιστα ὁμολογουμένων 'by the things above all assented to' (*Mem.* 4.6.15), cf. Aristotle's τῶν ὑπαρχόντων ὡς ἐνδοξοτάτων 'most generally accepted in existence' (*SE* 183a38, b6).[61]

---

59 *Cri.* 49d5-e4, *Chrm.* 165b, 166cd, *Rep.* 335e7, 349a8. *Ap.* 38a4-5, *Men.* 77a. For Irwin 1975: 69f and Vlastos 1983 Socrates himself believes in these premises. Cf. Bolton 1993 133, with references: *Cri.* 46d-47a, 48b-49b, *Euphr.* 12b, *Prt.* 330bc, 333c7-9, *Grg.* 472bc, 474b, 504c.

60 E.g. *Euphr.* 11c1-7, *Prt.* 331a7-8. We should remember here the unevenness in philosophical maturity between Socrates and his respondent. Aristotle reminds us, two ignorants may engage in a peirastic encounter (*SE* 11). However, Socrates is not ignorant in the same sense as his counterpart. Frede 1992: 206 concludes that the argument is the respondent's. I think this is a simplification ignoring the evidence given in the previous note.

61 Cf. also ref. to Xenophon in Ryle 1971b 101. Interestingly, there is at least one case where the conversation is threatened by failure to base it on generally accepted grounds (*Rep.* 348d). A particularly striking example of an *endoxon* that governs the discussion is found e.g. in *Meno* 87d:
    (1) virtue is good (*endoxon*)
    (2) good is knowledge
  ∴ (3) virtue is knowledge (*hypothesis*)
  ∴ (4) virtue is teachable

Aristotle says that a dialectical premise is 'a question which is *endoxos* either to everyone, or to the majority, or to the wise or philosophers (and either to all of them, or to the majority, or to the best-known, so long as it is not paradoxical).' (*Top*. 104a8-11).[62] *Endoxa* (dialectical premises) would then mean something like: 'important/plausible opinions', serving as starting points for discussions.

Aristotle's collection of *endoxa* (dialectical propositions) at *Top*.1.10:
(1) the generally acceptable
(2) what is like it
(3) what contradicts the contraries of it
(4) what is in accordance with the recognized arts

On 2: it being generally thought that knowledge of contraries is the same, it seems also generally thought that perception of contraries is the same. Similarly, if there be one science of grammar in general opinion, there will be one science of flute-playing as well. On 3: if it is generally believed that one ought to do good to friends, then one ought not to harm them or one ought not to do good to enemies or one ought to do evil to enemies (contrary predicates belong to contrary subjects). Finally, on 4: people generally assent to what a doctor or a geometrician says. The concept of plausibility is wide enough to embrace both the plain man's knowledge and the expert's (provided it is not outrageous in the plain man's eyes).

In brief, *endoxa* are plausible/important views. In indirect refutation they are the views that are adduced to help deduce absurdity from the thesis. In direct refutation they are simply the premises from which the negation of the thesis is deduced.

Let us then see what are the actual *endoxa* employed in Extended Reductio and in Direct Refutatio (the minor premise of a MTT does not count here[63]). Looking at the attached list[64] (which is not exhaustive), we find *general logical* or *semi-logicial views* like: 'every contrary has one contrary

---

[62] Probably best understood not as a definition of *endoxos* but as a clarification about *what kinds of endoxa there are* (cf. W. Wilkinson (2005) on reductio ad absurdum). Cf. Bolton (1993) for the relevance of Aristotle.
[63] It is arguable that the minor premise in a MTT is an added premise of its own kind. See note 50 above.
[64] Appendix E.

only', 'what comes to be comes to be because of a process', or 'what is done in the same manner is done by the same agency', or 'skills are for opposites' (Socrates obtains this generalisation by induction, whereas Aristotle offers it ready as an *endoxon*), and that 'craftsmen cannot use their skill to opposite effects' (note: 'skills [themselves] are for opposites'). Then there are views on *psychology*, e.g., that 'confidence requires knowledge' or that 'nobody wants to be harmed', on *morals or meta-morals,* e.g., that 'justice is a standard for man', or that 'justice is either an ability or knowledge or both', or that 'the fine is either pleasant or useful or both' and on *politics*, e.g., that 'good government requires division of labour'. Furthermore we find *religious views* about the likes and dislikes of various gods and *views on* and *respect for expertise.*

Not all of this is 'common knowledge'. Some is specialist knowledge. Knowledge here includes a few value statements such as that 'justice is the standard for man/virtue of soul', though most 'moral' premises are quite general about the meaning of 'good' and 'virtue' (e.g. *Men.* 87de), 'fine' (e.g. *Grg.* C) or 'justice' (e.g. *Rep.* D, *Grg.* E).[65] Socrates argues from this, together with the refutandum or alone (in direct refutation). It seems highly unlikely that he does not share at least some of these views. They are either philosophical insights or widely believed or in some cases even self-evident conceptual necessities (e.g. 'action answers to passion'), and when Socrates uses them to demonstrate either his own views, or views in which he is interested, he needs premises he himself shares.[66] E.g., when Socrates directly refutes Meletus (*Ap.* C), he relies on their shared religious background. Moreover, when directly refuting Gorgias's statement that the orator may abuse his art and showing that the orator never wants to do injustice, Socrates relies as he is wont on the craft analogy which he is exploring. The same applies to the direct refutations of Hippias' bourgeois views on morality that there is a difference between deceitful and honest persons or of Thrasymachus' view that justice is the advantage of the infallible stronger. It seems unlikely that these interlocutors are just refuted out of their own mouth.

---

65 This is in distinction from 'the minor premise' which is typically of the extensional form 'x is fine' or 'x is good'. E.g. 'temperance is beneficial and good' (*Chrm.* 169b), 'temperance is fine' (*Chrm.* A and B), 'the brave are good' (*La.* C), 'the brave are fine' (*La.* B), 'the just is useful' (*Rep.* A).

66 Cf. n. 59.

This is at most only partly true. In so far as they share Socrates' general ideas such as virtue being like a craft, the conversation is a 'common enterprise'.

Are the *endoxa* used together with the thesis in Extended Reductio different from *endoxa* used on their own in Direct Refutation? First of all, not surprisingly the sheer *number* of *endoxa* is far greater in direct refutation than in indirect refutation (83:21).[67] Second, and more important, *endoxa* in indirect refutation tend to be more of a *logical* (sometimes self-evident) kind such as 'opposites cannot be had by same subject', 'every contrary has one contrary only', 'what is done in same manner is done by same agency, what is done in contrary manner is done by a contrary agent' and the like. Conversely, *endoxa* in direct refutation tend to be more *empirical*, although this is not without exceptions: 'every action has an object', 'the function of heat is to heat, the dry to dry', 'the just is good'. These are all *endoxa* in direct refutation.

What is the reason for this difference in the use of *endoxa*? Here one must recall the findings mentioned above: out of a total of 71 registered arguments we have found *26 direct refutations* and *45 indirect* arguments including *34 without extra premises* (what I call 'Basic Reductios'). This reflects Socrates' predominant interest in indirect refutation which relies on the thesis proposed for examination. Ideally, this kind of argument would appear most forceful, indeed irresistible, if restricted in its premises to that thesis (and we have 34 of that kind), but second-best if assisted by more or less self-evident supporting *endoxa* (we have 11 Extended reductios of which many are with such more or less self-evident *endoxa*). I am far from claiming that this is demonstrably the explanation why *endoxa* and their kinds are distributed as they are, but the evidence seems to point in the direction that Socrates wants to create the most compelling arguments.

Will Wilkinson,[68] supported by R. Smith, provides a useful summary of Aristotelian dialectic:

> We can better understand the function of *endoxa* within dialectical arguments if we understand the function they play in gymnastic dialectical exchanges. In any sort of dialectical argument, the questioner must

---

67 Indirect refutation here is limited to 11 Extended Refutations in contrast to 26 Direct Refutations.
68 Will Wilkinson (2005).

construct an argument out of the responses elicited from the answerer by means of questions admitting of yes or no answers. As Robin Smith notes, success in this task requires that the premises put forward by the questioner satisfy two criteria: (1) the answerer must accept the premises, and (2) the premises must logically imply the conclusion the questioner wishes to establish.[69] The point of the *Topics* seems to be, in large part, to provide a method for this very purpose - the purpose of coming up with premises that satisfy these two criteria.

This is of course Aristotle, but it does apply to much argument in the early Plato. It tries to delimit the kind of premise to be expected in a dialectical encounter, and so far the description is valid for Socratic conversation as well. However, something is missing: it does not reflect the engagement of Socrates, the questioner, which is at least sometimes evident when stress is put on the conversation as a '*common* search'. It is significant that such stress is especially evident in the context of *indirect* argumentation where we perhaps would least expect it.[70]

Vlastos, who in his analysis of the elenchus relies heavily on the extra premises and who would be expected to take an interest in *endoxa*, surprisingly disregards them.[71] Socrates, we learn, appeals neither to self-certifying truths nor to *endoxa* (in the Aristotelian sense). He is not interested in 'common beliefs', in spite of Xenophon's report, which seems supported by Aristotle's analysis of peirastic. The standard elenchus is the only final support for Socrates' moral doctrine. However, in this way Vlastos has created his own 'problem of the elenchus', i.e. how a method that can only show up inconsistencies can prove the falsity or truth of anything.

Vlastos' defence of his view is that Socrates wants the personal opinion of the respondent. But this is entirely consistent with adopting a common opinion. It should be noted that Vlastos acknowledges that respondents have no constraints on what they can say if only they believe it.[72] The rest of Vlastos' argument is largely rhetorical: how could we believe Xenophon who

---

69 Smith 1994: 145.
70 Cf. *Cri.* 49d5-e4, cf. 46b-48d, *Chrm.* 165b, 166cd, *Prt.* 330c, 333c7-9, *Men.* 77a3-4, *Rep.* 335e7.
71 Vlastos 1994: 13-16.
72 Vlastos 1994: 17 n. 51.

missed so much of the depth of Socrates?[73] Quite apart from Xenophon it is difficult to disregard Aristotle in this connection. He gives the fullest available account of dialectic, also of the procedure which it is very likely that Socrates, too, took advantage of.[74] Vlastos also argues that Socrates could never have derived his 'outrageous' views from common sense, and that it would be impossible to reform ethics on that basis.[75] However, the point of the elenchus is perhaps not so much to provoke common sense as provoke the misguided views of the interlocutor. Also, the things most intensely assented to seem to be general views that Socrates *needs* to support his own 'revision' of specific moral concepts. Hence, it is a matter of systematization rather than wholesale rejection of common ideas.

Bolton thinks, rightly but unsurprisingly, that *endoxa* are themselves products of everyday experience. He has done a great service, however, in clarifying how relevant Aristotelian dialectic is for our understanding of Socratic dialectic[76] and in uncovering the epistemological basis of that dialectic.[77] Bolton's project is to argue that we should understand what Socrates does in terms of Aristotle's account of *peirastic*. The premises of that are things that are most *endoxon*. According to Bolton this suggests that experience is the basic source of the theory-independent knowledge which the practitioner of *peirastic* does not disavow. This is also the authoritative base for *elenctic* enquiry.[78] In this he disagrees with Vlastos who does not think that Socrates is at all empirical or uses induction as normally understood.[79]

---

73 Vlastos 1994: 13-17.
74 Cf. Ostenfeld (1996) and above on Aristotle's collection of *endoxa*.
75 Vlastos refers to passages where Plato rejects the recommendations of the majority for the advice of the expert in specific situations (*La.* 184e, *Cri.* 46d-47d). However, as Bolton has argued (cf. nn. 76 and 79), this is beside the point. *Endoxa* are background 'knowledge', not practical solutions to present problems. Positively, it may be argued, as I do, that Socrates would actually need common opinion if he aimed at revision and systematization rather than wholesale rejection of common opinion.
76 Bolton (1993). For instance, Socrates refutes the principle or rule that one should follow common opinion in *Crito* 47a-48a by an elenchus based on common opinions (123-24). Socrates is against just following common opinion, not against arguing from common opinion.
77 Bolton (1999).
78 Bolton 1993: 150-51.
79 It could be objected that there are cases where Socrates refuses to accept common opinion as premises. However, this is only if the respondent does not himself sub-

As for the epistemic basis of the *endoxa* the answer obviously depends on what *endoxon* we choose. Consequently, I would be somewhat hesitant simply to ascribe logical and conceptual truths to experience.

Vlastos cannot, then, be right that there is no appeal to *endoxa*. The situation is immediately obvious from a glance at the appended table of *endoxa* (app. E). Nor is he right that there is no attempt to establish the premises. There are admittedly a few, important, undocumented premises ('the good life is the just life' (*Cri.*), 'justice is the standard for man' (*Rep.* 1), 'justice is either an ability or knowledge or both' (*H.Mi.*), 'if x is fine, it is either pleasant or useful or both' (*Grg.*) or 'there is something good, something bad and something neither good nor bad' (*Grg.*)). However, *endoxa* range from *logical* truths ('every contrary has one contrary only', 'opposites cannot be had by the same object') via *conceptual* trivialities ('the function of heat is to heat', 'flourishing is the opposite of being miserable', 'one is capable if one does what one wants', 'the courageous is confident', 'every action has object' and 'its passion correlates to act of agent') to *psychological* truths ('nobody wants to be harmed', 'the bad harm their surroundings, the good improve them'), *political* truths ('in a well-governed city labour is divided', 'injustice causes civil war'), other *empirical* truths ('no craftsman wants to outdo another craftsman', 'other rulers demand pay'), and further on to *religious* truths ('the gods are in discord about just/unjust, etc.', 'the pious is loved because it is pious') and *value* statements ('one should esteem the good opinions', 'we cannot live with a spoiled body or soul', 'doing injustice is uglier than suffering injustice'). For obvious reasons there is no need to 'document' logical truths and conceptual trivialities, although Socrates does illustrate such statements by examples, sometimes amounting to induction (*epagoge*).[80] As for psychological truths many of them at least are too evident to need more support than normal adult experience. The same seems to apply

---

scribe to it. Socrates does not want simply to 'follow common opinion'. In the *Crito* 47a-48a he argues for the view that we should not follow public opinion, but the expert. But this is not a rule of elenctic method. Hence it does not stipulate as a rule that the elenchus shall start from expert knowledge in the premises. On the contrary, the elenchus in *Crito* is itself based on common opinion.

80 E.g., 'whatever comes to be/undergoes is a thing coming to be/something affected ... because of the process of coming into being/of affecting' (*Euthyphro* B), 'what is done in the same manner is done by the same agency' etc. (*Prt.* B), 'every contrary has one contrary only' (*Prt.* B), 'no art is deficient' (*Rep.* F).

to a great many other empirical truths. However, such truths are nevertheless sometimes supported by examples (*epagoge*). It is only when we enter the area of religious matters and value statements that justification becomes difficult and rare. However, this does not mean that there is no arguing for *endoxa* generally.

The employment of *endoxa* in direct refutation obviously ensures that Socrates can positively prove something. Here it is not a matter of showing up inconsistencies except incidentally. However, also in indirect refutation, where *endoxa* are involved in extended refutation, the result may be constructive, if we have grounds to think that Socrates accepts the *endoxa* (e.g. 'the bad harm their surroundings' (*Ap.* B), 'what is done in the same way is done by same agency', 'every contrary has one contrary only' (*Prt.* B), etc.

VII. *HYPOTHESIS* AND *EPAGOGE* (*LACHES, LYSIS, CHARMIDES, MENO*)

Are *epagoge* and *hypothesis* not separate and independent tools of proof? According to Vlastos, The Standard Elenchus is the *only final support* for Socrates' moral doctrine: analogies from the crafts are a part of, *not external* to the elenchus.[81] However, it is not true that Socrates has no other foundation than elenchus for his moral views. E.g., the view that one should not care for the opinion of the many about what is just, fine, good and their opposites (*Cri.* 48a) is reached by analogy independently of elenchus, the notion of self-knowledge is attacked if not refuted by *epagoge* (*Chrm.* 167b-169b), and the idea that injustice is impotent is also reached by *epagoge* (*Rep.* I 351a-352d). One might also suggest that Socrates' mission of testing is itself dictated by something other than elenchus (*Ap.* 21a-23b), Elenchus is just one of several methods. Other methods are: *inductive analogy* (e.g. *La.* 184d-185a, *Cri.* 46b-48b, cf. esp. the *techne* analogy), *inductive generalizations* (e.g. *Ap.* 27b3-c3, *H.Mi.* 366c, 369a, *Grg.* 460c), *sorites* (*Men.* 87d-89a), *dilemma* (e.g., *Ap.* 27c10-28a2 and *Rep.* C), argument by *elimination* (e.g., *Grg.* 475b5-c9), *hypothetical* syllogism (cf. all MT and MP arguments), *categorical* syllogism

---

81 Vlastos 1994: 17 n. 51.

(among many *La.* 194d1-195a). All these methods are available for either refutation or direct proof. Moreover, the dialectician has psychological refutatory tools at his disposal such as scolding, irony or shaming. However, *elenchus* is an overreaching strategy that utilizes a variety of these instruments.[82]

Vlastos' understanding of Socratic *epagoge* is that *epagoge* is *not true induction*, i.e. probable inference from empirical data.[83] Rather, it is 'intuitive induction' where the instances exemplify rather than prove the meaning of a general statement.[84] However, this analysis is unsatisfying in disregarding the actual procedure as demonstrated in, e.g., *Chrm.* 159c-160b, *Euphr.* 10a5-c6, *H.Mi.* 373c-375c, *Rep.* 341c4-342c7, 349d-350a. Vlastos denies that probable inference which can be falsified by experience and confirmed empirically is involved. The examples exemplify, rather than prove, the general statement.[85] Particular negative instances are not considered as disconfirming.[86] However, to take just a few examples, Laches' first attempt at defining courage (as remaining at one's post) is considered as disconfirmed by a negative instance (*La.* 190e-191c), and in *Lysis* the first proposal of a definition is refuted by a counter-example (*Lys.* 212de). It may be objected that for Aristotle, the author of 'Socratic epagogic arguments', *epagoge* is generally from species to genus. This is also the level (of types) at which moral thinking operates for Socrates. In the *Laches* example just mentioned the subject is ways of fighting, not specific incidents. Science does not deal directly with individuals. But species are of course founded on and consist of individuals. This means that moral discourse is based, in the end, on experience and has an empirical foundation. It also means that experience can confirm or falsify in a Socratic conversation.

Vlastos also holds that adopting the hypothetical method inspired by geometry in the *Meno* to deal with moral issues is to 'scuttle the elenchus'.[87]

---

82 Cf., e.g., Robinson (1966) ch. 3, and Woodruff (1987).
83 Vlastos (1991) additional note 3.2 'Epagogic arguments'.
84 Vlastos (1991), esp. p. 268. Cf. *Enc.Brit. Macropaedia* 1977 (15th ed.) vol. 16, 1004 s.v. 'Socrates'. But see Lacey (1976) s.v. 'induction' (96). In intuitive induction, instances are psychological causes. This is definitely not what Socrates produces. A favourite, genuinely inductive (and empirical) strategy adopted by him is analogy.
85 Vlastos 1991: 268.
86 Vlastos 1991: 269.
87 Vlastos 1991: 123.

But the use of hypothesis in the *Meno* mainly differs from the procedure of the early dialogues in taking its departure from 'a higher hypothesis' and would not in itself result in a transformation of argument into demonstration of 'necessary consequences of the axioms of the system'.[88] There are so far no axioms. The *Phaedo* (100a, 101de), which develops this new method, assures us of that.

Hypothesis is well integrated in the elenchus. It is in fact its most important element,[89] *epagoge* being another. This is not to say that both cannot be used independently of elenchus. But in the *Meno*, we witness the hypothetical method developing out of its use *in* elenchus into a method of its own, fully illustrated in the *Phaedo*. Here, and in *Republic*, elenchus has itself become an element of hypothesis (e.g., *Phd.* 92a-95a (refutation of the harmony of soul) and *Rep.* 532ab and 534b-d (on method)). To put it more simply, we see a development from hypothesis in elenchus to elenchus in hypothesis.

VIII. CONCLUSIONS

(a) Patterns of Argumentation

Is there then one or more patterns of argumentation to be found in the early dialogues? Vlastos has an answer: the argument pattern is mostly direct refutation which is used to establish doctrines, not merely to expose contradiction in interlocutor's belief-set. This is the only possible potential of the indirect elenchus. Socrates is not committed to the premises of indirect elenchus from which negation of thesis is deduced.[90] Robinson's indirect elenchus is 'not in the texts'.[91] Concerning indirect elenchus, Vlastos claims that 'in point of logic there is no substantial difference from Standard Elenchus'.[92]

---

88 Vlastos 1991: 124.
89 Cf. Ostenfeld (1999).
90 Vlastos 1983: 38-39.
91 Vlastos 1994: 3.
92 Vlastos 1994: 12 n. 34.

It must now be demonstrated that the logic of indirect and direct proof is substantially different. As Vlastos himself is well aware, in indirect proof the refutandum is part of its own refutation as opposed to direct proof. Secondly, reductio is a *proof of an inconsistency either internal and formal or with other beliefs*, whereas direct proof is *proof of the negation of the refutandum*. So far we have registered **four patterns of argument:**

(1) **Basic Reductio**
    1) p
    2) p→q
    3) ¬q
  ∴4) ¬p 1-3 MTT

Examples are: *Ap.* A, *La.* A-C and *Rep.*A and C. The interlocutor realizes that p clashes with common sense or general experience. P implies q, but we must also hold ¬q. As the latter is felt more basic p must go.

(2) **Extended Reductio**
    1) p
    2) r or r, s
    3) [p, r] or [p, r, s]→q
    4) ¬q
  ∴5) ¬p 1-4 MTT

The absurdity or impossibility is here derived from p and one or more additional premises. This is what I have described above as the fact that p 'with the help of extra premises' leads to contradiction (q and ¬q). The interlocutor's claim p and additional premise(s) are shown to be inconsistent with, e.g., general psychology (e.g., 'nobody wants to be harmed' *Ap.* B), common sense (e.g., good and bad are not equally good' *Grg.* K) or logic (e.g., 'the same things are not both pious and impious' *Euphr.* A, 'every contrary has one contrary only' *Prt.* B, 'the just is not a sort of thief' *Rep.* B). The additional premises are more basic and allow us to skip p. Note that the additional premises have a different status from the minor ¬q.

(3) **RAA**
    1) a=b

2) Fa
3) ¬Fb
4) [if a=b, then a and b have the same properties (Leibniz' law)]
5) [if a and b do not have the same properties, then a and b are not identical] 4 MT
6) [a and b do not have the same properties] 2,3
7) [a and b are not identical] 5,6 MP
8) [a is identical with b and a is not identical with b] 1,7 &I
∴9) a and b are not identical 1,8 RAA

Added premises are in square brackets. This is a reductio format found in modern logic text-books[93] and suited to formalizing many Socratic arguments, e.g. refutation of definition proposals (e.g., *Chrm*. A where some missing premises have been supplied). Depending on whether premises (2) and/or (3) are conceived as added premises or not we find this type of argument in either Extended Reductio or Basic Reductio. Examples are: *Chrm*. A and B, *Grg*. J, *La*. B, and *Euphr*. C. The interlocutor is shown to be inconsistent in merely uttering p (Strong Reductio). RAA shows similarity with Zenonian dialectic. Vlastos holds that there is no connection: refutands in Zeno's paradoxes are 'unasserted counterfactuals'.[94] It is difficult to find confirmation for this view in the sources. It appears from Plato's *Parmenides* (127d-128d) that the refutand (the *hypothesis*), pluralism, was categorically asserted by common sense and by the opponents of Parmenides.

(4) Direct Refutation
1) p
2) r, s
3) [r, s]→ ¬p
∴4) ¬p 2,3 MPP (modus ponendo ponens)

Here p does not at all enter the proof as a premise. It is only negated by it. Hence, no inconsistency is proved of p. What is proved is a negation of p entirely on the basis of common notions. However, in so far as the interlocutor agrees to both p and the common notions from which the contradiction of p is deduced *he* is contradicting himself. This must be declared a consid-

---

93 E.g., Lemmon (1965).
94 Vlastos 1994: 2 and 8-10.

erable difference in point of logic. Examples would be the proofs *Ap*. C (that Socrates does believe in gods) or *H.Mi*. B (that the deliberately failing person is better than one who fails undeliberately) or *Gorg*. A (that the orator never wants to do injustice).

(b) Aim, Scope and Value of Elenchus

Let us summarize by asking the following three questions:
1) What is the consequence of the fact that a Socratic refutation may be either indirect or direct? Does Socrates, e.g., use indirect elenchus *in different contexts* from and/or *on other subjects* than direct elenchus?
2) What is the consequence of the various kinds of *premises* in Socratic refutation? Is Socrates *committed* to any of these?
3) What is the *potential* and value of the different kinds of proof`? Are they merely destructive or is there a constructive potential?

First, then, does Socrates use indirect and direct refutations in different contexts and on different issues? This can be answered with a clear Yes. A look at a table of conclusions of indirect and direct refutations (appendix B) shows that definition issues are uniformly decided by indirect argument,[95] whereas other propositions are dealt with largely (with a few exceptions) by direct refutation. An explanation of this distribution may be that definitions are identity statements that can be queried simply by showing that definiendum and definiens do not share properties – without resort to external premises. A wrong definition defeats itself as it contains a self-contradiction.

Second, this outcome is connected with a matter of substance: the different *status of the premises* and their acceptance. Basic Reductios by definition have premises that are accepted only by the interlocutor. A special problem concerns the status of the minor premise of the MTT of the indirect refutation. The absurdity is not deduced from that premise. It is confronted with it. It is the responsibility of the interlocutor. *He* wants to uphold a basic assumption, such as that virtue is fine, that virtue is good or that the pious is loved because it is pious, at the expense of giving up a suggested definition.

---

[95] The few examples of non-definitional arguments that are indirect are: *Ap*. A and B, *Cri*. B, *Prt*. A and C, *Grg*. I and *Alc*. A-C.

But the minor premise of a MTT seems generally to be Socratic too (e.g., *Ap.* A, *Euphr.* D, *Lys.* A-C, *Prt.* A). We have seen (n. 59) how Socrates stresses that the search is 'common', particularly in the context of indirect argumentation.

Direct refutation, however, relies on external premises that must also be acceptable to Socrates, *if* he is to prove his own doctrines as he normally does in direct refutation (e.g., proofs *Grg.* B2 that 'orators have no power' and *Grg.* C that 'suffering injustice is preferable to doing injustice' rely on a number of Socratic premises). Extended Reductio has a mix of premises of both kinds, external and internal (e.g. *Euphr.* A and B, *Rep.* B).[96]

Third, what is the potential of the different kinds of proofs? Destructive or constructive? Do the *endoxa* entering the proofs detract from the value and strength of these proofs? *Endoxa* are only one factor affecting the strength of the proofs. Another is of course the very structure of the proofs themselves. Obviously, the strength of reductios relying solely on the refutandum are bound to be stronger than Extended Reductios and direct refutations relying partly and wholly respectively on *endoxa*. As said earlier, nothing can be stronger than a proof of inconsistency, whereas proofs depending on *endoxa* derive their strength from the strength (epistemic value) of the premises (the *endoxa*). And, as we have seen, these premises are of varying strength, some self-evidently true, others supported by empirical evidence of various kinds.

Clearly, the conclusions of a reductio are by definition negative. However, this does not mean that reductios lead to uninformative conclusions. E.g., when the thesis is itself negative the conclusion is equivalent to a positive proposition. E.g., 'holiness is justice' (*Prt.* A). Where there are only two possibilities (contradictories), which both make sense, the negative part of the pair is informative. E.g., 'Socrates does not corrupt', 'Socrates should not escape', 'Alcibiades does not know about justice'. Or 'the life of pleasure is not identical with the good'. The latter is in fact an important ethical doctrine denying another important ethical doctrine. So even Basic Reductio may lead to or imply positive insights, and when such a conclusion is reached by a Basic Reductio it is *the safest possible*, not relying on anything but the thesis stating the opposite (wrong) view.

---

96 In general, it is important to distinguish between agreement to premises and agreement to a derivation. Common assent to derivation is required in all refutations.

While indirect refutation is by definition negative, direct refutation need not be negative:[97] by disproving Polus' sophistic view that it is better to injure people than be injured by them, Socrates indirectly proves his own view that suffering injustice is better. And in refuting Meletus' claim that Socrates is an atheist, he proves that he does believe in gods.

Finally, according to Vlastos, elenchus in *Meno* 81c-82a is only used to correct mistakes, and it has a purely negative use in middle dialogues (*Phd.* 85c), neither discovery nor proof. The method of discovery in *Meno* is maieutic: the slave recovering knowledge from himself (85d).[98] I have grave reservations about most of this: first, the reference to *Phd.* 85c, where Simmias is briefly advocating elenchus, is hardly proof of its negative use by Socrates in that dialogue, and a fortiori of the general claim of negative use in middle dialogues. Vlastos seems right in so far as the elenchi are now generally indirect and so far negative. However, we have already seen that a negative use does not by itself mean that no positive results are produced.[99]

(c) Summing up

On the basis of a registration of the arguments to be found in the early dialogues,[100] the following results have been reached:

(A) We have found that Vlastos must be mistaken on several important points and that Robinson was much more right than his later critics have realized:

(1) Firstly, a closer and more systematic examination of the dialogues confirms that the overwhelming amount of refutation is indirect (almost twice

---

97 13 out of 26 conclusions of direct refutations are positive (see appendix B).
98 Vlastos 1994: 5, cf. 1991: ch. 4 n. 54
99 Other examples could be *Meno* 82e-84a (what is not the side of a double square), *Phd.* 92a-95a (against the soul conceived as a harmony), *Smp.* 199b-201d (*eros* is not beautiful), *Rep.* 534b8-d1, cf. 532a5-b2, 511b3-c2 (leading to the Good).
100 Of course the individual analyses are, and will always be, a matter of interpretation. However, the cumulative analysis is not, as far as I can see, to be doubted.

the number of direct refutation 45:26).[101] Hence, Vlastos' critique that Robinson's indirect elenchus is 'not in the texts'[102] is unwarranted.

(2) Secondly, it is notable that indirect refutation is used mainly to refute *definitions of moral terms*, whereas direct refutation focuses largely on *other positive moral theses* (e.g., 'listen to experts in morals', 'the deliberatively criminal is the only good person', 'it is worse to do wrong', 'correction is better than licence', 'the beautiful is identical with the good').[103]

However, there is no warrant for claiming that Socrates does not use indirect argument too for *establishing* moral theses ('justice is holiness', 'temperance is wisdom', 'might is not right', 'life of pleasure is not attractive and not the good'). This relates to Socrates' commitment to the arguments and the minor premises.

(3) Thirdly, contrary to what Vlastos claims, there is a clear dependence on *endoxa* in direct refutation and in Extended Reductio. Vlastos claims that none of the indirect arguments do not rely on external premises, where the analyses of the present study show that of 45 indirect refutations 34 are conducted without such support (Basic Reductio).

(4) Fourthly, we have noted a methodological development from *hypothesis* in elenchus to elenchus in *hypothesis*.

(B) We have also countered the prevalent rather despairing attitude as to finding a consistent method in Socrates' argumentation with a demonstration that we do have at least four logically distinct patterns in the texts that deserve the title 'elenchus'.

Hence what has been offered is an empirically more well-founded picture of what Socrates' procedure in his conversations is. At the same time this is a defence of R. Robinson against the still dominant influence of G. Vlastos

101 Only six of the ten theses mentioned by Vlastos 1994: 11-12 are in fact 'established' by direct refutation.
102 Vlastos 1994: 3.
103 The refutations listed as direct refutations are refutations even if the conclusion is not formulated in the negative. But the positive formulation helps incidentally to see that refutations can lead to constructive results.

and also a counter-argument against the recent scepticism of, e.g., Brickhouse/Smith.

BIBLIOGRAPHY

Allen, R.E. *Plato's Euthyphro and the Earlier Theory of Forms* (London 1970).
Benson, H. 'Problems with Socratic Method' in Scott (2002) 101-13.
Bolton, R. 'Aristotle's Account of the Socratic Elenchus' *Oxford Studies in Ancient Philosophy* (*OSAP*) 11 (Oxford 1993) 121-52.
Bolton, R. 'The Epistemological Basis of Aristotelian Dialectic' in *From Puzzles to Principles? Essays on Aristotle's Dialectics* (1999) (ed. M. Sim) 57-106.
Brickhouse, Th. and Smith, N.D. *Plato's Socrates* (Oxford 1994).
Brickhouse, Th.C. and Smith, N.D. 'The Socratic Elenchos?' in Scott (2002) 145-57.
The Cambridge Dictionary of Philosophy (ed. R. Audi) (Cambridge 1995).
Carpenter, M. and Polansky, R.M. 'Variety of Socratic Elenchi' in Scott (2002) 89-100.
Copi, I.M. *Introduction to Logic* third ed. (New York 1968).
A Dictionary of Philosophy (ed. A.R. Lacey) (London 1976).
Dictionary of Philosophy and Religion (ed. W.L. Reese) (Sussex 1980).
Encyclopaedia of Philosophy I-VIII (ed. P. Edwards) (London 1967).
Encyclopedia Britannica, Macropedia 15th ed. (London 1977).
Frede, M. 'Platonic Arguments and the Dialogue Form' *OSAP* Suppl. vol. 1992) (eds. J.C. Klagge & N.D. Smith) 201-19.
Hussey, E. 'Pythagoreans and Eleatics' in Taylor (ed.) (1997) 128-74.
The Internet Encyclopaedia of Philosophy.
Irwin, T. *Plato's Moral Theory, The Early and Middle Dialogues* (Oxford 1975).
Kneale, W. and Kneale, M. *The Development of Logic* (Oxford 1962).
Lemmon, E.J. *Beginning Logic* (London 1965).
Ostenfeld, E.N. 'Socrates' Argumentation Strategies and Aristotle's *Topics* and *Sophistical Refutations*' *Methexis* 9 (1996) 43-57.
Ostenfeld, E.N. 'Hypothetical Method in the *Charmides* and in the Elenchus' *C&M* 50 (1999) 67-80.

Owen, G.E.L. 'Zeno and the Mathematicians' *Proceedings of the Aristotelian Society (PAS)* 58 (1957-58) 199-222.
The Oxford Companion to Philosophy (ed. T. Honderich) (Oxford 1995).
Penguin Dictionary of Philosophy (ed. Th. Mautner) (London 1997).
Robinson, R. *Plato's Earlier Dialectic* (Oxford 1966) (corr. repr. of 2nd ed. 1953)
Ross, W. D. *Aristotle* (London 1949) (5th ed.).
Routledge Encyclopedia of Philosophy I-x (ed. E. Craig) (London 1998).
Ryle, G. 'Philosophical Arguments' (Inaugural Lecture 1945) in *Collected Papers* vol. I (1971a) 194-211.
Ryle, G. 'Academy and Dialectic' in *Collected Papers* vol. I (1971b) 89-115.
Santas, G.X. *Socrates* (London 1979).
Scott, G.A. (ed.) *Does Socrates Have a Method* (Philadelphia 2002).
Sim, M. (ed.) *From Puzzles to Principles? Essays on Aristotle's Dialectics* (Lanham 1999).
Smith, R. 'Dialectic and the Syllogism' *Ancient Philosophy* 14 (1994, special issue) 133-51.
Smith, R. *Aristotle: Topics, Books I and VIII* (Oxford 1997).
Taylor, C.C.W. *Plato: Protagoras* (Oxford 1976) .
Taylor, C.C.W. (ed.) *From the Beginning to Plato* (Routledge History of Philosophy, I) (London 1997).
Vlastos, G. 'The Socratic Elenchus' *OSAP* I (Oxford 1983).
Vlastos, G. *Socrates: Ironist and Moral Philosopher* (Cambridge 1991).
Vlastos, G. *Socratic Studies* (ed. M. Burnyeat) (Cambridge 1994).
Waterfield, R. *Plato, Gorgias* (Oxford 1994).
Wilkinson, W. 'Enlightenment: Aristotle on Dialectic and Demonstration' Internet article (2005) at www.enlightenment.supersaturated.com.
Woodruff, P. 'Expert Knowledge in the *Apology* and the *Laches*: What a General Needs to Know' *Proceedings of the Boston Area Colloquium in Ancient Philosophy* III (ed. J. Cleary 1987) 79-115.

APPENDIX A: OVERVIEW OF ARGUMENT TYPES

45 (34 B) indirect, 26 direct arguments (asterisk * = the argument is dealt with in this paper, MTT = modus tollendo tollens, RAA = reductio ad absurdum (Lemmon), B = Basic Reductio, AP = added premises = Extended Reductio, non-def. = non-definitory conclusion).

Apology
- A. indirect, MTT, B (24b3-25c4) non-def.*
- B. indirect, MTT, AP (25c5-26a7) non-def.*
- C. DIRECT (26a8-28a1)

Crito
- A. DIRECT (47a2-48a10)
- B. indirect, MTT, B (Laws: 48d-53a) non-def.

Euthyphro
- A. indirect, MTT, AP (7a-8b)*
- B. indirect, RAA, AP (9e-11a)*
- C. indirect, RAA, B (12d-13d)*
- D. indirect, MTT, B (13d-14b)*
- E. indirect, MTT, AP (14c-15c)

Charmides
- A. indirect, RAA, B (159b5-160d4)*
- B. indirect, RAA, B (160e2-161b4)
- C. indirect, MTT, AP (161b4-162b11)
- D. indirect, RAA, B (163d7-164d3)
- E. indirect, MTT, B (164d3-166e3)
- F. indirect, MTT, B (166e4-169c2)
- G. indirect, MTT, B (170a6-172c3)
- H. indirect, MTT, B (172c6-175a8)

Laches
- A. indirect, MTT, B (190d-192b)
- B. indirect, RAA, B (192b-193d)
- C. indirect, RAA, B (195a-199e)

Hippias Minor
- A. DIRECT (364c-369b)
- B. DIRECT (*epagoge*, analogy) (373c-375d)
- C. DIRECT (analogy) (375d-376c)

Lysis
- A. indirect, MTT, B (212d3-e5)*
- B. indirect, MTT, B (212e6-213b5)*
- C. indirect, MTT, B (213b5-213c5)*
- D. indirect, RAA, B (214b2-215c1)
- E. indirect, MTT, B (216a4-216b9)
- F. indirect, MTT, B (216e7-220e6)
- G. indirect, MTT, B (221e3-222e7)

Protagoras
- A. indirect, MTT, B (330a3-332a1) non-def.*
- B. indirect, MTT, AP (332a4-333b6)*
- C. indirect, MTT, B frg. (333d-334c) non-def.
- D. DIRECT (349d-351b2)
- E. DIRECT (351b3-357e8)
- F. DIRECT (358a5-360e5)

Gorgias
- A. DIRECT (458e3-461b)*
- B. B1) indirect, RAA, B (466a4-467c4)
  B2) DIRECT (467c5-468e5)
- C. DIRECT (474c5-475e6)
- D. DIRECT (476a-477a)
- E. DIRECT (477a8-477e6)
- F. DIRECT (477e7-479a4)
- G. DIRECT (488b2-489b6)
- H. DIRECT (489d5-491a3)
- I. indirect, MTT, B (492c4-494e8) non-def.
- J. indirect, RAA, AP (495d-497a)*
- K. indirect, MTT, AP (497e-498c)*
- L. indirect, MTT, AP (repet.) (498d-499b)*
- M. DIRECT (499b-505b)

Meno
- A. indirect, RAA, B (72e-73c)
- B. indirect, RAA, B (73d-77a)
- C. indirect, MTT, B (77b-78b)
- D. indirect, RAA, B (78b-79e)

Republic I
- A. indirect, MTT, B (331e1-333e2)*
- B. indirect, MTT, AP (333e3-334b7)*
- C. indirect, MTT, B (334b8-334e5)*
- D. DIRECT (334e5-335e6)
- E. indirect, RAA, AP (338c-340a2)
- F. DIRECT (341a-342e)
- G. DIRECT (345e-347d)
- H. DIRECT (348b-350d)
- I. DIRECT (*epagoge*) (352a-352d)
- J. DIRECT (352d-354a)

Alcibiades I
- A. indirect, MTT, B (106c4-110d4) non-def.
- B. indirect, MTT, B (110d5-112d10) non-def.
- C. indirect, MTT, B (113d9-114a6) non-def.
- D. DIRECT (115a1-116b1)
- E. DIRECT (116b2-116c6)
- F. DIRECT (116c7-116d7)

APPENDIX B: CONCLUSIONS OF ELENCHI

(Basic Reductio Indicated by CAPITALS)

Indirect (reductio) 45 (Basic 34)	Direct 26
SOCRATES DOES NOT CORRUPT *Ap*. A	
Socrates does not corrupt intentionally *Ap*. B	
	Socrates does believe in gods *Ap*. C
	Not listen to many, but to expert in morals *Cri*. A
SOCRATES SHOULD NOT ESCAPE *Cri*. B	
Pious is not what is dear to the gods *Euphr*. A	
Pious is not what is loved by all the gods *Euphr*. B	
PIETY IS NOT CARE OF THE GODS *Euphr*. C	
PIETY IS NOT SERVICE TO THE GODS *Euphr*. D	
Pious is not knowledge of how to sacrifice *Euphr*. E	
TEMPERANCE IS NOT QUIETNESS *Chrm*. A	
TEMPERANCE IS NOT MODESTY *Chrm*. B	
Temperance is not doing your own *Chrm*. C	
TEMPERANCE IS NOT DOING GOOD THINGS *Chrm*. D	
TEMPERANCE IS NOT SELF-KNOWLEDGE *Chrm*. E	
TEMPERANCE IS NOT SELF-KNOWLEDGE *Chrm*. F	
TEMPERANCE IS NOT SELF-KNOWLEDGE *Chrm*. G	
TEMPERANCE IS NOT LIVING SCIENTIFICALLY *Chrm*. H	
BRAVERY IS NOT REMAINING AT ONE'S POST *La*. A	
BRAVERY IS NOT ENDURANCE *La*. B	
BRAVERY IS NOT KNOWLEDGE OF FEARFUL AND HOPEFUL *La*. C	
	The same is deceitful and truthful in all fields *H.Mi*. A
	Odysseus and Achilles are alike *H.Mi*. A1
	The deliberately failing person is better than the undeliberately *H.Mi*. B
	The deliberate criminal is the good person *H.Mi*. C
THE FRIENDLY IS NOT WHAT CAN REPROCICATE *Lys*. A	

THE FRIENDLY IS NOT THE LOVED *Lys*. B	
THE FRIENDLY IS NOT THE LOVER *Lys*. C	
THE FRIENDLY IS NOT THE SIMILAR *Lys*. D	
THE FRIENDLY IS NOT THE DIFFERENT *Lys*. E	
THE FRIENDLY IS NOT THE NEUTRAL *Lys*. F	
THE FRIENDLY IS NOT WHAT IS AKIN *Lys*. G	
JUSTICE IS HOLINESS *Prt*. A	
Temperance is wisdom *Prt*. B	
JUSTICE IS TEMPERANCE *Prt*. C	
	Courage is knowledge *Prt*. D
	Being overpowered is *amathia Prt*. E
	Courage is wisdom *Prt*. F
	The orator is just / never wants to do injustice *Grg*. A
ORATORS DO NOT HAVE POWER *Grg*. B1	
	Orators do not have power *Grg*. B2
	It is worse to wrong than to be wronged *Grg*. C
	To be punished is to be freed from greatest evil *Grg*. D-E
	The unpunished is most unhappy *Grg*. F
	Not natural right that stronger seizes property *Grg*. G
	Not natural right that the better ought to have *Grg*. H
LIFE OF PLEASURE NOT ATTRACTIVE *Grg*. I	
Flourishing and pleasure are different *Grg*. J	
Pleasure is not identical with the good *Grg*. K	
Pleasure is not identical with the good *Grg*. L	
	Correction is better than licence *Grg*. M
VIRTUE IS NOT MANLY VIRTUE ETC. *Men*.A	
VIRTUE IS NOT CAPACITY TO GOVERN MEN *Men*. B	
VIRTUE IS NOT DESIRING AND BEING ABLE TO GET FINE THINGS *Men*. C	
VIRTUE IS NOT POWER OF GETTING GOODS *Men*. D	
JUSTICE IS NOT BENEFITING FRIENDS, HARMING ENEMY *Rep*. A	
Justice is not benefiting friends etc. *Rep*. B	

Justice is not benefiting those that seem to be good etc. *Rep.* C	
	It is never right to harm anyone *Rep.* D
Justice is not advantage of the stronger *Rep.* E	
	Justice is not advantage of infallible stronger *Rep.* F
	No one willingly chooses to rule *Rep.* G
	The unjust is bad and ignorant *Rep.* H
	The unjust is impotent *Rep.* I
	The unjust is unhappy *Rep.* J
Alcibiades does not know about justice *Alc.* A	
Alcibiades does not know about justice *Alc.* B	
Alcibiades does not know about the useful *Alc.* C	
	The fine is identical with the good *Alc.* D
	The fine is identical with the good *Alc.* E
	The just is useful *Alc.* F

APPENDIX C

Basic Reductio (MTT or RAA) is used to prove the following 34 theses:[104]
    Socrates does not corrupt the young (*Ap.* A)
    Socrates should not escape (*Cri.* B)
    Piety is not care of the gods (*Euphr.* C) RAA
    Piety is not service to the gods (*Euphr.* D)
    Temperance is not quietness *Chrm.* A RAA
    Temperance is not modesty *Chrm.* B RAA
    Temperance is not doing good things *Chrm.* D RAA
    Temperance is not self-knowledge (*Chrm.* E, F, G)
    Temperance is not living scientifically (*Chrm.* H)
    Bravery is not remaining at post (*La.* A)
    Bravery is not endurance (*La.* B1) RAA
    Bravery is not knowledge of fearful and hopeful (*La.* C) RAA
    The friendly is not what reciprocates (*Lys.* A)
    The friendly is not the loved regardless of his attitude (*Lys.* B)
    The friendly is not the lover (*Lys.* C)
    The friendly is not the similar (*Lys.* D) RAA
    The friendly is not the different (*Lys.* E)
    The friendly is not the neutral (*Lys.* F)
    The friendly is not the akin (*Lys.* G)
    Justice is identical with holiness (*Prt.* A)
    Temperance is identical with justice (*Prt.* C)
    Doing as you like unintelligently is not power (*Grg.* B1) RAA
    The life of constant pleasure is unattractive (*Grg.* I)
    Virtue is not being able to manage public affairs, the home, etc. (*Men.* A) RAA
    Virtue is not to be able to rule over men (*Men.* B) RAA
    Virtue is not desiring and being able to get fine things (*Men.* C)
    Virtue is not power of getting goods (*Men.* D) RAA
    Justice is not benefiting friends and harming enemies (*Rep.* I A)
    Justice is not benefiting those that seem to be good, etc. (*Rep.* I C)
    Alcibiades does not know about justice (*Alc.* A and B)
    Alcibiades does not know about the useful (*Alc.* C)

---

104 See Appendix A for identification of the arguments.

APPENDIX D

Conclusions of 11 *Extended* Reductios (MTT or RAA):

Socrates does not corrupt intentionally *Apol.* B
Pious is not what is dear to the gods *Euphr.* A x
Pious is not what is loved by all the gods *Euphr.* B x
Pious is not knowledge of how to sacrifice *Euphr.* E x
Temperance is not doing your own good *Chrm.* C x
No distinction between temperance and wisdom *Prt.* B
Flourishing and pleasure are different *Grg.* J x
Pleasure is not identical with the good *Grg.* K x
Pleasure is not identical with the good *Grg.* L x
Justice is not benefiting friends etc. *Rep.* B x
Justice is not advantage of the stronger *Rep.* E x

Negated definitions are marked by x.

APPENDIX E

Endoxa collected from early dialogues (refer to appendix A for identification of arguments):

Indirect refutation (Extended Reductio) 21	*Direct Refutation 83*
The bad harm their surroundings, the good improve them (*Ap.* B)	
Nobody wants to be harmed (universal desire for well-being) (*Ap.* B)	
	If one believes in human activities, then one believes in human beings (*Ap.* C)
	Daemons are either gods or children of gods (*Ap.* C)
	The sportsman regards only the knowledgeable (*Cri.* A)
	We cannot live with a spoiled body (*Cri.* A)
	The soul is more valuable than the body (*Cri.* A)
	The good life is the just life (*Cri.* A)
The gods are in discord about just/unjust, etc. (*Euphr.* A)	
The gods like the just, fine, etc., hate what is unjust, etc. (*Euphr.* A)	
What comes to be/undergoes is a thing coming to be/something affected … because of the process of… (*Euphr.* B)	
What is loved is either a coming into being or something affected… (*Euphr.* B)	
The pious is loved because it is [itself] pious (*Euphr.* B)	
Our gifts are honour, reverence and gratitude (*Euphr.* E)	
They are dear to the gods (*Euphr.* E)	
If a city is to be well governed, labour must be divided (*Chrm.* C)	
	The deceitful is capable… (*H.Mi.* A)
	One is capable if one does what one wants (*H.Mi.* A)

	The physically better achieves both results (*H.Mi.* B)
	In any field, better minds can deliberately produce bad results (*H.Mi.* B)
	We prefer better minds (*H.Mi.* B)
	Justice is either an ability or knowledge or both (*H.Mi.* C)
What is done in same manner is done by same agency, what is done in contrary manner is done by contrary agency (*Prt.* B)	
Every contrary has one contrary only (*Prt.* B)	
	The knowledgeable are more confident (*Prt.* D)
	The courageous are the confident (*Prt.* D)
	Being overcome by desire of food is evil only because of future disease (*Prt.* E)
	Pains are good only if resulting in pleasure (*Prt.* E)
	The same magnitudes seem greater from near than from a distance (*Prt.* E)
	Ignorance is having false opinion (*Prt.* F)
	Fear is expectation of evil (*Prt.* F)
	The brave are eager to go to something else than the cowards (*Prt.* F)
	The brave willingly enter battle, cowards do not (*Prt.* F)
	This is fine and good (*Prt.* F)
	The orator must know about right and wrong (*Grg.* A)
	One who has learnt something is such (*Grg.* A)
	If you do x for the sake of y, then you don't want x but y (*Grg.* B2)
	There is something good, something bad and something neither good nor bad (*Grg.* B2)
	The neutral is done for the sake of the good, our sole end (*Grg.* B2)
	Killing, bannings, etc. are neutral things (*Grg.* B2)
	Doing injustice is uglier than suffering injustice (*Grg.* C)

	If x is fine, it is either pleasant or useful or both (*Grg.* C)
	Doing injustice is not painful (for agent) (*Grg.* C)
	The worse and uglier is not preferred by anyone (*Grg.* C)
	Being punished is to suffer justly (*Grg.* D)
	If justly, then finely (*Grg.* D)
	Every action has an object (*Grg.* D)
	Its passion correlates to act of agent (*Grg.* D)
	Being punished is passive (*Grg.* D)
	The rightly punishing person does it justly (*Grg.* D)
	There are three kinds of evil (*Grg.* E)
	(Doing) injustice is the ugliest (*Grg.* E)
	The most harmful is the biggest evil (*Grg.* E)
	Poverty, illness and injustice are removed by finance, medicine and jurisdiction respectively (*Grg.* F)
	Jurisdiction is finest, i.e. most useful (*Grg.* F)
	Medicine is useful in removing physical evil (*Grg.* F)
	The better are the stronger (*Grg.* G)
	Mass of men naturally stronger (*Grg.* G)
	Also conventional belief of majority that equality is right and that it is baser to do wrong (*Grg.* G)
	One wise may be stronger than... (*Grg.* H)
Flourishing is opposite of being miserable (*Grg.* J)	
Opposites cannot be had by same object... (*Grg.* J)	
The intelligent and brave are good, the fools and cowards are bad (*Grg.* K)	
The intelligent can feel joy (*Grg.* K)	
The fools can feel joy (*Grg.* K)	
The good are good because they have good in them and the pleased are pleased because they have pleasure in them (*Grg.* L)	

SOCRATES' ARGUMENTATIVE STRATEGY 97

	Some pleasures are good, some are bad (*Grg*. M)
	Good pleasures bring benefit, bad bring harm (*Grg*. M)
	An expert is needed to discriminate between good and bad pleasures (*Grg*. M)
	Some occupations produce pleasure without discrimination, some are based on knowledge (*Grg*. M)
	Good craftsmen give order and proportion (*Grg*. M)
	The good soul is orderly and proportionate (*Grg*. M)
	The order of the body is health and strength (*Grg*. M)
	It is no good to live with miserable body (*Grg*. M)
	An invalid is not allowed to fill his desires (*Grg*. M)
Skill is for opposites (*Rep*. B)	
	If horses or dogs are harmed, they are made worse of their kind (*Rep*. D)
	Justice is standard for man (*Rep*. D)
	Crartsmen cannot use their craft to opposite effect (*Rep*. D)
	The function of heat is to heat, of the dry to dry (*Rep*. D)
	The just is good (*Rep*. D)
Rulers are fallible (*Rep*. E)	
Correct law is advantageous to ruler, incorrect law is disadvantageous (*Rep*. E)	
	No art seeks own advantage (*Rep*. F)
	The arts rule over/are stronger than their fields (*Rep*. F)
	Other rulers demand pay (*Rep*. G)
	Different crafts have different functions (*Rep*. G)
	They benefit us differently (*Rep*. G)
	Medicine is different from wage-earning (*Rep*. G)
	If craftsmen get benefit, it must be from wage-earning (*Rep*. G)

	A just person does not try to outdo a just person (*Rep.* H)
	He does try to outdo the unjust (*Rep.* H)
	The unjust person tries to outdo both (*Rep.* H)
	No craftsman wants to outdo another craftsman (*Rep.* H)
	An ignorant tries to outdo both knowledgeable and ignorant (*Rep.* H)
	A knowledgeable person is clever and good (*Rep.* H)
	Injustice causes civil war (*Rep.* I)
	Anything in which it comes to be is incapacitated (*Rep.* I)
	The unjust is the enemy of the gods (*Rep.* I)
	X's function is what one can do only or best with it (*Rep.* J)
	X's virtue enables it to perform its function well (*Rep.* J)
	The soul's function is care, ruling, deliberation and living (*Rep.* J)
	Justice is the virtue of soul (*Rep.* J)
	One who lives well is blessed and happy (*Rep.* J)
	It profits no one to be wretched (*Rep.* J)

A NOTE ON READING VELLEIUS PATERCULUS

By Sebastian Persson

Summary: This note tries to demonstrate that the now lost manuscript of Velleius Paterculus from the monastery Murbach (*M) was written in a (pre-)caroline minuscule in the last half of the eighth century or first half of the ninth century and tries to show how this knowledge might help the reader distinguish between the many emendations that have been made to the text.

Readers of ancient literature are only all too aware of the fact that the texts they read are *textus recepti*; and as such one is left with the task of making sense of conjectures made by readers, copyists and editors, not all of whom followed the editorial conventions to which we now adhere. Remembering this is paramount in the case of the *historia* of Velleius Paterculus, as our text is mainly based upon the *editio princeps* of Beatus Rhenanus (published in 1520) and the recensio of Rhenanus' friend and employee Albert Burer.[1] Rhenanus discovered a manuscript of the text at the Abbey of Murbach (*M) and had a friend make a copy of the manuscript. He then postponed the printing a couple of years, hoping that another manuscript of the text would come to light. During this time, a friend of Rhenanus made his own copy of the Rhenanus copy: A. When a new manuscript containing Velleius did not emerge, Rhenanus finished his editio princeps: P. During the printing of the text, Burer discovered some incongruities between the printed text and the manuscript, halted the press and collated the text with the manuscript *M. His findings were printed as an appendix to the editio princeps:

---

[1] L.D. Reynolds, ed. *Texts and Transmission* (Oxford 1983) 431-33; A.J. Woodman *Velleius Paterculus – the Tiberian Narrative* (Cambridge 1977) 3-28.

B. After the publication of the editio princeps, the manuscript appears to have stayed at Murbach. The last time we hear of the manuscript is in the letters of Martin Gerbert (1764-1793) abbot of St. Blasien in Schwarzwald. A letter, dated tenth of August 1786, directed to a P. Ribbele has the following:[2]

> L'abbé Grandidier avance beaucoup dans l'impression de son 1. volume de l'histoire d'Alsace, j'en ai vu une partie. Je viens de lui envoyer plusieurs actes de Murbach, non encore imprimés, et qui regardent Lucerne, ancien dépendant de cette abbaye. Vous savés que le couvent de S. Pirmin transmuté en chanoines imitant sans doute la règle bienfaisante et toute débonnaire des Héros du Lutrin chanté par Boileau a annoncé la vente de livres, surtout des Manuscrits parmi lesquels il y a des Sacramentaires, une collection des Epitres de St. Jérome de VIII siècle, un Velleius Paterculus du même temps et l'unique qui existe. M. l'abbé Grandidier m'en a mandé l'avis qui a été confirmé dans la Gazette de Bâle. Cette vente ne sera pas vraisemblablement avant octobre. J'ignore si le catalogue est imprimé. Ces trésors littéraires iront peut'être se perdre en Russie comme les Piastres dans la Chines, si les principales Bibliothèques n'ont l'attention d'empêcher cette étrange migration.

The Velleius Paterculus, 'l'unique qui existe' must be our *M, which Gerbert dates to the eighth century. This date is accepted by L.D. Reynolds in *Texts and Transmission* as well as by Woodman in his edition of and commentary to the end of Velleius' work. He especially draws attention to the open-a, »cc«, and the long-s written as an »l«.[3] In spite of these features, it has been suggested that the lost manuscript dated from the eleventh century.[4] Luckily letter forms are just one of the means by which we can date manuscripts. I write luckily, as the use of the different letter forms developed over time:

---

[2] Reynolds 1983: 431 n. 2; Arthur Allgeier 'Bibliotheksgeschichtliche Nachrichten im Briefwechsel des Kardinals Garampi mit Fürstabt Martin Gerbert von St. Blasien' in *Studi e Testi* 126 – *Miscellanea Giovanni Mercati* VI (Vatican 1946) 452; 457-58.

[3] Reynolds 1983: 431 n. 3; Woodman 1977: 3 n. 4.

[4] John F. D'Amico *Theory and Practice in Renaissance Textual Criticism – Beatus Rhenanus Between Conjecture and History* (Berkeley 1988) 58.

open-a gradually disappeared in the ninth century and the long-s was used at least until the eleventh century.[5]

What I intend in this note is to collect the information that Rhenanus and Burer explicitly give on the nature of the manuscript on which the editio princeps is based, and to compare this information with Lowe's *Codices Latini Antiquiores* (CLA) in order to create the most likely impression of the original manuscript. If we can form an idea of what the manuscript that Rhenanus based his edition on looked like, then we might be able to understand some of the misreadings Rhenanus made, and to better assess the more than 1500 emendations that have been proposed (between 1873 and 1933).[6] At the end of this note, I have supplied the statements of Rhenanus and Burer upon which I base my arguments. They are numbered Rx for Rhenanus statement x, and Bx for Burer statement x.

There has been one attempt at giving a description of *M by J.C.M. Laurent, who in 1847 in a remarkable and well structured study identified 12 different features of *M (I have paraphrased Laurent's findings and attempted to find the reference):[7]

1. *M had no punctuation ($R4^3$ & $B6^3$).
2. *Puncta divisibilia* was used to distinguish between words and numbers ($B2^2$).
3. As a rule, words were divided correctly, but sometimes wrongly.
4. *M was written in minuscule, except for words like *cons* which was written in Uncial ($B6^4$).
5. Sometimes *M had majuscule letters in the middle of sentences ($B15^1$ & 16^1).
6. The letter »a« was written as cc ($B9^2$).
7. »æ« was written as a and e ($B3^2$ & 10^2).
8. »i« had no markers ($R4^3$, $?B6^3$).
9. *M had the following abbreviations: & for et; horizontal stroke marking an abbreviation; (.) was used as a mark of abbreviation; *aliqn* for *aliquando* ($B7^1$, 11^2 & ?12).

---

5 Bernhard Bischoff *Latin Palaeography* (Cambridge 2001) 115; 120.
6 Woodman 1977: 3.
7 In the following, I use the question mark in front of a reference in order to designate my best assumption of which part of the *editio princeps* Laurent might have been thinking of.

10. Words that were not abbreviated: *cum*; *nisi*; *semper*; *et*; *numquam* (for semper B12²).
11. Some orthographical peculiarities: *adque*; *gratis* for grates; *contemptus* for contentus; *epistula*; *tricensimo*; *aditiam* for adiciam; *capatia* for capacia; *aspitiens* for aspiciens; *adiitiens* for adiiciens; *aties* for acies; *velud* for velut; *Fauio* for Fabio; *Theuanum* for Thebanum.
12. Some letters have changed places (B2²).

As a conclusion, Laurent writes:

> Eine reifliche Erwägung aller dieser Einzelheiten führt mich auf die Vermuthung, der Cod. Murb. (*M) sei spätestens ins 9. Jahrhundert zu setzen. Ob er aber nicht ins 7., 8. oder selbst früher zu stellen, ob hier an Merovingische Schrift zu denken sei, ist eine Frage, die ich hiermit den gelehrten Lesern dieser Zeitschrift bestens ans Herz gelegt haben will…[8]

As is obvious from Laurent's description, the information that Rhenanus and Burer provide is in no way unambiguous. Rhenanus states that *M had no punctuation marks, yet Burer identifies marks to distinguish between words and numbers (cp. R4³, B2²). Of the two (Rhenanus and Burer), Burer is the one who seems to have examined *M most thoroughly. Rhenanus found the manuscript, but had a friend make a copy for him (R1³), Burer collated *M with Rhenanus' edition by examining it word by word, even letter by letter, as he writes (B1²). Both Burer and Rhenanus agree that the poor quality of the text is due to the scribe's poor understanding of Latin and to the age of the manuscript, which has rendered parts of the text illegible. This underlines their great effort in editing Velleius (R4¹⁻⁵; B7², 8²⁻³, 10², 14², 16², 17³ & 18²).

That *M did not distinguish »i« with markers (no. 8), the way of marking and the use of abbreviations (no. 9) and the orthographical peculiarities are

---

[8] Eleven years earlier, Laurent had published a series of conjectures to Velleius in his *Loci Velleiani* (Altona 1838). Although he sometimes argues from a palaeographical point of view, cf., e.g., pp. 16, 27-28, 36-37, 52-53, 79, 84-85, 105-6, 117-19, 129, Laurent primarily deals with errors of a generic kind, such as misreadings of abbreviations, suspensions and with incorrect division of words; none of these features are specific for the period to which he later dates the Murbach manuscript.

features which are common in manuscripts from at least the seventh to the ninth centuries, as Laurant concludes. The writing of »a« as »cc« and »æ« as »a« and »e«, on the other hand, are features which can narrow down the dating of *M.

If we are to try to date and describe *M, then we have to identify the library in which Rhenanus found the manuscript. He states that he found it in the Abbey of Murbach (R1¹), and in fact the Murbach library catalogue is extant, in three versions (two originate from the same manuscript, Colmar, Archives départementales du Haut-Rhin, Cartulaire Abbaye Murbach Nr. 1, and one from Darmstadt, Hessische Landes- und Hochschulbibliothek, Hs 2760 foll. 133r-141v). The two versions from the same manuscript appear to originate from the time of Abbot Iskar, i.e. the ninth century.[9] When the third list was compiled is a matter of uncertainty, the extant manuscript being a fifteenth-century copy of an earlier catalogue.[10] Curiously enough, Velleius is not mentioned in these catalogues, which might be due to the circumstance that *M was a *Mutilus*, as the beginning and a large part in the middle of Book I was missing (R3⁸). Velleius Paterculus' historia is part of a group of manuscripts which Birger Munk Olsen describes as: '…mutilés du début souvent avec des lacunes supplémentaires à l'intérieur'.[11]

The manuscript might therefore have evaded the attention of the librarian as he made his catalogue. The catalogues show that besides auctores like Vergil and Cicero, the library contained some historians (Livy, Pompeius Trogus, Dares and Lucan): this historical interest could have prompted an interest in Velleius Paterculus. E.A. Lowe in his CLA (*Codices Latini Antiquiores*: an attempt at collecting a complete corpus of facsimiles of Latin manuscripts written before 800[12]) has identified twelve manuscripts originating from the vicinity of Murbach, six of which are positively traced to Murbach. The six manuscripts are (CLA vol. and no. with my paraphrase of Lowe's description):

---

9 Wolfgang Milde *Der Bibliothekskatalog des Klosters Murbach aus dem 9. Jahrhundert* (Heidelberg 1968) 8-9.

10 B.M. Olsen *L'Étude des Auteurs Classiques Latins aux XIe et XIIe Siècles* vol. 3.1-2 (Paris 1987) 167-69.

11 B.M. Olsen 'Le sort des mutili des œuvres classiques latines' in Pierre Lardet (ed.) *La tradition vive. Melanges d'histoire des textes en l'honneur de Louis Holtz* Bibliologia 20, (Paris & Turnhout 2003) 21-33: 22.

12 E.A. Lowe *Codices Latini Antiquiores* vol. I-XI, 2nd ed. (Oxford 1988) vol. I, p. vii.

CLA 2, 222 (Manchester, John Rylands Library 15, Cyprianus Epistulae, etc.): VIII ex., uses punctuation, open »a« prevails, the shaft of »h« bends to the left, »t« mostly cursive, »z« tall, numerous ligatures, even »nt« in mid-word.
CLA 2, 242-243 (Oxford, Bodleian Junius 25 [5137] Aethicus, Cosmographia & Glossarium Latino-Teutonicum): VIII ex., punctuation used freely (point, comma or oblique stroke), high »e« in ligature, insular »g«, open »a«, superscript »a« in ligature, subscript »i« in »mi« and »ni«, tall »z«.
CLA 6, 749: VIII-IX (Colmar, Bibliotheque Municipale 38), virgula marks main pause, medial point with an oblique line marks lesser pause, »a« and »d« have two forms, uncial »g«, »r« and »s«.
CLA 6, 751: VIII-IX (Colmar, Bibliotheque Municipale 39), main pause marked by one or several »;«, lesser pauses by point, spelling poor, »a« written as »cc«, broken back »c«, »ti» and »nt« form ligature even in mid-word.
CLA 6, 756: VIII-IX (Colmar, Bibliotheque Municipale 130), semicolon marks main pause, medial point lesser pause, »a« has two forms, »cc« and »a«, top of »t« looms to the left, and »ti« form ligature.
CLA 8, 1193: VIII-IX (Freiburg-im-Breisgau, Stadtarchiv S.N.), semicolon or ·.· marks main pause, medial point lesser pause, »a« and »d« have two forms, »cc« and »d« predominantly; »y« is dotted, ascenders and descenders are long, here and there the lower left limb of »x« in the ligature »ex« has an added knob to the left.

The other six manuscripts that Lowe has identified (CLA 6 731: VIII-IX, 753: VIII-IX, 755: VIII; CLA 9 1290: VIII-IX, 1296: VIII-IX, 1442: VIII-IX) share the common feature that »a« and »d« have two forms, of which the open »a« is one. Some of the manuscripts also have majuscule letters among the minuscule letters. The »cc-a« (open »a«) and the use of majuscule or a different type of letters combined with the minuscule script seem to be one of the defining characteristics of the Murbach scriptorium. Punctuation marks, on the other hand, seem to be used, but there is no apparent system.

According to Burer (B3², 10²) the diphtong »æ« was not written as e-caudata, which indicates that the manuscript was written before the tenth or eleventh century, as the e-caudata was used frequently in those centuries.[13] The Abbey of Murbach (founded in 727) was in contact with four other

---

13 Bischoff 2001: 122.

monasteries: Reichenau, Remiremont, St. Gall and St. Giulia/Brescia. Reichenau and St. Gall are known for their Alemannic style (broad rounded strokes and frequent ligature of »nt«), which was used well into the ninth century.[14] If the manuscript was written in *scriptura continua* (R4³ & B2²), it might narrow the dating of *M down. The habit of separating words by empty spaces originated in Ireland and came to Europe with the Irish monks. The first manuscripts written with any form of separation between words or word units are from the late seventh or early eighth centuries (found in insular manuscripts), but the practice did not become standard on the Continent until the mid-tenth century, yet insular centers like Fulda and St. Gall experimented with word separation as early as the eighth century.[15]

All in all, it seems reasonable to assume that *M was written in a (pre-)caroline minuscule in the last half of the eighth century or the first half of the ninth century.

EMENDATIONS

As mentioned above, more than 1500 emendations have been proposed. As an example one might consider 1.14.2 (all the following examples are taken from Watt's edition, Teubner 1988):

> Post septem annos quam Galli urbem ceperant (ceperant *Madvig* ceperunt **PA**).

In this instance Rhenanus must have misread an open–a for an »u« as the context requires the pluperfect *ceperant*, as Madvig noted. Further examples are:

> 1.17.7 praeteritoque eo in quo eminere non possumus aliquid in quo niteamus (niteamus *Cludius* (<e>niteamus iam *Heinsius*) nitamur **PA**) conquirimus

---

14 Bischoff 2001: 114; 118.
15 P. Saenger *Spaces Between Words* (Stanford 1997) 83-106.

It has been stated that the context requires a verb meaning to excel.[16] Niteamus can be defended by perceiving the »r« of nitamur as a misreading of a tall »s« and the »e« was taken as a part of the »cc« »a«.

> 2.2.3 simul etiam promulgatis agrariis legibus, omnibus agrum (factum **A** statum **P**) concupiscentibus, summa imis miscuit (sc. Ti. Gracchus) ...

Halm has proposed *statum novum* even though it, as Shackleton Bailey remarks, 'was the have-nots, not the whole population that wanted a new deal.'[17] The readings of A and P are very similar and can be explained as A being a misreading of *omnibusstatum*; the scribe of A divided the words before the first »t« and read it as an »f« and the »cc« »a« as a »c«. *Statum* can be defended as status has the connotation of political/civil status, yet given the historical context Watt's agrum is tempting.

> 2.3.1 Tum P. Scipio Nasica ... pronepos autem Cn. Sciponis, celeberrimi uiri P. Africani patrui, is (patrui is *Aldus*, patruus **PA**) priuatusque et togatus ...

Aldus' emendation is almost certainly the right reading, as we in the context would expect a genitive predicate and not a nominative predicate to Cn. Scipio denoting the relationship between Cn. Scipio and P. Scipio Africanus. The misreading is easily explained from a palaeographical point of view. We know that »i« did not have any markers (R4³) and that the manuscript was written in *scriptura continua* (R4³ & B2²), hence one would easily make the mistake of reading *patruiis* as *patruus*.

> 2.6.2 ... longe maiora et acriora petens (petens *Ruhnken* repetens **PA** re<i p.> petens *Watt*) dabat (*sc. Gaius Gracchus*) ciuitatem omnibus italicis ...

The emendation can be explained as an example of the scribe dividing the words incorrectly. Either he read the ending of *acriora* as the beginning of

---

16 D.R. Shackleton Bailey 'Notes on Velleius' *CQ* n.s. 34 (ii) p. 445.
17 Shackleton Bailey 1984: 445-46.

petens as well (Ruhnken) or overlooked an abbreviation of *rei publicae* (Watt). The second solution is alluring as it would present us with a dative describing to *whom* Gaius Gracchus' plan was *acriora*. It can be defended as we know of at least one instance where *rei publicae* had been abbreviated (B10²) and of at least two instances where the political terminology was abbreviated (B6 & B20). Furthermore we know that the *scriptura continua* was of inconvenience to Rhenanus (R4 & B2²) which makes it likely that he overlooked the abbreviation. Furthermore, the reading *rei publicae* would be part of a tricolon consisting of *tribunatum* from the previous sentence and *ciuitatem* of the main clause.

> 2.78.1 redierat ... Antonius ... in transmarinas provincias, quas magnis momentis (motibus (cf. 1.3.1) noluit Krause) Labienus ... concusserat.

In his commentary to his edition Woodman writes:[18]

> The text of this passage is problematic. Since concutere is regularly used with such nouns as bello, tumultu etc. (TLL 8.1393.59ff.), we might naturally expect the paradosis to mean 'with great disturbances'; yet despite Laurent, who compared 1.3.1 'Graecia maximis concussa est motibus' (cf. Curt. 4.14.20), *momentum* seems incapable of meaning 'disturbance'. One might suggest reading *motibus* here, but it is hard to see how the corruption would have arisen ... Prof. Goodyear thinks V. may have written magna moliens: this is indeed attractive (cf. 2.14.1 'quod cum moliens reuertisset', 26.1 'multa ... molitus', 129.2 'noua molientem'), but again it is hard to see how the corruption might have arisen. I have therefore obelised.

We as readers are left to decide what seems the most likely to us: is momentis a misreading of *motibus* or *magna moliens*? Burer shows one instance where *a militibus* has been corrupted into *ambitus* by a later scribe (B14² – another instance of a second scribe is B21). Considering this the conjecture to *motibus* might not be unlikely, especially not if the earlier scribe had suspended the vowels and the *-bus* ending (e.g. *motibus* → *mt·* / *mot·*). Good-

---

18 A.J. Woodman *Velleius Paterculus – the Caesarian and Augustan Narrative* (Cambridge 1983) 191.

year's emendation does not offer a similar explanation and is, in my view, not as attractive as *motibus*.

> 2.100.3 nihil quod facere aut pati turpiter potest femina luxuria <ac> (luxuria ac *Orelli*, luxuria **PA**, luxurians *Krohn*) libidine infectum reliquit (*sc. Iulia*),…

In his commentary Woodman writes:

> It will be seen that I have followed Orelli in supplying ac, thus avoiding the asyndeton of the two paired nouns which is found in the paradosis. In such cases it is often very difficult to decide what the correct reading should be, especially since some writers of the 'silver' age were fond of this type of asyndeton … and a scribe could very easily have omitted ac between these two nouns.[19]

If we could explain the omission of ac as a possible misreading by Rhenanus, then Orelli's emendation might be even more attractive. We know that the »cc-a« was predominant in manuscripts from Murbach and that *M was written in scriptura continua. The line may have read »luxuricccc« (= luxuriaac) which make it likely that Rhenanus' scribe read ac as the »a« in luxuria. Krohn's *luxurians* do not offer the same palaeographical explanation.

ALIAS (ALS)?

One last peculiar thing about the editio princeps is Rhenanus' use of *alias* to introduce alternative readings. They might be thought to be intended as manuscript readings, but as Woodman states: *Alias* is not a method of referring to the codex.[20]

On p. 9 of the editio princeps, for instance the text has *Ad quintum Fabioque*, with the marginal note *Al'as * At Q. Fabio quintum*. This exact spot prompts Burer (B6[1-5]) to explain that »d« for »t« is a common miswrit-

---

19 Woodman 1977: 122.
20 Woodman 1977: 5 n. 5.

ing in old manuscripts, and that the conjecture »at« is therefore right. Woodman's statement seems correct, as none of the places where Burer has registered variants made by the copyist or another scribe and deletion marks (B4², 5², 13², 14² & 21²) are commented on by Rhenanus with an *alias*. The *alias* notes must therefore be taken to present Rhenanus' own conjectures, and not to furnish more evidence for what the codex contained, even though it has been speculated that *alias* might be Rhenanus' way of introducing how he thought the manuscript might be read.[21] In a recent study of the philological language of Beatus Rhenanus, Pierre Petitmengin has noted that *Al.* (*Alias*) might be used by Rhenanus to introduce his own conjectures that he could not find evidence for in the manuscript, as he seems to have consulted the *exemplaria vetusta* whenever possible.[22] We could do worse than heed the concluding remarks of Petitmengin:[23]

> Et l' 'habillage' des données dans un vocabulaire foisonnant, plus littéraire que technique, n'était pas fait pour éliminer toute ambiguïté. Après tout, Rhenanus n'écrivait pas pour fournir des materiaux aux éditeurs d'aujourd'hui, mais pour render leur sens et leur beauté aux auteurs antiques.

Hopefully, this note has shed some light on some of the difficulties that follow when reading Velleius Paterculus. If one visualises a manuscript written in the late eighth or early ninth century, then it might be easier to decide on one of the many textual conjectures that have been suggested.

---

21 D'Amico 1988: 59-60.
22 P. Petitmengin 'La terminologie philologique de Beatus Rhenanus' in *Beatus Rhenanus – lecteur et editeur des textes anciens* (Turnhout 2000) 198.
23 Petitmengin 2000: 221.

APPENDIX

In this appendix I have tried to gather all the instances where either Rhenanus or Burer mention *M. For legibility, I have resolved abbreviations, introduced notation marks, and occasionally spelt »u« as »v«, mainly in the beginning of a word. I have kept the punctuation of the original, confusing as it may seem. I have inserted numbers in order to facilitate referring to the text.

Rhenanus

R1 p. ii [1]Equidem abhinc annos ut puto quinque, cum primum hunc in Murbacensi bibliotheca reperissem, [2]et viderem tam prodigiose corruptum, ut omnia restituere non foret humani ingenii, [3]properanter ac infeliciter ab amico quodam descriptum, [4]premendum plane censebam donec melioris nobis codicis fieret copia, quem acceperam haberi Mediolani inventum olim a Georgio Merula. [5]Verum dum frustra iam treis annos expectamus, [6]interim doctissimus quisque mecum expostulat, [7]cur tam insignem autorem studiosis communicare tamdiu differam.

R2 p. 1 [1]Qamquam puto magis hominum incuriam accusandam, quam ipsam vetustatem. [2]Poterant exemplaria ætatis vitio obsolescentia describi, poterant vitis instar ob senium iamiam emorituræ per novas propagines restitui, [3]si fuissent quos huius rei cura tetigisset. [4]Et certe fuerunt, qui tametsi parum docti, præstiterunt tamen quod potuerunt: quibus habendam gratiam censeo, quod horum saltem opera qualicunque miseras bonorum autorum reliquias licet mendosissime exceptas, conservatas videamus, si modo conservari est, tam depravate esse descriptum. [5]Utinam vero quidam autores extarent, quamlibet mendose scripti. [6]Possent in illis multa restitui per viros eruditos, ac iudicio præditos. [7]Egregie sudatum est in hac parte a Benedictinis olim, in asservandis inquam veterum monimentis. [8]At postquam ptochotyranni isti irrepserunt, conspiratum est in veteres autores, ut istorum somnia mundo commodius obtrudi possent.

R3 p. 5 [1]Nam bonam operis partem hoc loco deesse nullus dubitabit. [2]Porro omnis medendi spes in integro sita est exemplari. [3]Quale repertum iam olim aiunt a Georgio Merula inter eos libros, de quorum ille inventione magnopere gloriatur in epistola quadam, quæ inter Politianicas legitur. ⁴Sed isti rumori fidem non habeo. ⁵Scilicet tantus vir nugas ædidisset, sic enim quasdam veterum grammaticorum quisquilias ab illo publicatas non injuria vocavero, præsertim cum Velleio commissas, et hoc opus suppressisset nobis, unde plus ad illum gloriæ, et ad studiosos commodi rediturum erat, quam ex sexcentis istius generis grammaticorum schedis. ⁶Nos hac æditione nostra, tametsi mutila, provocabimus Italos, ut nobis quod nacti sumus in medium conferentibus, ipsi quoque sua candide studiosis impertiant. Sed de hac re plus satis iam loquuti sumus. ⁷Cæterum ut quasi viam tibi sternamus ad sequentis Velleiani fragmenti intelligentiam, quod in media ferme periodo sublatis anterioribus aliquot ternonibus abruptum est ... Velleius ... propemodum ad initium tertii belli Punici pervenit ...

R4 pp. 69-70 ¹'Nec propterea nullam mihi gratiam habebis amice lector, quod non omnia restituerim. ²Id enim absque emendatiori codice non erat possibile, at meus et unicus erat, et mendosissimus. ³Ausim jurare, eum, qui illum descripserat, ne verbum quidem intellexisse: adeo omnia erant confusa absque ullis punctis aut distinctionibus. ⁴Quod si tu scires quam ego laborarim in hiis fragmentis utcunque restituendis, credo fateberis te mihi nonnihil debere. ⁵Neque enim quia tu multa absque offensione legis, idcirco codex planus erat: imo nihil erat non depravatum: in singulis pene verbis hærebatur. ⁶Fatebuntur me vera dicere, quicunque vetustum codicem inspexerint, qui in Murbacensi bibliotheca adhuc asservatur... ⁷Cæterum optime lector videtur hic parum deesse in hac peroratiuncula notitia,[24] nam in exemplari versus aliquot erant erasi, forsan ab aliquo nebulone facturo periculum, an illitæ membranis notæ expungi possint.

Burer

I have followed the same editorial practice as above, but as there are no page numbers in Burer's appendix, I have retained his system which refers to the page numbering of the *editio princeps* (I have inserted the page number in angled brackets, as Burer lists all his emendations under the page number). Furthermore, I have placed quotations in ''.

24 uotitia B

B1 <Prol.> ¹Contuli itaque Velleium a capite (quod aiunt) usque ad calcem, atque hoc solo studiosorum nomine, cum nihil aliud spectarem, quam ut studiosos obsequio demererer, iisque pro mea virili gratificarer. ²Præterea cum hunc recentem vetusto Vellei codici conferrem, non modo versum versui, sed etiam syllabam syllabæ, et (quod alicui plus quam curiosum ac pene stultum videri queat) etiam literam literæ contuli, ne quid non ageretur in rem studiosorum.
[…]
B2 ¹Pagina eadem <2>, versu 23. 'imprudenter rixanincies,' 'tu rixam injiciens:' ego vero 'rixam ciens' legendum puto, literis vetusti exemplaris propius inspectis: ²sic enim vetustum habebat exemplar, 'rixam. ncies.' interposito inter 'rixam' et 'ncies' puncto divisibili, et transposita 'n' litera.
[…]
B3 ¹Pag. 3. ver. 15. 'alii nocturno æris sono.' exemplar vetustum habet, 'nocturno aeris sono:' nisi veteres aliter pinxerint diphthongum 'æ', quam hodie pingamus. ²Erat enim 'e' ab 'a' spacio divisum.
[…]
B4 ¹Pag. ea. <7> ver. 36. 'quicquid de Carthaginensibus dicebatur,' exemplar vetustum habet, 'quicquid de Carthaginiensibus diceretur.' ²'ba' ab alio quopiam additum videtur, nam non est chirographum scribæ veteris exemp.
[…]
B5 ¹Pag. 9. ver. 1. 'Nam militarium et causa et autores etc.' exemplar vetustum sic habuisse videtur. ²'Nam militarium et causæ,' apiculo illo quo fit diphthongus, abraso.
[…]
B6 ¹Pag. 9. vers. 15. 'Ad quintum Fabioque Decio Mure quarto Coss. quo anno Pyrrhus regnare coepit Sinuessam Minturnasque missi coloni.' Exemplar vetustum sic habet: 'ad quintum fabioque decio mure quarto CONS. quo anno pyrrhus regnare coepit etc.' ²Locum hunc veræ ac genuinæ lectioni suæ sic restituendum puto. Qui aliquando veterum exemplaria evolverunt, sæpicule imo ferme semper et ubique 't' pro 'd,' et rursum 'd' pro 't' positum legerunt: ut 'haut', pro 'haud': 'aput', pro 'apud': et 'at', pro 'ad': multaque huiusmodi. ³Noverunt item pleraque veterum exemplaria sine maiusculis literis, sine punctis, demum etiam sine omni sententiarum discrimine scripta. ⁴Nunc cum præsentem Vellei locum sic scriptum repererim ('ad quintum fabioq· decio mure quarto CONS. quo anno etc.') literis singulis ordine diligenter excussis atque perpensis, sic legendum hunc locum

exhibeo. 'Ad quintum Fabio Q. (fuit autem Q. Fabius, teste Livio, quinquies CONS. iccirco quintum pro quinto adverbialiter hic positum opinor) Decio Mure quarto cons.' ⁵'Ad' hic, ut dixi, pro 'At' positum est, nisi si cui videatur ad Sinuessam referri debere, quod tamen non est simile vero. 'Fabioq·' pro 'Fabio Q.' positum videtur, non pro 'Fabio' et 'que' coniunctione.
[…]
B7 ¹'Pag. 11. ver. 3. 'Huius ergo præcedentisque seculi ingeniorum similitudines congregantis, et in studium par, et in emolumentum, causas cum semper requiro, et cætera.' Exemplar vetustum sic habet, 'huius ergo recedentis mq. seculum ingeniorum similitudines congregantesq. se et in studium par et memolumentum causas cum semper requiro, et cætera.' ²Hic ideo vetusti codicis formam lectori proposuimus, ut videat quibus laboribus Velleius a mendis, quibus scatebat inumeris, fuerit repurgandus.
[…]
B8 ¹'Pa. 23. ver. 2. 'qua demendesmontem ti fata cum C. Norbano concurrerat Sylla.' Exemplar vetustum sic scriptum habet, 'posuit victoriam qua demendes montem tifata cum C. Norbano concurrerat Sylla.' ²Hic locus depravatissimus adeo omnium suffugit conjecturas, ut pene de eo quasi irrestituibili loco desperatum esset. ³Nihilominus ego (ceu solent canes venatici) odorari non destiti, donec lectionem aliquam, si non germanam, attamen germanæ simillimam deprehenderim. ⁴Ea hæc est, 'posuit victoriam qua demens de monte in Tifata cum C. Norbano concurrerat Sylla.' Fuit autem Tifata (teste Volaterrano) oppidum in Campania, non longe a Capua, ubi Sylla Norbanum acie vicerat.
[…]
B9 ¹'Pag. ea. <24> ver. 39. 'Hicce toga virili.' exemplar vetustum habet, 'Hic a toga virili adsuetus etc.' ²Is qui Velleium e vetusto descripsit, falsus est a litera in 'cc[c]', nam ut in hoc, sic etiam in quibusdam aliis veterum codicibus 'a' sic scribitur 'cc' quod iste pro 'ce' syllaba aspexit.
[…]
B10 ¹'Pa. ea. <25>. ver. 37. 'nimium iam liber ære.' exemplar vetustum sic habet, 'nimium iam liber aeret.' ²Mirum est si me literarum coniectura hoc loco fallit, nam ex aeret sic conjicio legi debere, 'nimium iam libere imperaret Reip. etc.' quod si cui hæc nostra coniectatio non placuerit, habeat is occasionem quærendæ melioris.
[…]

B11 ¹Pa. ea. <27> ver. 11. 'homo virtuti simillimus etc.' exemplar vetustum habet, 'non virtuti simillimus.' ²Sed (ut sunt varia chirographorum genera) suspicor librarium 'homo' sic 'hō' scriptum pro non aspexisse; nam si aspirationis caudam quam sursum erectam habet, non longule in altum protraxeris, n esse cuiuis non penitus introspicienti videtur.
[…]
B12 ¹Pa. 30. ver. 11. 'ita semper omne spacium.' exemplar vetustum habet, 'ita se per omne spatium etc.' ²Nec miror cur hic 'semper' pro 'se per' inoleverit, cum facile 'se per' vel sola <m>²⁵ literæ interpositione depravari poterat in 'semper.'
[…]
B13 ¹Pagina. eadem. <34> vers. 24. 'ac vicina ei urbi regio castris Pompeio retinetur.' Exemplar vetustum 'habet, ac vicinia ei urbi regio castris Pompei,' ²'o' literæ puncto deletili superscripto, sic '˙o'.
[…]
B14 ¹Pag. ea. <36> ver. 3. 'ei ambitus deferretur imperium.' exemplar vetustum habet, 'qui vir cum summum ei a militibus deferretur imperium etc.' ²'A militibus' in 'ambitus' depravatum est, vitio scribæ posterioris.
[…]
B15 ¹Pa. 43. ver. 6. 'ad quem et e Brutianis castris.' lectio Velleiana bene habet. In cetera codice sic scriptum erat, 'adque me T e brutianis castris etc.'
[…]
B16 ¹Pag. ea. <43> ver. 13 'post Antonianam fugam.' exemplar vetustum sic habet, 'post antonii A mutinam fugam.' ²Quid hic legendum conjiciam nescio, nisi sicui 'post Antonii a Mutina fugam,' legendum videatur.
[…]
B17 ¹Pa. ea. <47> ver. 19. 'illa marcebant omnia.' Exemplar vetustum habet, 'illam arcebant omnia.' ²Sed perinde 'm' ab 'arcebant' detractum, atque præcedenti dictioni est additum: ac si quis studiosissime id fecerit. ³Odoratur hic etiam inscitia librariorum non intelligentium ea quæ scribebant.
[…]
B18 ¹Pagina eadem <55>, versu 7. 'facere voluerat, atque vehementer repugnante Nerone erat inhibitus.' ²Ex vestigiis vetusti codicis apparebat pro atque, 'eoque, sive eo quod' scriptum: nam vestigia literarum vix poterant videri præ vetustate.

25 in B

[…]
B19 ¹'Pagina ea. <57> ver. 5. 'Data a Cæsare petenti facultas.' Exemplar vetustum habet, 'data petenti facultas.' ²Hoc 'a Cæsare' in vetusto cod. hoc loco non reperitur, vide[26] unde huc immigrarit.
[…]
B20 ¹'Pag. ea. <65> ver. 23. 'Pompeio Apuleioque COS.' pro 'cos' scribatur 'COSS.' ss duplici: nam sic solet scribi 'consules.' 'consul' vero unico 's'. ²In codice vetusto sic scriptum est, 'COS.' potest autem scribi 's' arcurato[27] vel erecto utcumque libebit, nec me fugit quomodo in veterum codicibus plerisque scribatur, in quibus 'consul' sic 'cos.' 'consules' vero sic 'CONS.' scriptum reperio.
[…]
B21 ¹'Pa. ea. <68> ver. 5. 'formam evocavit'. 'formam' sursum in tertium versum, unde incuria librarii decidit, reponatur: nam ut hic superest, sic isthic deest. ²Nec te multum moverit lectio, quæ paulo inferius in margine posita legitur: nam superiore illa, inferior hæc inducitur.

26 unde B
27 acurato B

ROMAN INSCRIPTIONS FROM FERRARA, MAZARA AND NÎMES IN THE PAPERS OF BØRGE THORLACIUS (1775-1829)

By Patrick Kragelund

Summary: The article presents three hitherto unpublished Roman inscriptions, seen in Ferrara in Italy, Mazara in Sicily and Nîmes in France by the Danish classical scholar Børge Thorlacius (1775-1829) during his travels in Italy and France in 1826-1828.

A professor of classical philology at the University of Copenhagen, Børge Thorlacius is in the eyes of posterity completely overshadowed by his renowned (and highly critical) successor, Johan Nicolai Madvig (1804-1886).

However, in the history celebrating the University of Copenhagen's fifth centenary, Ivan Boserup succeeded in bringing out the ideals of a scholar whose lifelong interest in antiquarian and aesthetic subjects was rekindled by travels in Italy and France which he visited in the final years of his life. The successes of Thorlacius' eminent pupil, Peter Oluf Brøndsted, may well have increased the old master's awareness of 'the potential value of the ancient monuments for the study of classical literature'.[1]

On his return to Denmark, Thorlacius began editing some of the results gathered on his travels, but, sadly, his new projects were cut short by his premature death. His family later solicited public support to edit the

---

1 Cf. B. Thorlacius *Monumentorum Siculorum specimen* I (Copenhagen 1829) 3 describing the aim of his travels 'ut monumenta classicae antiquitatis ... ad literarum usum, qua liceret, converterem'. I. Boserup 'Klassisk filologi efter 1800' in P.J. Jensen & S. Ellehøj *Københavns Universitet 1479-1979* vol. 8 (Copenhagen 1992) 241-476; on Thorlacius, ibid. 280-88.

detailed account of his journey in 1826-1828 – but for lack of subscribers the project fell through.

What remains are the diaries, now in the department of manuscripts in the Danish Royal Library.[2] Previously ignored, Boserup has drawn attention to the numerous notes on classical inscriptions, which Thorlacius had seen and deciphered, sometimes as the first. In letters, Thorlacius himself seems to have discussed his notes from Sicily with fellow epigraphists like Girolamo Amati, whom he befriended in Rome,[3] and the Berlin professor August Boeckh who – after the death of his friend and with the help of his pupil and successor F.C. Petersen – published or quoted a number of Thorlacius' transcripts from Syracuse and Acrae in the third volume of his monumental *Corpus Inscriptionum Graecarum* (1828-1877); for some of these entries, Thorlacius remains the only authority.[4] Presumably, Thorlacius had originally planned to publish this material himself, but he was only spared the time to edit two Greek items – and his transcripts of Latin inscriptions were subsequently completely forgotten. From this latter group three inscriptions are, apparently, hitherto unpublished.

Before turning to a discussion of the individual items, a brief comment on Thorlacius' travels and work as epigrapher seems in order. Setting out from Denmark in 1826, Thorlacius traveled extensively in France and Italy until the summer of 1828; wherever he came he was assiduous in visiting academies, museums and collections – and he described meticulously what he saw and whom he met. Many of his notes concern inscriptions. As for his interests in this field, his criteria were broad. A famous stone he would rarely pass by. When in Arles, it was for instance natural that he would take down the (fake) inscription referring to Marius, the 'conqueror of the Cimbri'

---

2 The diary is in *Ny kgl. Samling* 377k I-II, 4, Department of Manuscripts, the Royal Library, Copenhagen. In the manuscript's first volume is a printed prospectus for the planned edition.

3 On Amati (1768-1834), see A. Petrucci, 'Amati, Girolamo', *Dizionario biografico degli Italiani* 2 (Rome 1960) 673-75; Thorlacius met Amati in Rome: diary (cf. n. 2) 30 October 1826.

4 A. Boeckh, *Corpus inscriptionum Graecarum* 3 (Berlin 1853) no. 5369; 5390; 5400; 5401; 5404; 5408; 5409; 5411; 5413 and 5420 (all from Syracuse); 5424-5428; 5431; 5432 (all from Acrae); Thorlacius still the only authority: P.A. Hansen, *A Bibliography of Danish Contributions to Classical Scholarship* (Copenhagen 1977) no. 1167.

(CIMBROR(um) VICTRICI).⁵ The Cimbri were, after all, held to be the ancestors of the Danes. In other cases he may well have had his scholarly reasons for copying; or alternatively, he may simply have wanted to try what he could make of it.

What matters here is that a few of his notes preserve what seems to be the only trace of inscriptions later lost. Of course they also offer glimpses of items still in existence and/or previously published, sometimes again and again. When in Vienne, in April 1828, Thorlacius would for instance copy nine inscriptions which all can be found in Otto Hirschfeld's edition of the inscriptions from Gallia Narbonensis in the *Corpus Inscriptionum Latinarum*.⁶ In such cases the accuracy of Thorlacius can be checked – on the whole, to his advantage. But sometimes he abbreviates or normalizes (without specifying that he does so);⁷ in other cases he clearly had difficulty reading what was there – but all epigraphists have tried that.⁸

I

The first of the hitherto inedited inscriptions is from Ferrara, which Thorlacius visited in October 1826. Here, he copied a great number of inscriptions which all have been published many times.⁹ But he also took down an inscription which otherwise seems to have gone unrecorded and of

---

5   *CIL* XII.112*; copied in Thorlacius' diary (cf. n. 2) on 6 April 1828.
6   In his diary (cf. n. 2, 12 April 1828) Thorlacius lists the inscriptions he transcribed at Vienna from 1 to 9: No. 1 = *CIL* XII.1854; 2 = 1807; 3 = 1824; 4 = 1987; 5 = 5512; 6 = 1848; 7 = 1849; 8 = 1868 and 9 = 1976.
7   Inscriptions in Ferrara may illustrate the shortcomings of Thorlacius' approach: in *CIL* VI.9593 line 5 Thorlacius has B M (i.e. B(ene) M(erenti)) but the stone in fact has BENE MEREN/TI; similarly, in *CIL* VI.24867 line 3 Thorlacius has CARISSIMAE, but the stone has KARISSIMAE.
8   In *CIL* V.2441 lin. 12 Thorlacius has ERVCTVS, but the stone has FRVCTVS and in V.2415, which Thorlacius rightly notes was found in 1777 (his 'fundet 1777' mirrors the stone's 'efossa ... 1777'), he has EGNATVLEIAE, but the stone has EGNATIAE MAIAE; in both cases Thorlacius fails to indicate that he only quotes a single word from either inscription.
9   Inscriptions still in the *Museo lapidario* in Ferrara: *CIL* V.2385; 2392; 2395; 2396; 2415 (cf. n. 8); 2420; 2430; 2441 (cf. n. 8); 8008; VI.9593 (cf. n. 7); VI.24697 (cf. n. 7); XI.6378.

which there seems to be no trace, in Ferrara or elsewhere (Fig. 1). In his caption above the transcript, Thorlacius describes the item as 'a round discus, on which is sculpted a bird with a fish in its claws'[10] – to which he adds a drawing and a text:

M(agistri?)[11]
T(itus) AELLIENVS
CORVVS
[?][12] ARVILLIVS
MARCELL(us)
COLLEG(ii)
AVGG(ustalium)[13]

The nomen Aellienus is exceedingly rare. Apart from this instance, it seems significant that not so distant Rimini furnishes what seems to be the only parallel, a Q. AELLIENVS (*CIL* XI.434). The editors of the *CIL* were unhappy with this latter name, suggesting that it perhaps was the far more common Allienus.[14] But now we have a namesake, from an inscription once to be seen in the Museum in Ferrara.

If found in the area (as seems likely), this is apparently the only extant evidence for the local presence of a *collegium Augustalium*.

II

The second item is from Sicily, where Thorlacius likewise took down a great number of inscriptions, in Greek, Punic and Latin. But unlike his learned colleague Friedrich Münter (1761-1830), to whom Sicilian friends sent inscriptions from ancient Lilybaeum which still adorn the porch of the bishop's palace in Copenhagen, Thorlacius only brought home his diary.[15]

---

10 'En rund Discus, hvorpaa er udarbeidet en Fugl med Kløerne paa en Fisk'.
11 The *augustales* had *magistri*: cf. *CIL* V.7604; 7646; X.1055; 1209; 6114.
12 In Thorlacius' transcript there is no trace of the man's *praenomen*.
13 Not on record in *CIL* V, VI, IX, X, XI, XIV.
14 H. Solin & O. Salomies, *Repertorium nominum gentilicium et cognominum Latinorum* (Hildesheim, Zürich & New York 1994) 7 quote the *nomen* with an added (?).
15 *CIL* X.7224 and 7226 (Marsala) came to Copenhagen in the 1820 s.

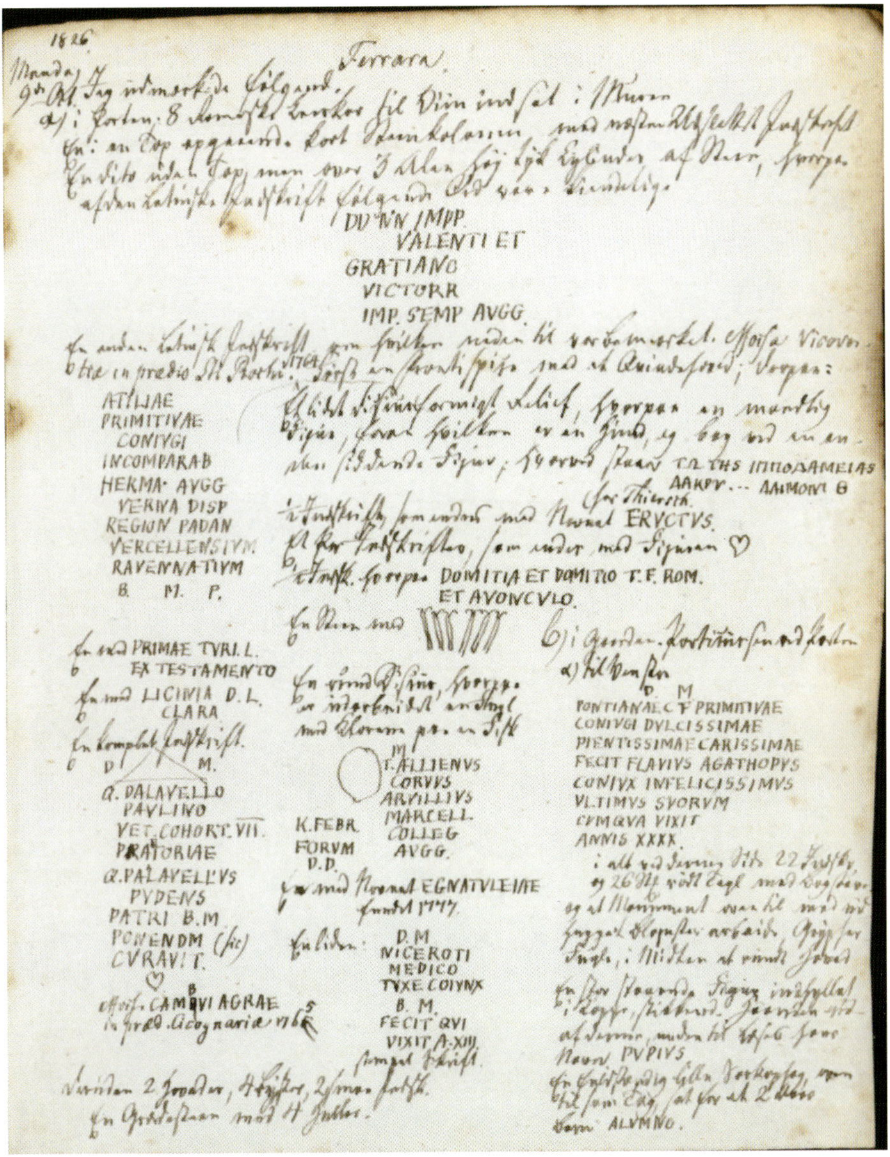

Fig. 1. A page from Thorlacius' diary showing the inscriptions he transcribed when visiting the Museum in Ferrara in 1826. The Royal Library, Copenhagen.

As mentioned above, the Greek items were later edited by August Boeckh. As for the Latin, Thorlacius in Marsala, which he visited on 9 June 1827, would take a brief look at *CIL* X.7230 (or 7229); similarly, he copied X.7013 and 7037 (both in the Museo Biscari in Catania). What matters here is his visit to Mazara on 9 June 1827, where in the Cathedral he spotted a sarcophagus with the following (apparently otherwise unrecorded)[16] inscription:

VALERIAE
MARCELLVS
CONIVGI CARISSIMAE

III

In Nîmes, finally, Thorlacius on 4 April 1828 visited the gardens of the renowned French epigraphist Jean-François Seguier (1703-1784), there copying some nineteen inscriptions, all distributed on two pages in his diary. Most of these inscriptions are still preserved and otherwise known.[17] But in his list there is one of which I have found no record in the standard works of reference.[18]

Thorlacius furnished a brief description: 'In the courtyard to the left lies among other fragments a long stone, without ornaments, with these large letters'.[19] Its inscription reads:

A(ulus) AGRIPPA L(ucii) F(ilius) C(ollegii) C(entonariorum)
[magister ?] ...

---

16 Not on record in *CIL* V, VI, IX, X, XI, XII, XIV.
17 In Thorlacius' drawing of inscriptions in the Seguier gardens in Nîmes no. 1 is *CIL* XII.3252; no. 2 = 3184; no. 3 = 3201; no. 4 = 3080; no. 5 = 3699; no. 6 = 4013; no. 7 = 3832; no. 8 = 3796; no. 9 = 3356; no. 11 = 3254; no. 12 = 3458; no. 13 = 3293; no. 14 = 3584; no. 15 = 3724; no. 16 is a renaissance inscription which is irrelevant here; no. 17 = 3232; no. 18 is a Greek inscription (= Boeckh, 1853 no. 6788B); no. 19 = *CIL* XII.3048.
18 Not on record in *CIL* V, VI, IX, X, XI, XII, XIV.
19 'I Gaarden ligger til Venstre blandt andre Fragmenter en lang Steen (?...) uden Ornamenter, med disse store Bogstaver'.

Rather than L(ucii) F(ilius), Thorlacius suggested reading LE(gatus), but the standard abbreviation is LEG(atus); since the following letters otherwise seem hard to integrate, it is a reasonable assumption that Thorlacius – here as elsewhere[20] – has mistaken an E for a F. On this reading Agrippa was a *magister* or *praefectus* of the local 'rag dealers' guild'[21] (pun un-intended).

---

20 Cf. *CIL* V.2441 (from Ferrara) where Thorlacius reads ERVCTVS for FRVCTVS.
21 *CIL* XII.3232 refers to a *patronus* of the *collegium* at Nîmes; such *collegia* had *praefecti* (*AE* 1934, 118) and *magistri* (*CIL* III.10335).

PERSIUS' RE-READING OF HORACE: THE CASE OF SOME PROPER NAMES

By Spyridon Tzounakas

Summary: By employing proper names already used by Horace (e.g., Pedius, Nerius, Craterus, Natta and Bestius), Persius does not merely exploit satirical commonplace, but attempts an implicit intertextual conversation with his predecessor, reshaping his model. Although he retains some of the previous traits of the Horatian personages, he gives them new characteristics which, as a rule, depict them more reproachable. In this way he protects his originality and allows himself to allude to a moral deterioration of his contemporary Roman society and thus to justify the abandonment of Horace's mild practices in favour of a harsher kind of censure.

Persius has frequently been accused of excessive mimesis of Horace and it is true that there are many Horatian echoes in his *Satires*.[1] On many occasions,

---

[1] For echoes of Horace in Persius the bibliography is extensive; see, e.g., G.C. Fiske 'Lucilius, the *Ars Poetica* of Horace, and Persius' *HSPh* 24 (1913) 1-36; G. Faranda 'Caratteristiche dello stile e del linguaggio poetico di Persio' *RIL* 88 (1955) 512-38, at 522-33; E. Paratore 'De Persio Horati interprete' *Latinitas* 17 (1969) 245-50; D. Henss 'Die Imitationstechnik des Persius' in D. Korzeniewski (ed.) *Die römische Satire*, WdF 238 (Darmstadt 1970) 365-83 (= *Philologus* 99 (1955) 277-94); A.L. Castelli 'La tecnica imitativa di Persio vista nelle sue caratteristiche e in riferimento alla II satira' *RAIB* 60 (1971-72) 42-60; D. de Venuto, F. Iengo and R. Scarcia *Gli auctores di Persio*, Studi su Persio e la scoliastica persiana 1 (Rome 1972) passim; N. Rudd *Lines of Enquiry: Studies in Latin Poetry* (Cambridge 1976) 54-83; D.M. Hooley '*Mutatis mutandis*: Imitations of Horace in Persius' First Satire' *Arethusa* 17 (1984) 81-95; id. 'Persius' Refractory Muse: Horatian Echoes in the Sixth Satire' *AJPh* 114 (1993) 137-54; id. *The Knotted Thong: Structures of Mimesis in Persius* (Ann Arbor 1997) passim; A. Cucchiarelli *La satira e il poeta: Orazio tra Epodi e Sermones* (Pisa 2001) 187-203. According to A. Cucchiarelli 'Speaking from Silence: The Stoic Paradoxes of Persius' in K. Freudenburg (ed.) *The Cambridge Companion to Roman*

the wealth of these literary imitations resulted in the undervaluation of Persius and his originality, a view that was predominant in the assessments of his poetry in the past.² However, since in most cases Persius reworked his Horatian prototypes and transformed them into something decidedly different with a new, vivid intensity,³ this older view is rightly discarded nowadays, and Persius' contribution to the evolution of the satiric genre begins to be appreciated on its own merits. Although Persius does not fail to recognize Horace's poetic worth and pays tribute to him, the later satirist wishes to lead Roman satire in new directions,⁴ while at the same time he attempts to free himself from the anxiety caused by the overpowering shadow of his predecessor, in a way that brings to mind Bloomian theory on the anxiety of influence.⁵

As is known, all the later satirists, despite their declarations that they would follow the example of Lucilius, abandoned his predecessor's practice of *ad hominem* attacks against socially prominent individuals, who were alive at the time.⁶ Horace turned his criticism mainly towards unknown people, a practice which was also followed to a certain extent by Persius, who moved more towards philosophical ideas, while Juvenal, at least according to his own declaration (1.170-71), attacked only the deceased. In his satires, Persius

---

Satire (Cambridge 2005) 62-80, the fact that the imitation of Horace is in conflict with Stoic philosophy, the other principal component of Persius' satire, is one of the chief reasons for his complexity.

2 See e.g. R.G.M. Nisbet 'Persius' in J.P. Sullivan (ed.) *Critical essays on Roman Literature: Satire* (London and Toronto 1963) 39-71, at 69: 'Persius is conventionally accused of unoriginality'; M. Morford *Persius* (Boston 1984), who in his preface notes: 'Yet even his positive qualities have been undervalued in recent centuries and his originality has been denied. It has often been said that he is a mere imitator of Lucilius and Horace'; G. Lee and W. Barr *The Satires of Persius* (Liverpool 1987) 3, where J.W. Mackail *Latin Literature* (London 1895) 179 is cited; cf. also the views cited by Hooley 1997 (above, n. 1) 19 ff.

3 See Hooley 1997 (above, n. 1) 30; cf. also Lee and Barr (above, n. 2) 1 ff., 88 and P. Connor 'The Satires of Persius: A Stretch of the Imagination' *Ramus* 16 (1987) 55-77, esp. at 55 and 75-76, where the opinion that Persius was a bookish poet is rightly rejected.

4 On Persius' attitude towards his predecessors, cf. 1.114-18 and see S. Tzounakas 'Persius on his Predecessors: A Re-examination' *CQ* n.s. 55 (2005) 559-71, with relevant bibliography.

5 Especially H. Bloom *The Anxiety of Influence: A Theory of Poetry* (Oxford 1973).

6 See, e.g., E.J. Kenney 'The First Satire of Juvenal' *PCPhS* 8 (1962) 29-40, esp. at 37-38; H.C. Fredricksmeyer 'An Observation on the Programmatic Satires of Juvenal, Horace and Persius' *Latomus* 49 (1990) 792-800; Tzounakas (above, n. 4) 559, with n. 7.

frequently borrows names of Horatian characters.7 According to Conington, this should be attributed partly to the existence of what could be called satirical commonplace and to Persius' intention to advertise to his readers that he was using the language of satire, partly to his lack of a wider worldly knowledge.8 He accuses Persius of 'not knowing or not remembering that satire is a kind of composition which of all others is kept alive not by antiquarian associations, but by contemporary interest – not by generalized conventionalities, but by direct individual portraiture' (xxxii) and does not hesitate to call him a plagiarist (xxxiii: 'He was what in modern parlance would be called a plagiarist – a charge which, later if not sooner, must have told fatally on an otherwise unsupported reputation').

In this paper, I shall try to demonstrate that by employing proper names already used by Horace, Persius does not merely exploit satirical commonplace but attempts an implicit intertextual conversation with his predecessor, reshaping his model. I argue that in this way he allows himself to allude to a moral deterioration of Roman society and thus to justify the abandonment of Horace's mild practices in favour of a harsher kind of censure. The cases of Pedius, Nerius, Craterus, Natta and Bestius are characteristic examples.9

7 Cf. E.S. Ramage 'Persius, the Philosopher-Satirist' in E.S. Ramage, D.L. Sigsbee and S.C. Fredericks (eds.) *Roman Satirists and their Satire: The Fine Art of Criticism in Ancient Rome* (Park Ridge, New Jersey 1974) 126, who briefly notes that 'Persius' debt to Horace is great' and that the latter's 'influence is most obvious in the characters that reappear in Persius' poems' to conclude that most of them 'crop up again in their original roles'. For an analysis and a classification of the names that appear in Horace's *Satires*, see especially N. Rudd 'The Names in Horace's *Satires*' *CQ* n.s. 10 (1960) 161-78; id. *The Satires of Horace* (Berkeley, Los Angeles and Bristol 1982²) 132-59, 291-96. On the names in Persius' *Satires* there is not such a work. The article of M. Seita, 'Uso e significato dei pronomi personali in Persio' *Paideia* 41 (1986) 25-34 examines the use of some personal pronouns by the satirist. Generally for names and naming in satire and other genres, see recently F. Jones *Juvenal and the Satiric Genre* Classical Literature and Society (London 2007) 48-75.
8 J. Conington and H. Nettleship *The Satires of A. Persius Flaccus* (Oxford 1893³, repr. Hildesheim 1967) xxxii-xxxiii; cf. also his statement that the borrowing, not only of Horatian images but also of Horatian names is 'not unnatural in a young writer and probably a recluse, who must have formed his notions of life as much from books as from experience' (37).
9 For the name of Crispinus in Pers. 5.126 and the possible Horatian background to the choice of this name, see N. Rudd, Review of J.P. Sullivan (ed.) *Critical Essays on Roman Literature: Satire* (London and Toronto 1963) *Phoenix* 19 (1965) 82-87, at 83; id. (above, n. 1) 79-80. For Labeo in Pers. 1.4 as a reminiscence of Hor. *Sat.* 1.3.82, against the informa-

Matters of literary criticism are frequently found in Roman verse satire, which defines itself among the 'low' poetic genres, turns against the *genus grande* of epic and tragedy, and is proud of its Roman origin. In his first satire, which is rightly regarded as programmatic,[10] Persius criticizes the literary production of his times and highlights the declining taste of both the writers and their audience. The neo-Callimachean movement, prevalent in that period, is the main target of Persius' attack and raises his indignation, *inter alia*, due to its affected and Graecicized style. According to the poet, this affected style is evident even in the Roman courts. He refers to a Pedius, who is accused of theft and replies to the judge *rasis antithetis*:

> 'fur es' ait Pedio. Pedius quid? crimina rasis
> librat in antithetis, doctas posuisse figuras
> laudatur: 'bellum hoc.' 'hoc bellum? an, Romule, ceves?' (1.85-87)

> 'You're a thief,' someone says to Pedius. What does Pedius say? He balances the accusations in smooth-shaven antitheses and is praised for composing clever expressions: 'That's lovely.' *That* – lovely? Are you wiggling your arse, Romulus?'[11]

Pedius, mentioned here, is sometimes identified with Pedius Blaesus, who, as Tacitus informs us (*Ann.* 14.18), was prosecuted for temple-robbery and cor-

---

tion of the *Scholia*, see V. Ferraro 'Accio Labeone: una creatura degli scoliasti di Persio' *SIFC* 43 (1971) 79-100.

10 J.C. Bramble *Persius and the Programmatic Satire: A Study in Form and Imagery* (Cambridge 1974) is an invaluable study on this subject.

11 All citations from Persius follow the OCT edition of W.V. Clausen *A. Persi Flacci et D. Iuni Iuvenalis Saturae* (Oxford 1992^2). The *Scholia* on his *Satires* are cited according to the recent Teubner edition of W.V. Clausen and J.E.G. Zetzel *Commentum Cornuti in Persium* (Munich and Leipzig 2004). All citations from Horace follow the Teubner edition of D.R. Shackleton Bailey *Q. Horati Flacci Opera* (Stuttgart 1991^2). The translations of Persius are based on those of S.M. Braund *Juvenal and Persius* (Cambridge, MA & London 2004) for Loeb. The translations of Horace are based on those of P.M. Brown *Horace: Satires I* (Warminster 1993, repr. with corrections 1995) and F. Muecke *Horace: Satires II* (Warminster 1993) in the case of his *Satires* and N. Rudd *Horace: Satires and Epistles; Persius: Satires* (Harmondsworth 1979^2, repr. with revisions 1997) for Penguin Classics in the case of his *Epistles*.

ruption in AD 59.[12] However, this would be the only exception from Persius' practice to avoid the satire of named and identifiable contemporaries; thus many scholars often attempt to interpret the choice of the name as a borrowing from Horatian satire 1.10,[13] a possibility that to me seems more plausible.

In three of his satires (1.4, 1.10, and 2.1), Horace comments upon Lucilius and expresses his objections to the style of his predecessor.[14] One of the accusations is that of frequent use of Greek words. While *Lucili fautores* justify the mixture of Greek and Latin words by comparing its stylistic effect to the *suavitas* that ensues of the mixture of Chian and Falernian wine, Horace employs the example of the court, where a linguistic impurity would be inappropriate:

scilicet oblitos patriaeque patrisque Latini,
cum Pedius causas exsudet Poplicola atque
Corvinus, patriis intermiscere petita
verba foris malis Canusini more bilinguis (*Sat.* 1.10.27-30)

---

12 *Scholia* ad 1.85: *Pedius quidam illo tempore damnatus est repetundarum; cui cum crimen obiectum fuisset furti, non se fortiter respondendo purgavit sed ex compositione versuum favorem quaerebat figuris dictionum serviens, securus criminum diversorum*; cf. also F. Villeneuve *Essai sur Perse* (Paris 1918) 207-8; N. Scivoletto *A. Persi Flacci Saturae*, Biblioteca di studi superiori 36 (Florence 1961², repr. 1964) 22; J.R. Jenkinson *Persius: the Satires* (Warminster 1980) 73; L. Mondin 'Gioco di specchi (tra Lucilio e Persio)' *Incontri triestini di filologia classica* 2 (2002-3) 91-113, at 107-8. However, in L. Canali and M. Pellegrini *Persio, Satire*, Oscar Classici Graeci e Latini 146 (Milan 2003) 62, n. 31 it is stated: 'È preferibile pensare a un nome di comodo, più che a un personaggio reale, come alcuni hanno supposto'.

13 See, e.g., W.S. Merwin and W.S. Anderson *The Satires of Persius*, Indiana University Greek and Latin Classics (Bloomington 1961) 107; Lee and Barr (above, n. 2) 78-79; cf. also Ferraro (above, n. 9) 85-86; R.A. Harvey *A Commentary on Persius*, Mnemosyne, Suppl. 64 (Leiden 1981) 41; W. Kissel *Aules Persius Flaccus: Satiren* (Heidelberg 1990) 223-25. According to P.A. Miller *Latin Verse Satire: An Anthology and Critical Reader* (London & New York 2005) 207, Persius' Pedius 'is a complicated figure embodying both a rare contemporary allusion and a borrowing from Horace'.

14 For Horace's criticism of Lucilius, see, e.g., Rudd *The Satires of Horace* (above, n. 7) 86-131; C.J. Classen 'Die Kritik des Horaz an Lucilius in den Satiren 1.4 und 1.5' *Hermes* 109 (1981) 339-60; R. Scodel 'Horace, Lucilius, and Callimachean Polemic' *HSPh* 91 (1987) 199-215.

> No doubt you'd prefer, whereas Pedius Poplicola and Corvinus sweat out their cases, them to forget their native land and father Latinus and to adulterate their native speech with foreign importations, like a bilingual from Canusium!

The Horatian Pedius is a pleader who exemplifies the meaning of *Latinitas* in the Roman court and is linked with M. Valerius Messalla Corvinus, another representative of pure *Latinitas*.[15] The satirist's view appears to be that as the court demands a pure, unaffected style that is free from Graecisms, the same could be said of Roman satiric poetry, which should not be bilingual. In Persius' first satire, the same proper name Pedius is also associated with the court. This sense is indicated by the accusation *fur es* and the words *crimina* and *librat*,[16] while the forensic atmosphere has possibly been prepared through the word *subsellia*[17] a few lines earlier (1.82). However, in Persius' text there is a remarkable refiguration. Now Pedius is not a pleader, but a defendant, who is more concerned with his elaborate style and the praise of his audience than with securing an acquittal.[18] He does not represent pure Latinity any more, as in the Horatian passage, since the Greek word *antithetis*, instead of the Latin *contrariis* (cf. Cic. *Orat.* 166), implies that he replies

---

15 On the two persons, see for instance E. Fraenkel *Horace* (Oxford 1957) 133-35; Brown (above, n. 11) 186. For a more recent view, see O. Knorr 'Three Orators and a Flawed Argument (Hor. *Sat.* 1.10.27-30)' *CJ* 100 (2004-5) 393-400.

16 Since *libra* is the symbol of justice, the verb here could be regarded as a parody which suggests the perversion of justice. The choice of the word brings to mind the imagery of the faulty pair of scales in 1.5-7: *non, si quid turbida Roma / elevet, accedas examenve inprobum in illa / castiges trutina nec te quaesiveris extra* ('If muddled Rome disparages something, don't step in to correct the faulty balance in those scales and don't search outside yourself'), where Persius attacks the popular standard at Rome. The proper balance that has disappeared from the judgment of the Romans is maintained in their rhetorical figures.

17 According to O. Jahn *Auli Persii Flacci Satirarum Liber, cum scholiis antiquis* (Leipzig 1843, repr. Hildesheim 1967) 100, the word *subsellia* refers to seats in a court of law, a view that is rejected in Conington and Nettleship (above, n. 8) 20, where it is interpreted as 'benches occupied during a recitation'; see further Harvey (above, n. 13) 40.

18 Lee and Barr (above, n. 2) 79. Contrary to Pedius' elegant and affected style, Persius' style here is not enjoyable; cf. W.S. Anderson 'Persius and the Rejection of Society' in id. (ed.) *Essays on Roman Satire* (Princeton, NJ 1982) 169-93 (=*Wissenschaftliche Zeitschrift der Wilhelm-Pieck-Universität Rostock, Gesellschafts und Sprachwissenschaftliche Reihe* 15 (1966) 409-16), at 187-90.

to the judge in a Graecicized style. Besides, the modification of this noun with *rasis* ('smooth-shaven') allows for further allusions. At a metaphorical level, it suggests the polished style of Persius' Pedius and could be interpreted as a hint at the reversal of the traditional appearance of the defendant in the court as *sordidatus*.[19] Furthermore, in the choice of *rasis* there is an implication of effeminacy,[20] which is also implied in the phrase *doctas posuisse figuras*.[21] The same charge is also directed to Pedius' audience (*an, Romule, ceves?*), which reacts to the delicacies of style in an unmanly way that does not befit the traditional Roman morality of the past and the status of Roman aristocrats.[22] Thus, while Horace's Pedius is associated with the Roman past (*patriaeque patrisque Latini, patriis ... foris*), Persius' Pedius is alienated from the Roman tradition and its morality.

The mention of Romulus is another indication of Persius' attempt to converse with Horace on the particular matter. Horace's reference to Pedius is followed by the warning he received in his dream by Quirinus (= deified Romulus) to stop composing poems in Greek:

> atque ego cum Graecos facerem, natus mare citra,
> versiculos, vetuit me tali voce Quirinus,
> post mediam noctem visus, cum somnia vera:
> 'in silvam non ligna feras insanius ac si
> magnas Graecorum malis implere catervas.' (*Sat.* 1.10.31-35)

> Indeed, when I, though born on this side of the ocean, was writing some little verses in Greek, Quirinus appeared to me after midnight, when dreams are true, and forbade me in tones like these: 'Carrying timber to a forest would be no crazier than your choosing to swell the packed ranks of the Greeks.'

In a parody of the motif of the poetic dream, Horace replaces Apollo, the

---

19 J.G.F. Powell 'Persius' First Satire: A Re-examination' in T. Woodman and J. Powell (eds.) *Author and Audience in Latin Literature* (Cambridge 1992) 150-72 and 248-51, at 157.
20 Cf. N. Rudd *Themes in Roman Satire* (Norman and London 1986) 180.
21 See D. Korzeniewski *Die erste Satire des Persius* in id. (ed.) *Die römische Satire*, WdF 238 (Darmstadt 1970) 384-438, at 416-17, who, in addition, connects the name of Pedius with the verb *pedicare* (416, n. 84); Bramble (above, n. 10) 124-25, n. 3.
22 Powell (above, n. 19) 157-58.

usual advisor of poets, with the deified Romulus, who appears as a symbol of Roman nationalism.[23] On the contrary, in Persius' passage not only does Romulus not appear as a champion of *Latinitas*, but he too seems to have succumbed to the literary affectation and effeminacy of the times. In this way, Persius underlines the extent of the corruption, since it includes even exemplary symbols of Latinity and of the honoured Roman past.[24]

In this framework, the very accusation of *furtum* possibly presents special interest. Persius' Pedius appropriates traits that are at odds with his previous appearance in Roman satire. His new persona suggests that he adopts a style alien to his nature in Horace. Thus it could be argued that he has 'stolen' a style that does not belong to him. This impression is further reinforced by the phrase *doctas posuisse figuras*, which points to the *doctrina* of the Callimachean programme and implies mimicry and lack of inspiration.[25] His stance brings to mind Persius' attack on his contemporary literature on the ground of its close imitation of Greek models.[26] In this sense, the excessive dependence upon the works and techniques of others could be equated with literary 'stealing' and accordingly it is heavily castigated by Persius.

Martial, who praises Persius,[27] could shed light on the particular case. In his epigrams 1.52, 53, and 66 he refers to a poet who recites some of Martial's poems as if they were his own compositions and calls him both *plagiarius* (1.52.9) and *fur* (1.53.12 and 66.1).[28] The case of line 1.53.12: *stat contra dicitque tibi tua pagina 'Fur es.'* is especially interesting here due to its verbal similarity with the accusation against Pedius in Persius. It indicates that the phrase *fur es* could equally apply to literary *furtum*.

When in *Sat.* 2.3.69 ff. Horace refers to a creditor who, in spite of his pre-

23 See Brown (above, n. 11) 187.
24 Cf. also *Titos* (1.20) and *Romulidae* (1.31).
25 Cf. S. Tzounakas '*Rusticitas* versus *Urbanitas* in the Literary Programmes of Tibullus and Persius' *Mnemosyne*[4] 59 (2006) 111-28, esp. at 116 and 118.
26 Cf., e.g., the imagery of the birds that imitate the Greek *chaere* in Prol. 8-11 as well as Persius' attack on Attius Labeo (1.4-5 and 50-51), who, according to the *Scholia* ad 1.4, translated Homer's *Iliad* and *Odyssey* word for word (*verbum ex verbo*).
27 Cf. Mart. 4.29.7-8: *saepius in libro numeratur Persius uno, / quam levis in tota Marsus Amazonide*.
28 For the particular epigrams as a classical example of the ancients' point of view on plagiarism, see, e.g., E. Stemplinger *Das Plagiat in der griechischen Literatur* (Leipzig & Berlin 1912, repr. Hildesheim, Zurich & New York 1990) 169-70; G.C. Fiske *Lucilius and Horace: A Study in the Classical Theory of Imitation* (Madison 1920, repr. Hildesheim 1966) 27.

cautions, can be tricked by his defaulting debtor, the name of Nerius is attributed to a banker or money-lender:[29]

> scribe decem a Nerio. non est satis; adde Cicutae
> nodosi tabulas; centum, mille adde catenas:
> effugiet tamen haec sceleratus vincula Proteus. (*Sat.* 2.3.69-71)
>
> Record ten thousand sesterces as lent through Nerius. That is not enough security, add Cicuta's knotty contract; add a hundred, a thousand chains. Nonetheless the blasted fellow will escape these fetters, a very Proteus.

The same name reoccurs in Persius' second satire, where Nerius appears to bury his third wife, in order to appropriate her fortune:

> Nerio iam tertia conditur[30] uxor. (2.14)
>
> Nerius is already burying his third wife.

In all probability, what we have here is another instance of borrowing from Horace. Persius seems to exploit the previous association of the name with the field of economics and presents his Nerius as a person who aims at financial profit.[31] But, as in the case of Pedius, there is again an implication of moral deterioration. While in Horace's passage Nerius' behaviour is not reproachable, Persius' Nerius figures in the passage with the examples of the impious prayers criticized by the poet, where his good fortune is the envy of the worshipper. In addition, while the Horatian character fails to force the devious debtor to refund the money, in Persius' satire Nerius is successful

---

29 On this character, see Rudd, *The Satires of Horace* (above, n. 7) 147; id. 'The Names ...' (above, n. 7) 170; Muecke (above, n. 11) 140 (on Hor. *Sat.* 2.3.69-76) with relevant bibliography.
30 The variant *ducitur* could mean that Nerius is marrying a third time, perhaps with the implication that he has just buried his second wife; see Conington and Nettleship (above, n. 8) 37. On this *varia lectio*, see also B.L. Gildersleeve *The Satires of A. Persius Flaccus*, Latin texts and commentaries (New York, Cincinnati & Chicago 1903, repr. New York 1979) 108; Harvey (above, n. 13) 61; Kissel (above, n. 13) 306-7.
31 Cf. Harvey (above, n. 13) 61.

and realizes his intentions. Moreover, his actions are no longer restricted to his clients, but are extended even to his family. The reference to his third wife implies that he has repeated the same practice twice previously.

The central section of the same Horatian satire 2.3 is devoted to the Stoic paradox that all men but the *sapiens* are mad, presented through a lecture of Stertinius. Medical imagery is frequently found in Stoic thought, which draws a parallel between passions and diseases and depicts the former as mental illness.[32] In accordance with the Stoic dogma that all sins are equal, Stertinius makes a transition from *avaritia* to another 'disease of the soul', that of *ambitio*.[33] In this framework, he exploits the analogy from physical illness to support his allegation that freedom from one *vitium* does not mean freedom from all.[34] Thus he uses the example of Craterus, a well-known practitioner of the time of Cicero, how if he claimed that a patient was not *cardiacus*,[35] that did not imply that the patient was not suffering from some other disease. Similarly, if the Stoic realizes that someone is not *avarus*, this does not automatically mean that he is not *ambitiosus et audax*. In this case he too is mad and needs to go to Anticyra to cure his madness with the hellebore that grows there:

> 'Quisnam igitur sanus?' 'qui non stultus.' 'quid avarus?'
> 'stultus et insanus.' 'quid? si quis non sit avarus,
> continuo sanus?' 'minime.' 'cur, Stoice?' 'dicam.
> non est cardiacus (Craterum dixisse putato)
> hic aeger. recte est igitur surgetque? negabit,
> quod latus aut renes morbo temptentur acuto.
> non est periurus neque sordidus: immolet aequis
> hic porcum Laribus. verum ambitiosus et audax:
> naviget Anticyram.' (*Sat.* 2.3.158-66)

---

32 On this Stoic analogy, cf., e.g., K.-H. Rolke *Die bildhaften Vergleiche in den Fragmenten der Stoiker von Zenon bis Panaitios* Spudasmata 32 (Hildesheim and New York 1975) 76-79, 315-26, 484-85; R.G.M. Nisbet and M. Hubbard *A Commentary on Horace, Odes, Book II* (Oxford 1978, repr. 1991) 44-45, with relevant bibliography.
33 On this transition, see Muecke (above, n. 11) 148.
34 See Muecke (above, n. 11) 148, who cites Hor. *Epist.* 2.2.205-12.
35 On Craterus and the controversy on the meaning of *cardiacus*, see Muecke (above, n. 11) 149.

'Who is sane then?' 'The man who is not a fool.' 'What about the lover of wealth?' 'A fool and a madman.' 'Tell me, if someone is not a lover of wealth, does it follow that he is sane?' 'By no means.' 'Why, Mr. Stoic?' 'I will tell you. It is not heart-burn (suppose Craterus to have been speaking) this sick man has. Is he all right, then, and will he get up? Craterus will say no, because an acute disease is attacking the chest or kidneys. He is not a cheat or a miser: let him, in that case, sacrifice a pig to the well-disposed Lares. But he is ambitious, and reckless: let him sail to Anticyra.'

The particular passage of Horace is the hypertext for interpreting Persius' lines 3.63-65,[36] where he again reworks his prototype:

elleborum frustra, cum iam cutis aegra tumebit,
poscentis videas; venienti occurrite morbo,
et quid opus Cratero magnos promittere montis?

You can see it's useless to ask for hellebore when the sickly skin is already getting bloated. Face the disease at its approach, and what need will you have to promise the earth to Craterus?

In Persius' passage the medical imagery remains, but there is a significant difference. Here, the speaker is not restricted to the highlighting of the disease, but suggests its prevention and timely cure.[37] Consequently hellebore,

---

[36] More generally, for Horatian satire 2.3 as a main model for Persius' third satire, see W.S. Smith 'Speakers in the Third Satire of Persius' *CJ* 64 (1968-69) 305-8; Lee and Barr (above n. 2) 101; Hooley 1997 (above, n. 1) 202-29; F. Bellandi 'Dogma e inquietudine: Persio, Orazio e la *vox docens* della satira' in L. Castagna and G. Vogt-Spira (eds.) Pervertere: *Ästhetik der Verkehrung. Literatur und Kultur neronischer Zeit und ihre Rezeption*, Beiträge zur Altertumskunde 151 (Munich & Leipzig 2002) 153-91, esp. at 163 ff.; Cucchiarelli 'Speaking from Silence ...' (above, n. 1) 70-71 with relevant bibliography. However, according to the *Scholia* ad 3.1, *hanc satiram poeta ex Lucilii libro quarto transtulit, castigantis luxuriam et vitia divitum*.

[37] This reflects a major difference between the two satirists, which is evident even in Persius' view on his predecessor (1.116-18: *omne vafer vitium ridenti Flaccus amico / tangit et admissus circum praecordia ludit, / callidus excusso populum suspendere naso* 'While his friend is laughing, the rascal Horace touches every fault in him and, once he's got in, he frolics around his heart, clever at dangling the public from his cleaned-out nose'). There, with

which is suggested in Horace's passage with the phrase *naviget Anticyram*, appears to be of no use when the problem has worsened and in this instance, Craterus' contribution proves not only pointless, but also costly. Thus we have to deal with a new reshaping and deterioration of a Horatian character, since in Persius' satire not only is Craterus not needed, but he is associated with material profit, something that is not implied in his predecessor's satire.

In satire 1.6 Horace is contrasted with a Natta, otherwise unknown; with an implication to his meanness, Natta is called dirty (*immundus*) and appears to use lamp-oil on his body:[38]

> ad quartam iaceo; post hanc vagor aut ego lecto
> aut scripto quod me tacitum iuvet unguor olivo,
> non quo fraudatis immundus Natta lucernis. (*Sat.* 1.6.122-24)

> I lie in bed till ten, and then take a stroll; or, after reading or writing for my own private enjoyment, I have oil applied, though not the sort that dirty fellow Natta uses, robbing his lamps.

This brief reference to Natta is exploited and elaborated by Persius, who attributes to him different traits:

> non pudet ad morem discincti vivere Nattae.
> sed stupet hic vitio et fibris increvit opimum
> pingue, caret culpa, nescit quid perdat, et alto
> demersus summa rursus non bullit in unda. (3.31-34)

> You're not embarrassed to live like that dissolute Natta. But he's paralysed with vice, and thick fat has grown over his liver. He has no sense of guilt or of what he's lost. He's sunk so deep that he makes no more bubbles on the surface.

---

his phrase *vafer vitium ridenti Flaccus amico / tangit*, Persius suggests that Horace is restricted to the diagnosis of a problem, while he himself proceeds to its treatment; cf. F. Bellandi *Persio: dai «verba togae» al solipsismo stilistico (Studi sui* Choliambi *e la poetica di Aulo Persio Flacco)*, Testi e manuali per l'insegnamento Universitario del Latino 25 (Bologna 1996²) 58, n. 67; Tzounakas (above, n. 4) 566.

38 See Brown (above, n. 11) 164.

Persius abandons Horace's implication of Natta's meanness.[39] Now the criticism of this character is not restricted to his physical appearance and his personal habits, but, given the moral implications of *discincti*,[40] it is extended on a moral level.[41] In addition, he is so ignorant of his vices and so insensible that he has no feeling of guilt, shame or remorse; thus he could be regarded as morally dead.[42] Once again, we have to deal with a significant deterioration in a Horatian character and a stricter censure on the part of Persius. He implies that even the mean Natta now leads a dissolute life.

Similarly, Hor. *Epist.* 1.15.33-37 seems to be Persius' main model for his Bestius in 6.37. In Horace, this name is attributed to an unidentifiable reformed spendthrift who makes himself out to be a savage moralist[43] and attacks the prodigals for their insatiable appetite:

> hic ubi nequitiae fautoribus et timidis nil
> aut paulum abstulerat, patinas cenabat omasi
> vilis et agninae, tribus ursis quod satis esset;
> scilicet ut ventres lamna candente nepotum
> diceret urendos, correctus Bestius. (*Epist.* 1.15.33-37)

---

39 Rudd (above, n. 11) 287 remarks that the name occurs in Hor. *Sat.* 1.6.124, 'but there the character is mean rather than extravagant'.

40 For the moral implications of *discincti*, see e.g. Lee and Barr (above, n. 2) 106 and Harvey (above, n. 13) 87, who cite 4.22; cf. also M. Coffey *Roman Satire* (Bristol 1989², repr. 1991) 239, n. 72.

41 In Conington and Nettleship (above, n. 8) 56 the choice of the name is also connected with Tacitus' information (*Ann.* 4.34) that Natta appears as a cognomen of the Pinarian *gens*. In the light of this evidence it is noted: 'There may then be something in a view mentioned by the *Scholia*, "Nattam fuisse quendam luxuriosum, qui … *nobilitatem suam male vivendo exturpaverit*".'; cf. also Villeneuve (above, n. 12) 233-34; Scivoletto (above, n. 12) 61; D. Bo, *A. Persi Flacci Saturarum Liber, Praecedit Vita*, Corpus Scriptorum Latinorum Paravianum (Turin 1969) 55-56. This view is rejected by Coffey (above, n. 40) 239, n. 72.

42 Cf. R. Jenkinson 'Interpretations of Persius' Satires III and IV' *Latomus* 32 (1973) 521-49, at 543; Harvey (above, n. 13) 87. According to M. Squillante *Persio. Il linguaggio della malinconia*, Storie e testi 6 (Naples 1995) 33, Natta is implicitly equated with a swine; cf. also G. L. Hendrickson 'The Third Satire of Persius' *CPh* 23 (1928) 332-42, at 337, who characterizes his fate 'merely bestial'.

43 R. Mayer *Horace, Epistles: Book I*, Cambridge Greek and Latin Classics (Cambridge 1994) 217; cf. K. Freudenburg *Satires of Rome: Threatening Poses from Lucilius to Juvenal* (Cambridge 2001) 200.

> When he had extracted little or nothing from those who applauded
> or dreaded his spite, he used to devour platefuls of tripe
> or cheap lamb – enough to fill a trio of bears.
> He would even assert, like Bruty when he had changed his ways,
> that wastrels should have their bellies burnt with red-hot plates.

When Bestius, whose name seems to be a proverbial and significant one,[44] reappears in Persius, he retains the main traits of his previous image. He again criticizes extravagancies in food in a moralistic way, but now he is strongly associated with the practices of the past and blames the Greek philosophers with the implication that they imported exotic luxury and thus they are responsible for the decadence and the corruption of his day:

> 'tune bona incolumis minuas?' et Bestius urguet
> doctores Graios: 'ita fit; postquam sapere urbi
> cum pipere et palmis venit nostrum hoc maris expers,
> fenisecae crasso vitiarunt unguine pultes.' (6.37-40)

> 'Are you going to diminish your fortune–and get away with it?' And Bestius blames the Greek professors: 'That's the trouble. Ever since this emasculated know-how of ours arrived in Rome along with pepper and dates, the haycutters have spoiled their porridge with thick oil'.

By attributing to his Bestius an attack on Greek philosophy[45] and an anti-Hellenism, Persius gives this person new characteristics and elaborates his

---

44 Cf. C.W. Mendell *Latin Poetry: The Age of Rhetoric and Satire* (Hamden, Conn. 1967) 63; C. Cowherd *Persius, Saturae*, Bryn Mawr Latin Commentaries (Bryn Mawr 1986) 122; Lee and Barr (above, n. 2) 162. More generally on Bestius, see A. Kiessling, R. Heinze and E. Burck *Q. Horatius Flaccus: Briefe* (Hildesheim & Zurich 1984¹¹) 131-32; C. S. Dessen *The Satires of Persius: Iunctura Callidus Acri* (London 1996²) 89-90; H. Beikircher *Kommentar zur VI. Satire des A. Persius Flaccus*, Wiener Studien, Beiheft 1 (Vienna, Cologne & Graz 1969) 65; G. Stégen 'Perse, Satire VI, 37-40' *AC* 44 (1975) 204-9; Jenkinson (above, n. 12) 94, 116-18. On Persius' text here, see also A.E. Housman 'Notes on Persius' in J. Diggle & F.R.D. Goodyear (eds.) *The Classical Papers of A.E. Housman*, II: *1897-1914* (Cambridge 1972) 845-66 (= *CQ* 7 (1913) 12-32), at 861-62.
45 The use of *sapere* encapsulates both the meaning of 'philosophy' and the meaning of 'taste'; cf., e.g., Nisbet (above, n. 2) 68; Beikircher (above, n. 44) 67 with n. 5; Harvey (above, n. 13) 194; Lee and Barr (above, n. 2) 162.

image. In particular, Bestius is depicted as narrow-minded with insular prejudices, despising intellectual pursuits and new habits. Besides, compared to his previous appearance in Horace, he is now more concerned with the change in nutrition, rather than with the quantity of the food, while it is worth noting that in Persius' description he lacks the positive modification *correctus* of the Horatian text.

While Lucilius and Horace are directly involved in the urban context they satirize, Persius turns his back on Roman society and rejects its morality.[46] He presents himself as a *semipaganus*,[47] who stands outside the corrupted society (1.114: *discedo*) and heavily castigates its vices. Consequently, by reshaping Horatian personages and depicting them as degenerate, Persius not only attempts an *aemulatio* of the great Augustan satirist that protects his originality, but also gives good reason for his differentiation from his predecessor's amiable approach to the *vitia*. With his famous phrase *ridentem dicere verum* (*Sat.* 1.1.24) Horace presents the smile as one of the most characteristic traits of his *Satires*. Persius does not espouse his predecessor's practice. He realizes the different needs of the age of Nero and seems to believe that the *vitia* of his time demand a more drastic castigation.[48] Thus, through the use of proper names that occur in Horace, Persius implies the moral deterioration of his contemporary society and justifies the choice of a different kind of satiric attack.

---

46 For the rejection of society in Persius' *Satires*, see, e.g., H. Bardon 'Perse, ou l'homme du refus' *RBPh* 53 (1975) 24-47; Bramble (above, n. 10) 134-35; Anderson (above, n. 18); M. Malamud 'Out of Circulation? An Essay on Exchange in Persius' *Satires*' *Ramus* 25 (1996) 39-64, at 43-44; Tzounakas (above, n. 4) 567 ff.

47 Prol. 6-7: *ipse semipaganus / ad sacra vatum carmen adfero nostrum* ('It's as a half-caste that I bring my song to the bards' rites'). On the meaning of *semipaganus* the bibliography is extensive. For a very good treatment of its meaning, see Bellandi (above, n. 37), esp. 33-71.

48 See K.J. Reckford 'Studies in Persius' *Hermes* 90 (1962) 476-504, at 500, who remarks that 'a non-Horatian age deserved non-Horatian satire'; Tzounakas (above, n. 4) 566-67.

BEMERKUNGEN ZU ZWEI EPIGRAMMEN

By Elias Sverkos

Summary: This paper comments on two funerary epigrams from Catania and Rome. The first (Peek, *GV* 1936) records the name of the legendary Persian queen Rhodogune given to Epagatho (obviously after her death). This name is probably to be associated with the literary interest of the deceased's social circle, and is employed either to signal a comparison of personal characteristics and qualities of the deceased Epagatho to those of the queen, or as a *consolatio per exemplum* that works by alluding to the fate all humans have in common. The humorous style of the second epigram (*IGUR* 1181) strongly suggests that the nick-name Petrokorax refers to the deceased's physical characteristics, and if so it was no doubt a name coined by his friends.

I

Mit dem Namen Rhodogune werden in den literarischen Quellen sechs Personen bezeichnet, die in Zusammenhang mit der Geschichte des Perser- bzw. des Partherreichs stehen.[1] Es handelt sich um die mythische Rhodogu-

---

[1] Für epigraphische Publikationen werden im Folgenden die in *SEG* verwendeten Abkürzungen benutzt. Wenn nicht anders angegeben, sind alle Datierungen n. Chr. Für wertvolle Hinweise bedanke ich mich herzlich bei Prof. Dr. A. Chaniotis (Oxford), J. Georgiou und Prof. Dr. D. Panagiotopoulos (Heidelberg). Großen Dank schulde ich schließlich auch Prof. Dr. Th. Corsten (Heidelberg/Oxford) für die kritische Lektüre des Manuskripts. Sprachlich wurde der Text von Dr. S. Schmidt-Hofner und A. Tata (Heidelberg) verbessert.

ne; die Gattin des Hystaspes und Mutter Dareios' I; die Tochter des Dareios I; die des Xerxes I; die des Artaxerxes II, Gattin des Orontes; und die Tochter des Königs Mithradates I von Parthien, Gemahlin des Demetrios II Nikator.[2] Mit der ersten, die in Gegensatz zu den historischen Frauen häufig erwähnt wird und in den einschlägigen Quellen besonders wegen ihrer Tapferkeit bekannt ist,[3] lässt sich ein Grabepigramm aus Katane (mod. Catania) verbinden, das allem Anschein nach in das 2./3. Jh. n. Chr. datiert. Der Text der Inschrift lautet wie folgt:[4]

Τύμβον ὁρᾷς, παροδεῖτα, περικλειτῆς Ῥοδογούνης,
ἣν κτάνεν οὐχ ὁσίως λάεσι δεινὸς ἀνήρ·
κλαῦσε δὲ καὶ τάρχυσε Ἀβιάνιος ἣν παράκοιτιν
4 καὶ βαιὴν στήλη τήνδ' ἀπέδωκες χάριν.
οὔνομα τὸ πρίν με πᾶς ἔκληζεν Ἐπαγαθώ,
νῦν δὲ Ῥοδογούνη[ν], βασιλίδος τὸ ἐπώνυμον.

Wie aus dem Inschriftentext hervorgeht, zählt das Epigramm zu den 'sprechenden' Grabmonumenten, in denen der Verstorbene oder das Grabmal

---

2 Für Trägerinnen dieses Namens in griechischen Quellen s. F. Justi *Iranisches Namenbuch* (Hildesheim 1963, 2. Ausg), 261 s.v. Ῥοδογούνη, G. Plaumann *RE* I A.1 (1914) 956-957 und zuletzt J. Wiesehöfer *DnP* 10 (2001) 995-96. Vgl. M. Karras-Klapproth *Prosopographische Studien zur Geschichte des Partherreiches auf der Grundlage antiker literarischer Überlieferung* (Bonn 1988) 155-57.

3 Siehe H. Dittmar *Aischines von Sphettos. Studien zur Literaturgeschichte der Sokratiker,* Philologische Untersuchungen 21 (Berlin 1912) 41-45, P. Bernard 'Un nouveau livre sur les Parthes' *Studia Iranica* 8 (1979) 129-33 und zuletzt T. Polanski 'Two Persian princesses in the paintings of the Greek "orientalists"' *CB* 24 (2005) 197-212 (bes. 202 ff.).

4 'Das Grabmal siehst Du, Wanderer, der berühmten Rhodogune, die ein schrecklicher Mann frevelnd zu Tode steinigte. Avianios beweinte und bestattete seine Ehefrau und erweis ihr mit dem Grabmal den mindesten Dank. Früher nannten mich alle Epagatho, nun aber Rhodogune, mit dem Namen der Königin'. *CIG* 5724, Kaibel, *EG* 685, *IG* XIV 499, Peek, *GV* 1936 und zuletzt G. Manganaro 'Iscrizioni, epitaffi ed epigrammi in greco della Sicilia centro-orientale di epoca romana' *MEFRA* 106 (1994) 94 no. 6 (= *SEG* XLIV 738 (6)). 'Das Grabmal siehst Du, Wanderer, der berühmten Rhodogune, die ein schrecklicher Mann frevelnd zu Tode steinigte. Avianios beweinte und bestattete seine Ehefrau und erweis ihr mit dem Grabmal den mindesten Dank. Früher nannten mich alle Epagatho, nun aber Rhodogune, mit dem Namen der Königin'.

selbst den Betrachter anspricht.⁵ Am Anfang des Epigramms wird angegeben, dass es sich dabei um das Grab (hier τύμβος bzw. στήλη genannt) der berühmten Rhodogune (περικλειτῆς Ῥοδογούνης) handelte, das der Gemahl der Verstorbenen, Avianios, errichten ließ. In den beiden letzten Zeilen wird allerdings erläutert, dass die Verstorbene in ihrem Umfeld unter dem Namen Ἐπαγαθώ bekannt war und den Namen (ἐπώνυμον) der Königin Rhodogune erst postum erhalten hat.

Die Frage ist, ob der Name Rhodogune hier als *agnomen* der Verstorbenen aus Katane verwendet wird,⁶ wie bereits I. Kajanto in seinem Beitrag zu *Supernomina* vermutete (allerdings mit folgender Bemerkung: 'it is naturally impossible to tell, why this Sicilian woman bore her name as an agnomen'),⁷ und wie zusätzlich die Erwähnung der persischen Königin gerechtfertigt werden könnte.⁸

Die Verwendung von Personennamen, die mit der Geschichte des persischen bzw. assyrischen Reiches verbunden waren, ist in der griechischen und römischen Welt ein gängiges Phänomen. Als Beispiel sei hier das häufige Vorkommen der Namen Dareios und Kyros in der römischen Kaiserzeit erwähnt.⁹ Der Name Rhodogune selbst begegnet in einer Inschrift des 3. Jh. aus Beroia und möglicherweise in einer Inschrift des 3./4. Jh. aus Syrakus¹⁰

---

5   Siehe dazu M. Burzachechi 'Oggetti parlanti nelle epigrafi greche' *Epigraphica* 24 (1962) 3-54 und P. Herrmann Τέρας θανόντων. Totenruhm und Totenehrung im städtischen Leben der hellenistischen Zeit' in: M. Wörrle, P. Zanker (Hsg.) *Stadtbild und Bürgerbild im Hellenismus. Kolloquium, München, 24. bis 26. Juni 1993*, Vestigia 47 (München 1995) 190.
6   Die Herausgeber des *LGPN* erachten den Namen als Personennamen (*LGPN* III A s.v. Nr. 1).
7   I. Kajanto *Supernomina. A Study in Latin Epigraphy*, Comm. Hum. Litt. 40 (Helsinki 1966) 11, 19. Vgl. hierzu M. Lambertz 'Zur Ausbreitung des Supernomen oder Signum im römischen Reiche' *Glotta* 4 (1913) 84, 86, W. Kubitschek 'Signum' *RE* II A 2 (1923) 2449.
8   Vgl. Kaibel *EG* 685 app. cr.: *ipsam defunctam Asianam fuisse utrumque nomen docet*. Vgl. dennoche H. Solin 'Die Namen der orientalischen Sklaven in Rom' *L'onomastique Latine* (Paris 1977) 219.
9   *LGPN* I-IV s.v. Zur Verbreitung iranischer Namen in Rom, H. Solin *Die griechischen Personennamen in Rom. Ein Namenbuch* (Berlin & New York 2003 2. Ausg.) 240-44, ders. *Die Stadtrömischen Sklavennamen. Ein Namenbuch* (Stuttgart 1996) 253-55, 606.
10 Zum Namen s. auch R. Schmitt 'Βαγώνη' *ZPE* 15 (1974) 169-71, *Bull. épigr.* 1974, 155 und zuletzt R. Schmitt *Iranische Antroponymie in den erhaltenen Resten von Ktesias' Werk* (Wien 2006) 183-85. Zur Inschrift aus Beroia *Bull. épigr.* 1959, 542, *I. Beroia* 278, *LGPN* IV s.v. Der Name in der Inschrift aus Syrakus ist ergänzt ([Ῥοδο]γύνη?) *LGPN* IIIA s.v. Nr. 2.

sowie in zwei lateinischen Inschriften aus Rom.[11] Nicht minder bekannt ist die Verwendung nichtgriechischer historischer Namen als *agnomina*.[12] In einer Grabinschrift der Kaiserzeit aus Histiaia ist eine gewisse [A]ἰλία Εὔνοια ἡ καὶ Σεμίραμις bezeugt.[13] Der Name der berühmten assyrischen Königin kommt ferner in einem Epigramm aus Itanos wie auch in einer weiteren kretischen Grabinschrift aus Sybrita vor[14] und ist auch aus Inschriften aus Rom bekannt.[15] In diesen Fällen lässt sich vermuten, dass zumindest in der Kaiserzeit die Wahl dieser Namen die literarischen Vorlieben oder das geistige Klima widerspiegelt, die in der sozialen Umwelt der Namensträger vorherrschten.[16]

Doch der Gegensatz, der im Epigramm aus Katane in den Worten πρίν με πᾶς ἔκληζεν ... νῦν δέ zum Ausdruck kommt, spricht gegen die Deutung des Namens Rhodogune als Personennamen oder *agnomen* bzw. *Supernomen*.[17] Ein Epigramm der *Anthologia Palatina* (7.691) lautet wie folgt: 'Ich

---

11 Solin *Personennamen* (Anm. 8) 242.
12 Kajanto (Anm. 6) 18-19.
13 *IG* XII 9, 1213, *LGPN* I *s.v.* Zur Königin Semiramis, Th. Lenschau, *RE* Suppl. VII (1940) 1204-12. Für die Bedeutung des Namens der Königin, Diod. 2.4.6: τὸ παιδίον τρέφειν (sc. Σίμμαν) ὡς θυγάτριον μετὰ πάσης ἐπιμελείας, ὄνομα θέμενον Σεμίραμιν, ὅπερ ἐστὶ κατὰ τὴν τῶν Σύρων διάλεκτον παρωνομασμένον ἀπὸ τῶν περιστερῶν (…und so zog er (sc. Simmas) das Mädchen mit aller Sorgfalt wie seine eigene Tochter auf. Als Name gabe er ihr Semiramis, was in der syrischen Sprache 'Taube' bedeutet (Übers. G. Wirth, Stuttgart 1992)).
14 *IC* II X 19 (= Peek, *GV* 678); *IC* II xxvi 19. Siehe auch *LGPN* I *s.v.* Σαμήραμις.
15 Beispiele bei H. Solin 'Analecta epigraphica' *Arctos* 11 (1977) 123-24, 16 (1982) 206 (= H. Solin *Analecta Epigraphica 1970-1997* (Rom 1998) 88, 163, ders. *Personennamen* (Anm. 8) 605.
16 Über die Eigenschaften der Semiramis s. z.B. Diod., 2.4-6 ἐπιφανεστάτην ἁπασῶν τῶν γυναικῶν ... διαφέρον τῷ κάλλει ... τῷ κάλλει πολὺ τὰς ἄλλας παρθένους διαφερούσης ... ἡ δὲ συνέσει καὶ τόλμῃ καὶ τοῖς ἄλλοις τοῖς πρὸς ἐπιφάνειαν συντείνουσιν κεχορηγημένη καιρὸν ἔλαβε ἐπιδείξασθαι τὴν ἰδίαν ἀρετήν ... . Vgl. Dio Chrysostomos (Anm. 26), Polyaenus *Strategemata*, 8.26, Iulian *Orationes*, 3.126D, Anonymus *De mulieribus*, I (Hsg. A. Westermann *Paradoxographi scriptores rerum mirabilium graeci* (London 1839) 231) Suidas, s.v., *AP* 5.252, 7.748 (= Merkelbach-Stauber, *SGO* II, 09/11/01), Merkelbach-Stauber, *SGO* I, 01/12/01 (Halikarnass, späthellenistisch?). Siehe dazu ebenfalls Dittmar (Anm. 2) 28-29.
17 Siehe dazu Kajanto *Supernomina* (Anm. 6) 5-6. Vgl. z.B. Peek, *GV* 874 (= A-M. Vérilhac Παῖδες ἄωροι. *Poésie funéraire. Vol. I. Textes* (Athen 1978), Nr. 61, Merkelbach-Stauber, *SGO* I, 05/01/36): ὅ<ς> τὸ πρὶν ἐν ζωῇ Διονύσιος ἦν πανάρεστος, υἱὸς Ἀπολλωνίου

bin eine neue Alkestis; ich starb um des herrlichen Mannes Zenon willen, den einzig in meinem Herzen ich hegte, den meine Seele noch mehr als das Licht und die Kindlein geliebt hat, Kallikrateia geheißen, ringsum von den Menschen bewundert'.[18] Die verstorbene Ehefrau des Zenon rühmt sich hier, dass sie wegen ihres Todes die neue Alkestis sei (Z. 1: Ἄλκηστις νέη εἰμί), erklärt allerdings in den nachfolgenden Zeilen, dass ihr eigentlicher Name Kallikrateia ist (Z. 4: οὔνομα Καλλικράτεια).[19]

Was die Nennung der Verstorbenen als Rhodogune im behandelten Epigramm angeht, vertritt K. Lehmann-Hartleben die Meinung, 'the reason for this adoption of the name of a legendary queen is undoubtedly to be sought in the strange circumstances of the death of this woman who, as the epigram says at the beginning, was stoned to death by a man'.[20] G. Manganaro ist der Auffassung, dass dies in Zusammenhang mit dem, durch den Dialog *Aspasia* des Sokratikers Aischines von Sphettos, bekannten Bild der persischen Königin steht und im Epigramm der Mut der Verstorbenen gegenüber ihrem tragischen Tod mit der Tapferkeit der legendären Königin verglichen wird.[21] P. Bernand ist gleicher Ansicht wie K. Lehmann-Hartleben.[22]

(Smyrna, 2. Jh.); Peek, *GV* 1029: οὔνομα Θεσμοφάνην με πατὴρ ἠδ᾽ ἅμα μήτηρ | κίκλησκον, δυεροῦ πρὶν θανάτοιο τυχεῖν (Athen, 2. Jh.?); Peek, *GV* 1083 (= Merkelbach-Stauber, *SGO* IV, 18/13/06) Z. 3: Μαρκιανὴ δ᾽ ἦν μοι τὸ πρὶν οὔνομα (Perge, Kaiserzeit); Merkelbach-Stauber, *SGO* II, 08/01/31 Z. 9: οὔνομα δ᾽ἦν μοι τὸ πρὶν Διονύσιος (Kyzikos, spätere Kaiserzeit).

18 Siehe auch Peek, *GV* 1738.

19 Als Gegenbeispiel kann hier der Fall der Mevia Victoria erwähnt werden. Die entsprechende Inschrift *CIL* IX 2893 (Histonium) lautet folgendermaßen: *hic abitat Mevia Victoria qe at superos sinnu abebat Cassandra*. Siehe dazu Lambertz (Anm. 6) 86 und Kajanto (Anm. 6) 54, 57.

20 K. Lehmann-Hartleben 'The Imagines of the Elder Philostratus' *Art Bulletin* 23 (1941) 31 Anm. 43; die Verbindung des Todes der Königin Rhodogune mit ihrer Feindlichkeit gegen die Männer und die Liebe ist nicht zwingend und passt ferner nicht zu dem Inhalt des Epigramms (Z. 3/4: Bestattung durch ihren dankbaren Ehemann). Aus demselben Grund muss die Meinung Polanskis, (Anm. 2) 204 ('Epagatho was stoned to death by her rejected suitor') ausgeschlossen werden.

21 G. Manganaro 'Novella e romanzo (a proposito di una recente pubblicazione)' *RFIC* 36 (1958) 390-92: 'Proprio il coraggio dimostrato nell'evento della orribile morte, incontrata sotto i colpi di un bruto, dalla sventurata donna, cui fu dedicato dal marito Avianio questo epigramma, credo le abbia fatto attribuire il soprannome di Rodogune, la famosa regina' (392). Siehe auch *Bull. épigr.* 1959, 542.

22 Bernard (Anm. 2) 131 Anm. 18: 'c'est cette mort, et non pas n'importe quelle autre, qui

Mit dem Dativ λάεσι werden tatsächlich die Umstände des Todes der Epagatho beschrieben. Dennoch bezieht sich der Ausdruck δεινὸς ἀνήρ vermutlich nicht auf einen bestimmten Mann, sondern steht in Zusammenhang mit der negativen Vorstellung vom Hades bzw. dem Tod.[23] In Grabepigrammen begegnet die Formulierung οὐχ ὁσίως ἔκτανε bzw. ἥρπασε etc. hauptsächlich verbunden mit Moira, Hades oder dem Tod[24] und wird verwendet in Grabinschriften von Minderjährigen bzw. Menschen, die zu Unrecht (ἀδίκως) den Tod fanden.[25]

Aus diesen Beobachtungen ergeben sich zwei Möglichkeiten, das Epigramm aus Katane zu deuten: Entweder liegt ein Vergleich der verstorbenen Epagatho, die höchstwahrscheinlich ein vorzeitiges oder tragisches Ende fand, mit Rhodogune vor, die für ihre ἀνδρεία ἐν τοῖς ἔργοις,[26] πολεμική und ihre Schönheit (τὸ ἐν αὐτῇ κάλλος) bekannt war;[27] oder es ist als eine

---

vaut à Epagathô d'être désormais appelée du nom de la reine'; siehe auch *Bull.épigr.* 1980, 593.

23 Siehe dazu A-M Vérilhac Παῖδες ἄωροι, Poésie funéraire vol II commentaire (Athen 1982) 149ff. und zuletzt M.C. Barrigón 'El Más Allá en las inscripciones funerarias griegas' in A. Alonso Avila et al. (Hsg.) *Homenaje al Profesor Montenegro.* Estudios de historia antigua, Historia y Sociedad 76 (Valladolid 1999) 133-49, *SEG* XLIX 2421. Als δεινός wird Hades in einem Grabepigramm aus Megalopolis bezeichnet, : Peek, *GV* 793 (3. Jh.). Vgl. Peek, *GV* 947 (= Peek, *GG* 158): δεινή μ᾽ εἰς Ἀίδην μοιρ᾽ ἤγαγεν (2.-1. Jh.); 606 (Grabepigramm für Bassos): ὃν ἔκτανε δύσφορος ἀνήρ (Tusculum, 2./3. Jh.).

24 Siehe z.B. für Hades: Peek, *GV* 1595 (= *IGUR* 1344): οὐχ ὁσίως ἥρπαξες ὑπὸ [χθόνα], | κοίρανε Πλουτεῦ (Rom, 2. Jh.?); 1547 (= Peek, *GG* 345): (θάνατος) ἥρπασεν οὐκ ὁσίως (Rom, 2. Jh.); *SEG* XXX 291: οὐχ ὁσίω[ς Ἀίδης ἥρπασε] (Athen, 400-350 v.Chr.); *SEG* LIV 961: εἰς θάνατον τὸν ἄωρον ἀνάξιον ἥρπασε Πλούτων ... ἐξείρπασε βάρβαρος Ἅ<ι>δης (Petelia, 1. Jh.); vgl. Peek, *GV* 968 (= Merkelbach-Stauber, *SGO* II, 09/04/11): Ἀίδης μὲν σύλησεν ἐμῆς νεότητος ὀπώρην (Prusa ad Olympum, 5./6. Jh.); Moira: Peek, *GV* 1300 (= Vérilhac I, Nr. 158): νῦν δέ | με Μοῖρα ἥρπασεν οὐχ ὁσίως (Athen, 2./3 Jh.). Vgl. Peek, *GV* 618: ἔκτανε Μοῖρα (Argolis, 1. Jh. v.Chr.); 729 (= *I.Perinthos* 218): οὐχ ὁσίως μίτος ἤγαγε Μοιρῶν (Perinthos, 3. Jh.?); 961 (= Merkelbach-Stauber, *SGO* II, 08/06/09): ἀμείλικτο|ς κτάνε Μοίρη (Hadrianuthera, etwa 3. Jh.). Weitere Beispiele bei R. Lattimore *Themes in Greek and Latin Epitaphs* (Urbana 1942) 142-58 und Vérilhac II 173ff. und besonders in 201-3 §96 (zum Audruck οὐχ ὁσίως).

25 Siehe z. B. Peek, *GV* 126: Ἀίδης δὲ ἀδίκως μὲ ἥρπασεν νηπίαχον (Cures, Frühe Kaiserzeit); *SEG* XXXVIII 440 (Grabepigramm für Sosikrates): ὃς θάν᾽ ο<ὐ>χ ὁσί|ως ἀλλ᾽ ἀδίκωι θανάτωι (Gonnoi, 4. Jh. v. Chr.).

26 So bei Anonymus *De mulieribus*, VIII (Westermann (Anm. 15) 215-16), mit dem Zitat ὥς φησιν Αἰσχίνης ὁ φιλόσοφος. Siehe auch die bei Anm. 2 angeführten Aufsätze.

27 Dio Chrysostomos *Oratio* 64.2: ἤνεγκεν ὁ παλαιὸς βίος καὶ ἐνδόξους γυναῖκας,

consolatio per exemplum zu verstehen, die indirekt auf ihr gemeinsames Schicksal verweist.

Die Parallelisierung bzw. die Angleichung der körperlichen und moralischen Eigenschaften von Menschen an die von Göttern oder Gestalten der Mythologie ist ein bereits seit der klassischen und hellenistischen Periode vertrautes Phänomen in Grabinschriften.[28] Als beliebteste weibliche Vorbilder treten hierbei Aphrodite, Athena und Hera auf.[29] Unter den Heldinnen der Mythologie begegnen Alkestis, Penelope und Laodameia am häufigsten.[30] Es lohnt sich an dieser Stelle, näher auf eine Grabinschrift aus dem

---

Ῥοδογούνην πολεμικήν, Σεμίραμιν βασιλικήν, Σαπφὼ μουσικήν, Τιμάνδραν καλήν (vgl. *Oratio* 21.6-7; dazu T. Szepessy 'Rhodogune and Ninyas: Comments on Dio Chrysostomus' 21st discourse' *AAntHung* 30 (1982-1984) 355-57). Über ihre kriegerische Energie, siehe Polyaenus *Strategemata* 8.27, Iulian *Orationes* 3.127 B. Für ihre Schönheit s. die Beschreibung von Philostratos, *Imagines* 2.5.

28 Vgl. z.B. den Ausdruck [ἡ] φιλανδρίας | ἀρχαῖον ἐζήλωσεν ἦθος in dem Epigramm Peek, *GV* 2028 Z. 8/9 (Tainaron, 2./3. Jh.). Für das Lob der Frauen in griechischen Epigrammen J. Pircher *Das Lob der Frau im vorchristlichen Grabepigramm der Griechen*, Commentationes Aenipontanae 26 (Innsbruck 1979), Vérilhac II, *passim*, dies. 'L'image de la femme dans les épigrammes funéraires grecques' in A.M. Vérilhac (Hsg.) *La femme dans le monde méditerranéen I. Antiquité* (Lyon 1985) 85-112 und zuletzt P. Grandinetti 'Virtù femminili negli epigrammi greci', in *XI Congresso Internazionale di Epigrafia Greca e Latina Roma 18-24 sett. 1997* (Rom 1999) 721-27.

29 Siehe z.B. Peek, *GV* 924 (= Peek, *GG* 318, Aphrodite, Athena; Boiai/Lakonien, 2./3. Jh. ?); 1164 (= Peek, *GG* 392, *IGUR* 1268, Aphrodite; Rom, 2./3. Jh.); 1323 (= Merkelbach-Stauber, *SGO* I, 05/01/33, Hera, Aphrodite ; Smyrna 1. Jh.?); 1528 (Hera-Athena-Erato ; Sikinos, 3./4. Jh.); 1925 (= *I. Napoli* II 130, Aphrodite-Athena-Musa; Napoli-Nola, 1. Jh.); 2032 (= Merkelbach-Stauber, *SGO* I, 01/14/01, Aphrodite; Iasos, Kaiserzeit); *IG* V 599 (Athena; Sparta, 3. Jh.), Merkelbach-Stauber, *SGO* III, 16/43/03 (Athena; Territorium von Amorion, 3. Jh.). Vgl. Peek, *GV* 675 (= *I.Aquileia*, 710, die verstorbene Vassilla als 10. Muse; 3. Jh.), *SEG* XLVIII 1770 C (Vergleich mit der Muse Kalliope; Karallia/Kilikien, undatiert).

30 Siehe z.B. Claudius Aelianus, *VH* 14.45: Γυναῖκας τῶν Ἑλλήνων ἐπαινοῦμεν Πηνελόπην καὶ Ἄλκηστιν καὶ τὴν Πρωτεσιλάου. Zu relevanten Beispielen s. Vérilhac, 'L'image de la femme' 108-12, Grandinetti (Anm. 27) 724-25 und zuletzt P. Grandinetti 'Gli epigrammi della Grotta delle Vipere a Cagliari: confronti per l'assimilazione al mito' *L'Africa Romana* 14 (2002) 1757-69 mit den Zusätzen von R. Tybout in *SEG* LII 942, 1672 app.cr. Vgl. ebenfalls Peek, *GV* 1737a (= T.B. Mitford *The Inscriptions of Kourion* (Philadelphia 1971) 68, Laodameia, Alkestis, Eurydike; Kourion, 1. Jh.). Zur Alkestis s. ebenfalls Fr. Mosino 'Il mito di Alcesti in un'iscrizione di Fere (Tessaglia)' *MEP* 4 Nr 5 (2001) 71-72.

kaiserzeitlichen Rom einzugehen, die auch im Hinblick auf den Namen besonders interessant ist. Die Verstorbene heißt Alkestis (Ἄλκηστις τοὔνομα) und stammt aus Aphrodisias (Karien). Sie berichtet sogar über sich selbst Folgendes: καὶ γέγονα Ἀλ|κηστις ἐκείνη ἡ πάλαι φί|λανδρος ἦν καὶ θεοὶ καὶ βρο|τοὶ ἐμαρτύρησαν σω|φροσύνης εἵνεκα.[31] Ebenso häufig sind die Beispiele, die männliche Vorbilder betreffen, unter anderem Atlas, Eros, Adonis, Herakles, Hyakinthos[32] und die homerischen Helden Aias, Achilleus und Nestor.[33] Noch interessanter sind die Fälle, in denen ein Vergleich mit historischen Persönlichkeiten vorkommt. Als Beispiel sei hier ein Epigramm aus Rheneia des 2./1. Jh. v. Chr. erwähnt, in dem der Verstorbene Themistokles, Sohn des Themison aus Antiocheia, mit dem Sieger von Salamis verglichen wird (ὃς βουλὰς καὶ θάρσος ἔχων ἴσ' ὁμωνύμωι ἀνδρί),[34] sowie ein Epigramm aus Athen, in dem der Verstorbene sich selbst mit dem spartanischen König Leonidas vergleicht (ἄμφω γὰρ πάτρῃσιν ἀμύνετον αἷμα

---

31 *IGUR* 322.
32 Siehe dazu Vérilhac II, 26-27 §14. Für Beispiele s. z. B. Atlas: *AP* 7, 692; Eros: *AP* 7, 628 (Krinagoras = Vérilhac, I, Nr. 45, 1. Jh. v./n. Chr.), Peek, *GV* 409 (= Vérilhac I, Nr. 44, Amaseia, 2./3. Jh.), 2045 (= Vérilhac I, Nr. 46, P.J. Sijpesteijn 'SEG IV 157: A correction' *ZPE* 87 (1991) 255-56, *Bull. épigr.* 1992, 32, Sutrium, 1 Jh. v./n. Chr.); s. auch dazu Vérilhac II, 39-41 §22; Adonis: Peek, *GV* 815 (= Merkelbach-Stauber, *SGO* IV, 18/12/02, hier mit Hyakinthos; Attaleia in Pamphylien, etwa 2. Jh.), Merkelbach-Stauber, *SGO* IV, 22/18/01 (Lahitha/Nabataea, unbestimmte Zeit); s. dazu auch *Bull. épigr.* 1964, 593 und 1978, 285; Herakles: Peek, *GV* 1247 (= É. Bernand *Inscriptions métriques de l'Égypte gréco-romaine. Recherches sur la poésie épigrammatique des Grecs en Égypte* (Paris 1969) 82, Karmoûz, Kaiserzeit), 1280 (= Peek, *GG* 323, Vérilhac I Nr. 47, *SEG* XLVI 1344, hier mit Dionysos und Endymion; Arcesicca, 2./3. Jh.), 1969 (= Vérilhac I, Nr. 66, *I.Perinthos* 214, 1./2 Jh.), Merkelbach-Stauber, *SGO* IV, 23/11 (= *SEG* LI 1691, Ilion, 2./3. Jh.). Vgl. *SEG* XXXV 1026 (Nereus-Dioskouroi; Canusium 2./3. Jh.).
33 Siehe z.B. Aias: Merkelbach-Stauber, *SGO* IV, 17/17/01 (Choma/Lykien, 4./3 Jh. v. Chr.), Peek, *GV* 1811 (hier mit Achilleus; Telos, 2. Jh. v. Chr.); Nestor: Peek, *GV* 1809 (= Peek, *GG* 364, Vérilhac I, Nr. 56, Merkelbach-Stauber, *SGO* II, 10/06/09, *I.Sinope* 170, 2. Hälfte des 2. Jh.); s. dazu Vérilhac II, 27-28 §15; Achilleus: Peek, *GV* 1804 (= *I. Laodikeia* 81, Merkelbach-Stauber, *SGO* I, 02/14/11, hier mit Hippolytos; 1. Jh. v. Chr.); Merkelbach-Stauber, *SGO* II, 10/02/28 (hier mit Hektor; Kaisareia/Hadrianupolis, Zeit Trajans/Hadrians).
34 Peek, *GV* 556 (= Peek, *GG* 131, *CD* 473, Vérilhac I, Nr. 48). Siehe auch zuletzt S. Schmidt *Hellenistische Grabreliefs. Typologische und chronologische Beobachtungen* (Köln-Wien 1991) 136-37.

τ[ε χεῦαν]|, ἀλλ᾽ ὁ μὲν ἐν βαιοῖς, ὃς [δ]ὲ τ[ρι]η[κο]σίο[ις]).³⁵ In einem Epigramm aus Attika vergleicht sich ferner der Bildhauer Eutychides, Sohn des Zoilos aus Milet, mit dem bekannten Bildhauer Praxiteles: Πραξιτέλους ἤνθουν λαοξόος οὔτι χερείων.³⁶

Ebenso häufig ist in Grabepigrammen die *consolatio per exemplum*, nämlich der Trost durch den Bezug auf das gemeinsame Schicksal von Menschen und Helden bzw. Königen.³⁷ In diesen Fällen dienen als Vorbilder hauptsächlich Aias, Achilleus, Adonis, Archemoros, Astyanax, Herakles und Phaethon³⁸ sowie – auf der Seite der Hinterbliebenen – die Mutter von Herakles (Alkmene), Thetis und Niobe.³⁹ Ein Epigramm aus Rom für Severa, Enkelin des Strymonios, erwähnt Folgendes: ἀθάνατ<ος> μερόπων οὐδεὶς ἔφυ·

---

35 Peek, *GV* 1731 (Athen, 2. Jh.?).
36 Peek, *GV* 1109 (= Vérilhac I, Nr. 75; 2. Jh.?); s. dazu Vérilhac II, 27-28 §15. Ebenso häufig ist in Grabepigrammen die Parallelisierung mit berühmten Vorgängern im Beruf, wie z.B. des Arztes Glykon mit Hippokrates in einem Epigramm aus Pergamon, Merkelbach-Stauber, *SGO* I, 06/02/32; s. auch H. Bernsdorff 'Ein Pferdearzt namens Hippokrates (SEG XLVII 1836)' *ZPE* 136 (2001) 49-50 [*SEG* LI 1849 bis].
37 Siehe z.B. Menander (der Rhetor, 3. Jh.), Περὶ παραμυθητικοῦ: πέρας ἐστὶν ἅπασιν ἀνθρώποις τοῦ βίου ὁ θάνατος, καὶ ὅτι ἥρωες καὶ θεῶν παῖδες οὐ διέφυγον (L. Spengel (Hsg.) *Rhetores Graeci* III, Leipzig 1856 [1966] 414, 4-6). Vgl. z. B. Merkelbach-Stauber, *SGO* IV, 18/18/01 Z. 22-23: καὶ γὰρ ἄριστοι | παῖδες ἐπουρανίων ἤλυθον εἰς Ἀΐδην (Kolybrassos, 3./4. Jh.) und Peek *GV* 2035 Z. 6-8: ἄστατος αἰών, | οὐκ ἀνέδραστον ἔχων ἴδιον δρόμον· ἧς δ᾽ ἔλαχέν τις μοίρης, ταύτην ἐκτελέσει· καὶ γὰρ βασιλῆες (Theben, 3./4. Jh.). Relevante Beispiele bei Bernand *Inscriptions métriques* 71 (Kommentar bei Z. 19). Siehe dazu Lattimore (Anm. 23) 250-56, H. Wankel. '"Alle Menschen müssen sterben". Variationen eines Topos der griechischen Literatur' *Hermes* 111 (1983) 129-154, L. Rossi 'Lamentazioni su pietra e letteratura "trenodica": motivi topici dei canti funerari' *ZPE* 126 (1999) 40 (= *SEG* XLIX 2422) und J.M. Strubbe 'Epigrams and consolation decrees for deseased youths' *AC* 67 (1998) 57.
38 Siehe z.B. Achilleus: Peek, *GV* 1197 (Thera, 1./2. Jh.), 1481 (Gytheion, 2./3. Jh.), 1695 (Thera, 1. Jh.?), 1811 (hier mit Aias; Telos, 2. Jh. v. Chr.); Archemoros-Astyanax: Merkelbach-Stauber, *SGO* I, 04/12/06 (Saittai, 182/3 n. Chr.); Herakles: Peek, *GV* 1249 (hier mit Minos; Itanos, 2./1. Jh.), *IGUR* 743 (Rom, Datierung unklar); 2023 (Mytilene, 1./2. Jh.); Nestor: Merkelbach-Stauber, *SGO* IV, 19/07/02, (Olba-Diokaisareia, nicht älter als 1. Jh. v. Chr.); zu Phaethon s. die relevanten Beispiele in *SEG* L 1060 und Anm. 40. Siehe auch, Peek, *GV* 766 (= *GG* 135, Homer; Tithoreia, 1. Jh. v.Chr.); 1010 (=Peek, *GG* 299, Peleus-Pheres; Thera, 1. Jh. ?).
39 Zu Thetis und Alkmene Anm. 37 (Achilleus/Herakles). Für Niobe Peek, *GV* 1545 (= *GG* 335, Merkelbach-Stauber, *SGO* I, 05/01/55, Smyrna, wohl 2. Jh.). Siehe weiterhin Peek, *GV* 1010 (Peek, *GG* 299, Peleus-Pheres; Thera, 1. Jh. ?).

τοῦδε, Σεβήρα, Θησεύς, Αἰακίδαι μάρτυρές εἰσι λόγου (3. Jh. n. Chr.).⁴⁰

Besonders bezeichnend sind in diesem Zusammenhang, vor allem auch wegen ihrer Ausführlichkeit, zwei Epigramme aus Alexandria und Nikopolis in Ägypten: Das erste, für einen 18-jährigen Jungen, besagt Folgendes (Z. 15-18): οὐδεὶς γὰρ ἐξέλυξε τὸν μίτον Μοιρῶν, | οὐ θνητός, οὐκ ἀθάνατος, | οὐδ᾽ ὁ δεσμώτης, | οὐδ᾽ αὖ ὁ τύραννος βασιλικὴν λαχὼν τιμὴν | θεσμοὺς ἀτρέπτους διαφυγεῖν ποτ᾽ ᾠήθη (Niemand ist dem Faden der Todesgöttinnen entronnen; weder Sterblicher noch Unsterblicher, weder der Gefangene noch der Tyrann, dem Ehren zuteil wurden, hat geglaubt, den unwiderruflichen Gesetzten entrinnen zu können). Als *exempla consolationis* werden hier Phaethon, Myrtillos, Achilleus, Sarpedon, aber auch der makedonische König Alexander der Große herangezogen.⁴¹ Im zweiten Epigramm vergleicht der Verstorbene Herakleides sein Schicksal mit dem von Osiris, Adonis, Endymion und Herakles.⁴²

Auf jeden Fall kann die Auswahl der persischen Königin Rhodogune als Vorbild bzw. Trostmittel als sehr ungewöhnliches und seltenes Zeugnis betrachtet werden. In einem Grabepigramm (*AP* 7 538), das der Anyte zugewiesen wird (um die Wende vom 4. zum 3. Jh. v. Chr.),⁴³ vergleicht der ver-

---

40 Peek, *GV* 1937 (= *IGUR* 1328).
41 Peek, *GV* 1935 (= Bernand, *Inscriptions métriques* 71) Z. 19-28: Φαέθοντα Τιτάν οὐκ ἔκλαυσ᾽, ὅτ᾽ ἐκ δίφρων | ἀπὸ οὐρανοῦ κατέπεσεν εἰς πέδον γαίης; | Ἑρμῆς δ᾽ ὁ Μαίας οὐκ ἔκλαυσ᾽ ἑὸν παῖδα | Μυρτίλον ἀπὸ δίφρων κύμασιν φορούμενον; | οὐδ᾽ αὖ Θέτις τὸν στεναρὸν ἔστενεν παῖδα, | ὅτ᾽ ἐκ βελέμνων θνῆσκε τῶν Ἀπόλλωνος; | ὁ δ᾽ αὖ βροτῶν τε καὶ θεῶν πάντων ἄναξ | Σαρπηδόν᾽ οὐκ ἔκλαυσεν, οὐκ ἐκώκυσεν; | οὐδ᾽ αὖ Μακηδὼν ὁ βασιλεὺς Ἀλέξανδρος, | ὃν τίκτεν Ἄμμων θέμενος εἰς ὄφιν μορφήν; (Alexandria, Kaiserzeit). Vgl. dazu auch *SEG* L 1060. (Hat nicht der Titan Phaethon beweint, als dieser aus seinem Wagen vom Himmel auf den Erdboden gestürzt war? Hat nicht Hermes, Maias Sohn, sein Kind Myrthilos beweint, als dieser aus seinem Wagen von den Wellen davongetragen wurde? Hat nicht auch Thetis ihren starken Sohn beklagt, als dieser von Apollons Pfeilen getötet wurde? Und hat nicht auch der König aller Sterblichen und Unsterblichen Sarpedon beweint und laut geklagt? Ähnlich wie der König von Makedonien, Alexander, den Ammon gezeugt hat, nachdem er die Gestalt einer Schlange angenommen hatte?)
42 Peek, *GV* 2028a, Bernand, *Inscriptions métriques* 76: Ἡρακλείδης ὁ καλὸς κεῖτ᾽ ἐνθάδε, ὡς Ὄσειρις | ἢ Παφίης ὁ Ἄδωνις | ἢ Ἐνδυμίων ὁ Σελήνης, | ἢ τῆς Ἀλκμήνης Ἡρακλῆς δωδεκάεθλος πάντων (Nikopolis, Kaiserzeit); s. dazu Vérilhac II, 26-27 §14.
43 Siehe ebenfalls Peek, *GV* 597. Für die Epigramme von Anyte, D. Geoghegan, *Anyte. The Epigrams. A Critical Edition with Commentary*, (Rom 1979) und Peek, *GV* 2035 (Anm. 36).

storbene Manes, offensichtlich ein Sklave phrygischer Abstammung,[44] mit Dareios verglichen: Μάνης οὗτος ἀνὴρ ἦν ζῶν ποτε· νῦν δὲ τεθνηκὼς ἴσον Δαρείῳ τῷ μεγάλῳ δύναται. In der behandelten Inschrift spiegeln sich mit Sicherheit die literarischen Vorlieben des Umfeldes der Verstorbenen wider, die, wie bereits erwähnt, mit dem Bild von Rhodogune im Einklang stehen, das durch die Überlieferung des Dialogs *Aspasia* des Aischines von Sphettos bekannt war.[45]

II

Das zweite Epigramm stammt aus Rom und datiert allem Anschein nach in das 2./3. Jh. n. Chr. Hier sollen zwei Aspekte herausgegriffen werden: Der erste bezieht sich auf den Spitznamen des Verstorbenen Geminas, Πετροκόραξ, der zweite auf die Personen, die dieses Denkmal errichtet haben und als οἱ σοὶ ἀδελφοί bezeichnet werden. Der Inschriftentext lautet wie folgt:[46]

[----------] Γεμινᾶν ἐκάλεσαν·
ἔσχε δὲ καὶ ἄλ<λ>᾿ ὄνομα χαριέστατον ὅν ποθ᾿
ἑταῖροι Πετροκόρακαν ἔκ<λ>ῃζον· οὐ ταχὺ βρ-
4 οτῶν τις τοίαν ἐκτήσατο γνώμην· ἤσκι τὴ-
ν ἁπλότητα, φίλους ὑπὲρ ἁτὸν ἐτίμα· διὰ τοῦτο
μνήμης ἕνεκεν, χάριτος δὲ ἀπάσης οἱ σοὶ ἀδελφοὶ
ἔθηκαν γνωστὸν πολλοῖσι βροτοῖσι, ἵνα

---

44 Zur Herkunft des Namens Manes s. F. Papazoglou 'Deorum nomina hominibus imposita', *Recueil travaux Fac. Philos. (Belgrad)* 14.1 (1979) 12 (vgl. *SEG* XXX 1833). Zum Gebrauch dieses Namens für Sklaven s. O. Masson 'Les noms des esclaves dans la Grèce antique' in *Actes colloque 1971 sur l'esclavage* (Paris 1973) 15, 19 (*OGS* I, 153, 157).

45 Siehe Anm. 20.

46 '...Gemeinas nannten (sie) ihn. Er besaß aber noch einen anderen sehr anmutigen Namen; einst nannten ihn die Gefährten Petrokorax. Kein Sterblicher hat so schnell solches Ansehen erworben. Er übte sich in Bescheidenheit und ehrte Freunde mehr als sich selbst. Deshalb, zur Erinnerung und voller Dank, haben dich deine Brüder unter vielen Sterblichen bekannt gemacht, damit jeder Wanderer dich "guter Petrokorax" nennt. Er lebte dreißig Jahre.' *CIG* III 6219, Kaibel, *EG* 716, *IG* XIV 1517, *IGUR* 1181 und zuletzt G. Dareggi 'Antichità romane nel Palazzo Gallegna Stuart a Perugia' *AFLPer* 14 (1990/1991) [1996] 116-120 Nr. 48 (= *SEG* XLVI 1340).

8 σε πᾶς παράγων ὀνομ<ά>ζῃ ἀγαθὲ Πετροκόραξ
   ἔζη ἔτη XXX

Die besondere Bedeutung der Inschrift besteht zunächst im humoristischen Grundtenor des Textes durch den Bezug auf den Spitznamen des Toten, Πετροκόραξ. Der Name ist, wie I. Kajanto richtig bemerkt, 'a hapaxlegomenon, but it is useless to try to divine the original implications of the name'.[47] Komposita mit dem Wort -κόραξ als zweiter Komponente, wie z.B. νυκτικόραξ, ὀστοκόραξ, πυρροκόραξ, bezeichnen in den meisten Fällen eine bestimmte Vogelart.[48] Darüber hinaus drückt der Stamm πετρ- der ersten Komponente bei Adjektiven in erster Linie einen Bezug zu Stein aus.[49] Als charakteristische Beispiele seien hier die zusammengesetzten Pflanzennamen πετρολάπαθον und πετροσέλινον erwähnt.[50] Letzterer begegnet sogar auch als Personenname.[51] Demzufolge könnte man vermuten, dass der Name Πετροκόραξ in Entsprechung zu den bereits bekannten Tiernamen entstanden ist, welche das Substantiv κόραξ als zweite Komponente haben. Darüberhinaus erlaubt ein Passus des Odyssee-Kommentars des Eustathios (1502.27) eine weitere Vermutung: Das Scholion betrifft die Lykier und erwähnt Folgendes: οἱ (Λύκιοι) χελιδόνας τινὰς ἃς οἱ ἰδιῶται πετροχελιδόνας φασίν, ἐκεῖνοι καλοῦσιν ἄποδας, οὐ διὰ παντελῆ

---

[47] Kajanto (Anm. 6) 21. Siehe hierzu Lambertz (Anm. 6) 84-85 und A. Hug 'Spitznamen' *RE* III A2 (1929) 1822. Der Aufsatz von G. Dareggi, 'Petrokorax (IGUR III, 1181): un hapax linguistico problematico' *AFLPer* 20 (2002-2004) 65-78, ist mir nach dem Abschluss des vorliegenden Aufsätzes durch die Anzeige in *AE.* 2005 (2008) 198 bekannt geworden: Danach wird der Name von Dareggi erklärt 'non comme un nom commun désignant le cormoran, mais comme un nom propre faisant reference a un être mythologique, le corbeau de la falaise d'Ithaque (Plutarch, Moralia, 776d), et, par consequent, comme une allusion au pays d'origine du défunt'. Siehe dazu hier Anm. 48.

[48] *TLG* s.v. Dazu D'Arcy W. Thompson *A Glossary of Greek Birds* (Hildesheim 1966) s.v.

[49] *TLG* s.v.; s. z.B. πετραῖος ὄρνις bei Aischylos, Fragm. 304 (Hsg. A. Nauck). Vgl. auch das Ethnikon Κορακοπετραῖος bei Stephan von Byzanz, L. Bürchner 'Κόρακος πέτρα' *RE* XI 2 (1922) 1372.

[50] *TLG* s.v. Vgl. z. B. Dioscurides, 3.66: πετροσέλινον· φύεται ἐν Μακεδονίᾳ ἐν ἀποκρήμνοις τόποις. Siehe dazu M. Aufmesser *Etymologische und wortgeschichtliche Erläuterungen zu* De materia medica *des Pedanius Dioscurides Anazarbeus* (Hildesheim – Zürich – New York 2000) 141.

[51] *CIL* IV 10246 (c, j), *LGPN* III A s.v. *Petroselinus*. Für Pflanzennamen als Personennamen s. Solin *Personennamen* (Anm. 8)1152-1200 und ders. *Sklavennamen* (Anm. 8) 511-26.

στέρησιν ποδῶν ἀλλ᾽ ὀλιγότητα ἤτοι σμικρότητα.⁵² Gerade, wenn man die Existenz des Namens Κόραξ wie auch anderer Tiernamen sowohl als Personen- als auch als Spitznamen bedenkt,⁵³ ist es docher nicht auszuschließen dass das Kompositum Πετροκόραξ ein Spitzname (ἕτερον χαριέστατον ὄνομα) des Geminas bei seinen ἑταῖροι war, der mit einem besonderen körperlichen Merkmal und, konkreter, seinen kurzen Beinen zu tun hatte,⁵⁴ was vermutlich die ironischen Kommentare seiner Freunde bzw. Kameraden veranlasst haben könnte.⁵⁵

Was die Personen anbelangt, die dieses Denkmal errichtet haben und als οἱ σοὶ ἀδελφοί bezeichnet werden, schließt der Inhalt des Textes selbst die Vermutung kategorisch aus, dass es sich dabei um die leiblichen Brüder des Geminas handelte. Der Text ist folgender thematischer Gliederung unter-

52 'Die (Lykier) bezeichnen eine Schwalbenart, welche die Bürger Steinschwalben nennen, fußlos, nicht wegen des gänzlichen Fehlens der Füße, sondern wegen deren geringen Größe.' Siehe dazu Thompson (Anm. 47), s.v. ἄπους.
53 Siehe z.B. *LGPN* I-IV s.v. Ἔλαφος, Κόραξ, Κόσσυφος/Κοσσύφα/η/ιον, Ὄρτυξ, Πιθήκη, Χελιδών/Χελιδόνιον, Χελώνη/Χελωνίων; s. ebenfalls dazu L. Robert *Noms indigènes dans l'Asie-Mineure grèco-romaine* (Paris 1963) 22-33 (Βούβαλος/Βουβάλιον etc.), O. Masson 'A propos de la plus ancienne inscription rhodienne (Inscr. Lindos, 710)' *Arch. Class.* 25-26 (1973-1974) 429-31 (= *OGS* I, 184-86), ders. 'Remarques sur les noms de femmes en grec' *MH* 47 (1990) 137 (= *OGS* III, 101), H. Solin 'Analecta Epigraphica' *Arctos* 34 (2000) 158-159 (= *SEG* L 1727). Für Beispiele aus Rom, s. Solin *Personennamen* (Anm. 8) 1125-51, ders. *Sklavennamen*, 503-10. Zum Gebrauch von Tiernamen als Spitznamen s. z.B. Fr. Bechtel *Die einstämmigen männlichen Personennamen des Griechischen die aus Spitznamen hervorgegangen sind* (Berlin 1898) *passim* und Solin, *Personennamen* 1471-81. Für die Verbreitung des Namens Κόραξ s. Bechtel 28, 42.
54 Als eine mögliche Parallele sei hier der Beiname Στραβέλαφος ('der mit den leicht schielenden Hirschaugen') erwähnt, der in einer Inschrift aus Ephesos begegnet, *GIBM* 574, *I.Ephesos* 1574; s. dazu Robert (Anm. 52) 150 Anm. 3 und O. Masson 'Remarques sur l'onomastique d'Ephese (A propos de l'Index Ephesos VIII.2)' *ZPE* 64 (1986) 179 (= *OGS* II 503). Vgl. also die Namen Ταυρέλαφος (Masson, a.O., Solin *Analecta* (Amn. 14) 402), Cercopithecus (Sueton *Nero*, 30, Solin *Personennamen* (Anm. 8) 1130) und Cynisculus (*CIL* IV 3784, *LGPN* IIIA, s.v.). Siehe auch O. Masson 'Quelques anthroponymes grecs et leur morphologie: Noms composés et noms simples' *Verbum* 18 (1995-1996) 286-87 (= *OGS* III, 320-21).
55 Vgl. z. B. den Namen Μύσκελ(λ)ος ('Krummbeinig'), O. Masson 'Myskellos, fondateur de Crotone, et le nom Μύσκελ(λ)ος' *RPh* 63 (1989) 61-65 (= *OGS* III 55-59), *Bull. épigr.* 1991, 198. Zum Gebrauch von Personennamen die auf körperliche Eigenschaften Bezug nehmen s. Bechtel (Anm. 52) 34, Solin *Personennamen* (Anm. 8) 711-55 und *Sklavennamen* 390-402.

worfen: Nach der Erwähnung des Geburtsnamens des Verstorbenen in der ersten Zeile (--------Γεμινᾶν ἐκάλεσαν)[56] schlägt der Text einen humoristischen Ton an mit der Erwähnung des Spitznamens Petrokorax, mit dem die Personen, die als ἑταῖροι bezeichnet werden, ihn nannten (ἔκληζον).[57] Anschließend werden, in einem sehr ernsten Ton, die Tugenden des Verstorbenen gepriesen: Betont wird nämlich seine Bescheidenheit (ἁπλότης /*simplicitas*), ein Begriff, der verhältnismäßig selten in griechischen Inschriften vorkommt,[58] sowie die Liebe für seine Freunde (der Ausdruck φίλους ὑπὲρ ἁτὸν ἐτίμα verweist auf das aus der klassischen und frühchristlichen literarischen Überlieferung bekannte Vorbild des Freundes als *alter ego*).[59] In diesem Kontext erklärt sich findet auch die Errichtung des Denkmals (Z. 5:

---

56 [Ὅν κεύθει τόδε σῆμα, βροτοὶ etc.] *GIG*, Kaibel, *EG* app.cr.; s. z.B. Peek, *GV* 1027: οὔνομά μοι θέσα[ν Ἰσιγ]όνα καλέεσθαι τοκῆες (Chersonesos, 2. Jh.); 1028 (= *IG* X 2.1, 454, Vérilhac I, Nr. 26): οὔνομα μ' ἐν γονέεσσι Δρόσον οἴδ' ἐκάλεσσ‹α›ν (Thessaloniki, 2./3. Jh.); 1029 (= Vérilhac I, Nr. 190): οὔνομα Θεσμοφάνην με πατὴρ φίλος ἠδ' ἅμα μήτηρ κίκλησκον (Athen, 2. Jh.?).
57 Zur Bedeutung des Begriff ἑταῖρος s. J.P.A. Eernstman Οἰκεῖος, ἑταῖρος, ἐπιτήδειος, φίλος (Groningen 1932) 26-51. Wie schon Lambertz (Anm. 6) 83, 85, bemerkt hat, kann hier als Parallele der Fall des L. Domitius Euaristus angeführt werden. Nach der Erwähnung des Namens und des Todesalters sagt die Inschrift (*CIL* VI 16932), dass Domitius Euaristus und Domitia Festa das Grabmonument errichtet haben *f(ilio) s(uo) Benedicto, hoc nomen imposuerunt sodales*, d. h. dass Euaristus von seinen Kameraden 'Benedictus' genavnt wurde. Siehe dazu auch Kajanto (Anm. 6) 10.
58 Vgl. ebenfalls den Ausdruck καὶ ψυχῆς ἀρετὴν ἤσκησεν ἐν αὐτοῖς in *IGF* 143 (Lyon, 3. Jh.). Zur ζηλότης als moralischem Wert s. O. Hiltbrunner *Latina Graeca. Semasiologische Studien über lateinische Wörter im Hinblick auf ihr Verhältnis zu griechischen Vorbildern* (Bern 1958) 15ff., H. Bacht 'Einfalt', *RAC* 4 (1959) 821-40, J. Amstutz Ἁπλότης. *Eine begriffsgeschichtliche Studie zum jüdisch-christlichen Griechisch,* (Bonn 1968). Die Verbindung des Gebrauchs des Adjektivs ἁπλοῦς wie auch des Begriffs ἁπλότης mit dem 'lateinischen Sprachgebiet' (so Hiltbrunner 81-82(Anm. 49)), ist nicht zwingend. s. z.B. *I.Priene* 112 (*SEG* XXXIX 1264, Ehrendekret für Aulus Aemilius Zosimos) Z. 10-12 : καλὸ[ς ὢν καὶ ἀγαθὸς ἀνήρ] | [καὶ] βίον μὲν οὐκ ἀφιλότι[μον] εἰς δόξ[αν, κ]ρίσιν δὲ τιμῆς [ἀ]ξίαν ἁπλότη[τά τε καὶ γενναῖον ἐ]|[ζη]λωκὼς ἦθος (nach 84 v. Chr.). Weitere Belege bei L. Robert *Hellenica* XIII (1965) 36 Anm. 1, ders. 'Documents d' Asie Mineure' *BCH* 101 (1977) 90 Anm. 1.
59 Siehe Fr. Dirlmeier Φίλος *und* φιλία *im vorhellenistischen Griechentum* (München 1931) und zuletzt R. Metzner 'In aller Freundschaft. Ein frühchristlicher Fall freundschaftlicher Gemeinschaft (Phil 2.25-30)' *NTS* 48 (2002) 111-31 bes. 111-13, 119-26 (mit der älteren Literatur).

διὰ τοῦτο). Dessen Ziel ist, die Identität des Verstorbenen bekannt zu machen, die – und an dieser Stelle erhält der Text wieder einen humoristischen Ton– direkt mit dem Spitznamen Πετροκόραξ verknüpft ist, mit dem der Wanderer ihn anreden soll (ἵνα σε πᾶς παράγων ὀνομ<ά>ζῃ ἀγαθὲ Πετροκόραξ). Der Text endet mit der Erwähnung von Geminas' Todesalter, allerdings mit lateinischen Ziffern.[60]

Nach den obigen Beobachtungen – und mit der Ausnahme der ersten Zeile, deren genauer Inhalt unklar bleibt – scheint es in der Inschrift keinerlei Bezug auf den familiären Kreis des Geminas zu geben. Im Gegensatz dazu setzt die doppelte Erwähnung des Beinamens des Verstorbenen, einen Freundes- und keinen Familienkreis voraus. Demzufolge sind mit dem Begriff ἀδελφοί dieselben Personen gemeint, die in der Inschrift auch φίλοι *(amici)* oder ἑταῖροι genannt werden.[61] Die Verwendung des Begriffs ἀδελφός zur Angabe eines freundschaftlichen Verhältnisses ist aus der griechisch-römischen Literatur und insbesondere den antiken Briefen wohlbekannt.[62] Ebenso ist auch die Errichtung von Ehren- bzw. Grabdenkmälern

---

60 Zur Erwähnung des Todesalters in Inschriften s. A. Degrassi 'L' indicazioni dell' età nelle iscrizioni latine' in *Akte des IV. Internationalen Kongresses für griechische und lateinische Epigraphik (Wien, 17. bis 22. September 1962)*, (Wien 1964) 72-98 und M. Clauss 'Probleme der Lebensalterstatistiken aufgrund römischer Grabinschriften' *Chiron* 3 (1973) 395-417. Mit lateinischen Ziffern wird die Anzahl der Lebensjahre in einer Grabinschrift aus Herakleia Lynkestis angegeben; s. *IG* X 2.2 76: [A]ντίγονος | ἐτῶν LV (1. Jh.). Zu diesem Phänomen s. M. Leiwo 'The mixed languages in Roman inscriptions' in H. Solin, O. Salomies & U.-M. Liertz (Hsg.) *Acta Colloquii Epigraphici Latini, Helsingiae 3.-6. sept. 1991 habiti*, Comm. Hum. Litt. 104 (Helsinki 1995) 293-301, *SEG* XLV 2269.
61 Vgl. z.B. Peek, *GV* 300 (*IGUR* 1299, Rom 2./3. Jh.) wo die Person, die das Monument errichtet hat, als φίλος erwähnt wird, der Verstorbene jedoch als ἑταῖρος; *I.Rhod.Peraia* 153 (Epigramm mit Weihung an Herakles): Κοιν[ῆι τοὶ] δύο τόνδ᾽ ἀν[ε]θή[καμ]εν ὄντες ἑταῖροι | πιστο[ὶ] τε ἀλλήλοι[ς], μνημόσυνον φιλίας (Thyssanus, 3. Jh. v.Chr.); *IG* I³ 1329: κύκλωι στεφανοῦσ<ι>ν ἑταῖροι μνημείων ἀρετῆς οὕνεκα καὶ φιλίας (Piraeus, 420-400 v.Chr.), *IG* X 2.1, 630 Z. 7: πολλοὺς ἐς φιλίην ἐκτησάμην ἄνδρας ἑταίρους (Thessaloniki, 2./3. Jh.); Merkelbach-Stauber, *SGO* III, 13/05/01 (Komana, 2./3. Jh.).
62 Siehe dazu Metzner (Anm. 58) 122. Zur Koexistenz der Begriffe *amicus-collega* in Inschriften aus Rom, M.L. Caldelli 'Amicus/a nelle iscrizioni di Roma: l'apporto dell'epigrafia al chiarimento di un sentimento sociale' in M. Peachin (Hsg.) *Aspects of Friendship in the Graeco-Roman World. Proceedings of a conference held at the Seminar für Alte Geschichte, Heidelberg, on 10-11 June, 2000*, *JRA* Suppl. 43 (Portsmouth 2001) 27-28.

durch Personen, die als φίλοι/*amici*[63] bzw. ἑταῖροι[64] bezeichnet werden, bekannt. Nicht minder häufig ist ferner die Verwendung dieser Begriffe für die Angabe von Mitgliedern religiöser oder beruflicher Vereine.[65] Jedenfalls ist es schwer, im Kontext von Grabinschriften und insbesondere Epigrammen den semantischen Unterschied zwischen den drei Begriffen klar zu fassen. Außerdem ist es auch schwierig, die präzise Bedeutung der Adjektive φιλέταιρος und φιλάδελφος zu bestimmen, mit denen Apollodoros, Sohn des Gaios, und Maximos in einer Inschrift aus Pautalia bezeichnet werden.[66] Mit einem konkreten und voneinander deutlich unterschiedlichen semantischen Gehalt werden die Begriffe in einem Grabepigramm aus Herakleia an der Salbake verwendet.[67] Der verfrühte Tod des Apollonides wurde von seinen gleichaltrigen Gefährten laut beklagt (μέγα στενάχουσιν δ᾽ ἑταῖροι ὀκτωκαιδεκέτες ἄνθος ὁμηλικίης);[68] das Denkmal (βωμός) selbst wurde von Menandros errichtet, 'der als Freund des Verstorbenen keinem Bruder nachsteht' (φείλος ἀδελφειοῦ μηδενὶ λειπόμενος).

---

63 Siehe dazu Chr. Veligianni 'Philos und *philos*-Komposita in den griechischen Inschriften der Kaiserzeit', in M. Peachin (Hsg.) 2001 (Anm. 61) 64. Belege in lateinischen Inschriften bei M. Reali *Il contributo dell'epigrafia latina alla studio dell'amicitia: il caso della Cisalpina* (Firenze 1998) und ders. 'Supplementum amicorum' *Epigraphica* 64 (2002) 232-44.
64 Siehe z.B. *I.Iasos* 116 (Totenehren für Isokrates) Z. 8-12: κα[ὶ] συν[α]|γαγών (sc. Θράσυλλος) τούς τε οἰκείους καὶ τοὺς | ἑταίρους καὶ τοὺς φίλους παρεκά[λε]|σεν συναγαγεῖν τιμῶντας | Ἰσοκράτην δαίμονα ἀγαθόν; Peek, *GV* 1086 (Athen, Mi. 2. Jh.), *I.Smyrna* 512 (= Merkelbach-Stauber, *SGO* I, 05/01/42 (Smyrna, 3. Jh. v. Chr.).
65 Siehe F. Poland *Geschichte des griechischen Vereinswesens* (Leipzig 1909) 53 ff., Veligianni (Amn. 62) 64-65.
66 *IGBulg* IV 2055: τοὺς φιλεταίρους | καὶ φιλαδέλφους | Ἀπολλόδωρον Γαΐου καὶ Μάξιμ[ο](ν) (der weitere Text fehlt).
67 Merkelbach-Stauber, *SGO* I, 02/13/01 (2. Jh.).
68 Vgl. den Ausdruck πᾶσ[ί] τε ἑταίροισιν σύντροφον ἡλικίας Peek, *GV* 544 (Athen, Mi. 4. Jh. v. Chr.).

'THE EXAMPLES OF THE SAINTS' READING EUGIPPIUS' ACCOUNT OF SAINT SEVERIN

By Carl I. Hammer

Summary: In 511 Eugippius wrote a Commemoratorium or 'Account' of the holy man, Severin, who was active from about 460 until his death in 482 in the frontier province of Noricum (now Austria). Eugippius was abbot of Severin's community, resettled near Naples in Italy, and his 'Account' has been used extensively by historians to reconstruct conditions along the Danubian frontier during the last years of the Western Roman Empire. But, beyond the distortions normally associated with hagiography – Eugippius was clearly concerned to portray Severin as a suitable founder-saint for his community – the author may also purposely have altered the historical information for other, more ideological purposes. This paper looks at two episodes which describe Severin's reception of relics: Saints Gervasius and Protasius (chapter 9) and St John the Baptist (chapter 23). Their common 'message' is to oppose the Arianism espoused by Theoderich's contemporary Gothic regime in Italy and to condemn the disputed papal election of 498 which ended through Theoderich's support of Symmachus. But the paper concludes that the short narratives of the relics embedded as pericopes within these chapters are historically credible. Thus, it appears that Eugippius' 'Account' is best contextualized and interpreted for historical information at the level of such discrete pericopes rather than the longer chapters where Eugippius may have reconfigured authentic historical information to advance his agenda.

DOES EUGIPPIUS' ACCOUNT OF SAINT SEVERIN HAVE AN 'UNDERSIDE'?

In 511 Eugippius wrote a *Commemoratorium*, a 'Catalogue' or an 'Account[ing]', of the wonders worked in the Danubian frontier province of *Noricum Ripense* by the late fifth-century saint, Severin.[1] Eugippius seems to have joined Severin's community there only shortly before or possibly even after Severin's death in 482, and he accompanied the saint's body on the provincial evacuation south to Italy in 488 where the community was re-established near Naples with Eugippius eventually as its head.[2] His 'Account' has long been valued by Central European, particularly Austrian historians for its vivid description of conditions and events during the final years of Roman rule there. In the nineteenth century the MGH in Berlin published two separate critical editions, one by Theodor Mommsen, and at the same time in Vienna the *Corpus Scriptorum* produced its own edition by Pius Knöll.[3] Indeed, in modern times the text became an Austrian touchstone for patriotic sentiment and religious piety. This was evidenced by the numerous publications, ceremonies and major exhibition marking the 1500th anniver-

---

* Completion of this article was facilitated by the fine collection and helpful staff of the Barbour Library at Pittsburgh Theological Seminary.
1 For literary commentary and the translation of the term 'Commemoratorium' see W. Berschin *Biographie und Epochenstil im lateinischen Mittelalter I* Quellen und Untersuchungen zur lateinische Philologie des Mittelalters 8 (Stuttgart 1986), 174-88, here: 176: 'Verzeichnis'.
2 For Eugippius, his other literary works and social circle see the still-useful account by M. Büdinger 'Eugipius [sic], eine Untersuchung', Kaiserl. Akad. Wiss., Phil.-hist. Kl., Sitzungsberichte 91 (Vienna 1878), 793-814; the major issues are rehearsed with references to modern editions and secondary literature by J. Hofmann 'Das Werk des Abtes Eugippius. Zum literarischen Vermächtnis eines spätantiken Augustinus-Kenners an die frühmittelalterliche Kirche des Abendlandes' *Zeitschrift für Kirchengeschichte* 109 (1998) 293-305.
3 *Eugippii Vita Sancti Severini*, ed. H. Sauppe, Monumenta Germaniae Historica, Auctores Antiquissimi 12 (Berlin 1877); *Eugippii Vita Sancti Severini*, ed. T. Mommsen, MGH, Scriptores Rerum Germanicarum in Usum Scholarum [26] (Berlin 1898); *Eugippii Vita Sancti Severini*, ed. P. Knöll, Corpus Scriptorum Ecclesiasticorum Latinorum 9,2 (Vienna 1886).

sary of the saint's death in 1982, which provided the occasion for the reissue of a bi-lingual edition of the *Commemoratorium* by Rudolf Noll which still serves as the scholarly standard.[4]

Despite two excellent translations into English, significant Anglo-American interest in this unique source has been only very recent.[5] I believe this new attention can be traced to a lecture published in 1982 by the distinguished English historian E.A. Thompson, which took energetic exception to a major re-evaluation of Eugippius' work published only six years earlier by the German historian Friedrich Lotter.[6] Thompson's aggressive application of Anglo-Saxon 'common sense' (p. 115) against (what he considered) German academic obfuscation resulted in a learned, nuanced and highly-intelligent but essentially literal historical reading of Eugippius' 'Account' against Lotter's (at times, controversial) reading of the text as a problematic piece of hagiography only incidentally concerned with historical issues. Thompson's vigorous advocacy of 'common sense' has directly influenced major new narratives of (depending upon preference) the 'Transformation'

---

4 *Severin zwischen Römerzeit und Völkerwanderung. Katalog* (Linz 1982); *Eugippius. Das Leben des Heiligen Severin. Lateinisch und Deutsch*, ed. R. Noll (Passau 1981), based on Mommsen's MGH edition with new critical, textual notes by E. Vetter; the first edition appeared in an East German series 'Schriften und Quellen der Alten Welt' (Berlin 1963). The more recent and accessible edition by Philippe Régerat, *Vie de Saint Séverin*, Sources Chrétiennes 374 (Paris 1991), while presenting excellent commentary, indices and French translation, does not contain a much-needed new, critical edition of the Latin text and is unsatisfactory for scholarly use (see review by F. Lotter in *Francia* 21/1 (1994), 307-11).

5 G. Robinson *The Life of Saint Severinus by Eugippius* (Cambridge, MA 1914); L. Bieler and L. Krestan *Eugippius, The Life of Saint Severin*, The Fathers of the Church 55 (Washington 1965), with excellent notes; both are based on Mommsen's MGH edition, but Bieler provides his own textual notes on p. 10, n. 38. See the autobiographical remarks prefacing Walter Goffart's 'Does the *Vita S. Severini* Have an Underside?' in *Eugippius und Severin. Der Autor, der Text und der Heilige*, ed. W. Pohl and M. Diesenberger, Forschungen zur Geschichte des Mittelalters 2, Österr. Akad. Wiss., Phil.-hist. Kl., Denk-schriften 297 (Vienna, 2001), 33-39.

6 E.A. Thompson *Romans and Barbarians: The Decline of the Western Empire* (Madison 1982), here: Chapter 7, 'The End of Noricum', 113-33; F. Lotter *Severinus von Noricum. Legende und historische Wirklichkeit. Untersuchungen zur Phase des Übergangs von spätantiken zu mittelalterlichen Denk- und Lebensformen*, Monographien zur Geschichte des Mittelalters 12 (Stuttgart 1976).

or the 'Fall' of Rome by English historians as diverse in their concerns as Peter Brown, Bryan Ward-Perkins, and Peter Heather.[7]

Nevertheless, as we learn more about Eugippius and the contemporary concerns which formed the immediate context and motivation for his 'Account', it becomes increasingly difficult to credit his historical objectivity without significant critical reservations. This is signaled immediately by the uniform organization of the chapters around individual miracles and their total number, forty six, a mystical number explicated by Eugippius' theological mentor, Augustine, which exposes the chapters as artful constructs arranged consciously within Eugippius' overall design.[8] It is clear that Eugippius constructed his 'Account' skillfully with a close regard to his contemporary audiences both within and outside the monastery, and it is now impossible to view the *Commemoratorium* as a naïve and – in Peter Heather's words – 'disjointed account' from which to extract colorful historical incidents.[9] Harald Dickerhof, in a finely crafted but neglected essay, has demonstrated the immense trouble, skill and sophistication Eugippius applied to remake his saintly hero, Severin, from a questionable anchorite into a proper coenobite suitable as the founder saint for a respectable monastery.[10] Beyond

---

7 P. Brown *The Rise of Western Christendom; Triumph and Diversity,* AD *200-1000,* 2nd ed. (Oxford 2003), here: 'A Saint of the Open Frontier: Severinus of Noricum', 123-25, citing Thompson but omitting Lotter on p. 502, n. 2; B. Ward-Perkins *The Fall of Rome and the End of Civilization* (Oxford 2005), here: 'Living through Invasion', 17-20, 134-36, 194, n. 9; P. Heather *The Fall of the Roman Empire; A New History of Rome and the Barbarians* (New York 2006), here: 'The Unravelling of Empire 468-476: The Frontier', 407-15, 531, n. 42. Severin merited only a footnote in Brown's seminal 1971 essay, 'The Rise and Function of the Holy Man in Late Antiquity', reprinted with his other essays in the same year as Thompson's lecture: *Society and the Holy in Late Antiquity* (Berkeley & Los Angeles 1982), 103-52, here 132, n. 143.

8 For the number 46, see Berschin, *Biographie und Epochenstil,* 182.

9 Heather, 2006 (n. 7), 407: 'What Eugippius produced was a disjointed account of Severinus' life and miracles – hardly a biography, but it is packed with incidents that vividly evoke life in a frontier region as the tide of Empire ebbed away.' For discussions of Eugippius' possible audiences, lay and monastic, see P. Amory *People and Identity in Ostrogothic Italy, 489-554* (Cambridge 1997), 120-27; and J.-N. Saint-Laurent 'Early Christian Hagiography in Late Antique Austria: Eugippius and Severinus' in *Papers Presented at the Fourteenth International Conference on Patristic Studies held in Oxford 2003,* ed. F. Young et al., Studia Patristica 39 (Leuven 2006), 429-34.

10 H. Dickerhof 'De Instituto Sancti Severini. Zur Genese der Klostergemeinschaft des Hl. Severin' *Zeitschrift für bayerische Landesgeschichte* 46 (1983), 3-36, p. 30; fortunately, back

this, Walter Goffart, in a characteristically-provocative essay, has asked whether Eugippius' 'Account' – far from being merely historical – has an 'underside', an ideological agenda, and is hardly even an, 'innocent and disinterested specimen of hagiography.'[11]

There can be little doubt that issues around accommodation with the contemporary barbarian regime in Italy were much on Eugippius' mind when he wrote the 'Account'. However Severin's own relations with his barbarian neighbors may have been – and Thompson argues, persuasively, that they were embarrassingly close and good – Goffart suggests, equally persuasively, that alienation from and resentment against Theoderich's Gothic and Arian rule in Italy was the essence of Eugippius' message, the 'underside' of his 'Account' of St Severin.[12] But Goffart fails to cite the best evidence for his hypothesis. In a letter commending the *Commemoratorium*, the deacon, Paschasius, refers to a passage in the First Book of Maccabees where the dying Jewish priest and rebel, Mattathias, urges his sons to continue his fight against the gentile dynasty of the Seleucids (I Macc. 2.49-69):

> Arrogance now stands secure and gives judgment against us; these are days of calamity and raging fury. Now, my sons, be zealous for the Law, and give your lives for the Covenant made with your forefathers. If you keep in mind the deeds they did in their generations, great glory and everlasting fame will be yours. [Leaders from Israel's history are then cited, from Abraham to Daniel]… So bear in mind how in the history of the generations, no one who trusts in Heaven ever lacks strength. Do not fear a wicked man's threats; his success will turn to filth and worms.

---

issues of this somewhat inaccessible journal now can be consulted through the Bavarian State Library's excellent website: www.bayerische-landesbibliothek-online.de. Dickerhof's essay is cited and his argument extended in I. Wood 'The Monastic Frontiers of the Vita Severini', in *Eugippius und Severin*, 41-51, which quite correctly notes, p. 42: '… however useful the image of a decaying frontier province may be for anyone trying to understand fifth-century Noricum or its neighbours, the *Vita Severini* cannot be read as a straightforward account which can be plundered for pure information, without any consideration of the nature of the source.'

11 Goffart 2001 (n. 5), 38.
12 However, and in sharp contrast, J. Moorhead *Theoderic in Italy* (Oxford 1992), 93-94: '… while Eugippius' *Life of Severin* is hostile to the Arianism of the Rugians, we have no reason to believe that this author would have felt similarly about the Ostrogoths.'

Today he may be high in honour, but tomorrow not a trace of him will be found: he will have returned to the dust and his schemes will have come to naught... Assemble to your side all who observe the Law, and avenge your people's wrongs. Repay the Gentiles in their own coin, and always heed the Law's decrees... (*REB* translation)

To which Paschasius comments approvingly to Eugippius:[13]

Thus, also, that model of faith, Mattathias, as his glorious death drew near, left to his sons as an inheritance, the examples of the saints (*sanctorum exempla*), in order that they, stimulated by their admirable struggle, might despise their own lives for the holy fervor of the eternal laws. Not in vain had the father's instruction been imparted to his children; the deeds of their elders bore so much fruit in them that, confessing openly their faith, they frightened armed princes, stormed the camps of the blasphemers, destroyed far and wide the cults and altars of the demons, and, decorated with eternal crowns, they provided a wreath of civic honor (*corona civica*) for their glorious country.

The intent of this passage can hardly be in doubt: it is an unmistakable call to resistance against Theoderich and his Amal regime, the 'Seleucid' dynasty imposing its gentile barbarism and its heretical Arianism on Rome. On this basis, Istvan Bóna argued that the relationship to Paschasius 'lifts the veil from Eugippius' true ideology'.[14] We shall return to this point – and Goffart's *gravamen* – at the end.

Eugippius and Paschasius surely shared a strong resentment against Theo-

---

[13] Citation based upon Bieler's translation, p. 102.
[14] I. Bóna 'Sever[in]iana' *Acta Antiqua Academiae Scientiarum Hungaricae* 21 (1973), 281-338, here 285: 'Den Schleier von der wahren Ideologie des Eugippius lüftet seine Beziehung, sein Verhältnis zu jenem Paschasius...'; see also R. Bratoz *Severinus von Noricum und seine Zeit. Geschichtliche Anmerkungen*, Österr. Akad. Wiss., Phil.-hist. Kl., Denkschriften 165 (Vienna 1983), 10-12. Bóna's excellent study, incidentally, provides for me the most convincing solution to Severin's numerous connections with important historical figures which bothers Goffart (2005 (n. 5) 34-36: 'Splashy historical information' ... 'Who would have thought Orestes had friends?' ... 'too good to be the casual celebration of a miracle-working monk from an abandoned, remote province'); he was active at Attila's court before coming to Noricum (Bóna, 325).

derich. The most egregious source of complaint was the Goth's intervention in the papal schism resulting from the elections in 498 of two rival popes, Symmachus and Laurentius.[15] Eugippius and Paschasius were partisans of the saintly Laurentius in this bitter and protracted conflict; Theoderich, however, had supported Symmachus, a Sardinian and a man (in their eyes) of questionable piety and dubious morals. Castellum Lucullanum in the diocese of Naples, the site of Eugippius' monastic community, was a prominent center for the losing, Laurentian party.[16] Thus, as Eugippius was writing his *Commemoratorium*, the sitting pope, Symmachus (d. 514), was the creature of a barbarian and a heretic. The message of the Maccabees was highly topical but, at the same time, extremely sensitive. It could only be addressed in indirect terms and through this less-charged biblical analogy.

The critical issue here is the extent to which Eugippius has migrated this or any other 'true ideology' or 'underside' into both the overall structure and the specific incidents reported in the 'Account' and, thus, reformulated them consistently for ideological rather than conventional historical and hagiographical purposes? Lotter has shown quite clearly that Eugippius took a variety of short narratives – 'pericopes' in the language of biblical exegesis – provided by his sources, sometimes conflated them into longer episodes, and then fitted these largely-discrete episodes (always including a miracle as proof of sanctity) into an overall structure that is both chronological/biographical and thematic.[17] We can explore this problem of an embedded 'underside' by looking more closely at two related episodes: Severin's reception of the relics of Saints Gervasius and Protasius in Chapter 9 and the relics of Saint John the Baptist in Chapters 22 and 23.

---

15 A good general narrative in English is Moorhead, *Theoderic*, Chapter 4: 'Schism in Rome' 114-39. Many fundamental critical issues including chronology, are discussed persuasively by E. Wirbelauer *Zwei Päpste in Rom. Der Konflikt zwischen Laurentius und Symmachus (498-514), Studien und Texte* Quellen und Forschungen zur Antiken Welt 16 (Munich 1993).

16 For Eugippius and Castellum Lucullanum see G. Nathan 'The Last Emperor: The Fate of Romulus Augustulus' *C&M* 43 (1992), 261-71.

17 Lotter 1976 (n. 6), 59-77: 'II.3. Komposition und Struktur der Vita Severini'; Berschin refers to these basic elements as 'exempla' 1986 (n. 1), 182.

REDEEMING THE SAINTS

The narrative structure of both episodes is so similar that they can be regarded formally as a literary 'doublet' which suggests that a similar intent underlies both episodes (App. 1-2).[18] One prominent and common element in both is the manner in which the relics are brought to Severin. In both cases the saint has a revelation that the relics are in the care of an unnamed stranger who has just arrived in barbarian territory across the Danube from Severin's main monastery at Favianis in search of the holy man. Accordingly, the relics come into Severin's possession through a double act of divine will which – as the Chapter 9 points out – is a certain guaranty of their authenticity despite the unconventional mode of translation. Quite possibly, all of the relics reached Severin together but were remembered in separate and distinct narratives by Eugippius' various informants, or, perhaps, more likely, Eugippius himself split a single recorded narrative into two parts. In either event, we may safely assume that his final arrangement of the material served his underlying narrative purposes.

Although Eugippius provides no further information on the relics' previous whereabouts, the fact that he begins the narrative of Saints Gervasius and Protasius with a reference to Severin's tireless efforts to redeem captives from the barbarians indicates that the relics too are the objects of an act of redemption. The redemption of captives from barbarians was a common *topos* in contemporary hagiographical literature but was normally ascribed to the pious acts of saintly Gallic bishops.[19] Similarly, mediation between oppressed Roman populations and barbarians was a typical episcopal activity there and also a prominent characteristic of Severin's ministry. It is, therefore, not surprising that the episode of Saints Gervasius and Protasius immediately prefaces the offer from an unknown source to consecrate Severin

---

18 The Latin texts follow Knöll's edition and the English translations Bieler with alterations. The doublet motif is brought out together with other examples in Lotter 1976, 146-47. Linguistic issues are discussed in F. Losek 'Die Latinität des Eugippius und das Latein des Heiligen Severin', in *Eugippius und Severin*, 99-107, here 100-2.

19 R. Mathisen *Roman Aristocrats in Barbarian Gaul; Strategies for Survival in an Age of Transition* (Austin 1993), 98-102; W. Klingshirn 'Charity and Power: Caesarius of Arles and the Ransoming of Captives in sub-Roman Gaul' *JRS* 75 (1988), 183-203.

as bishop.[20] It is notable, however, that he not only declines the offer but that Eugippius uses the opportunity to insert an admonition disparaging monks who are attracted from their vocations by worldly office. This unexpected elaboration would have been understood quite clearly by contemporary readers: Severin's sanctity was very different from that of the most famous subject of late-Antique hagiography, Martin of Tours. This reading is confirmed by the chapter summary which Eugippius provides at the beginning of the 'Account': the point of Chapter 9 is not liturgical reception of the relics but, rather, the quasi-episcopal authority ascribed to the saint without the dangers – both moral and canonical – of the office.[21]

Thus, the relic narrative in Chapter 9 contains an artful commentary on contemporary models of sanctity by conjoining elements – pericopes – which probably had no substantive biographical connection. The narrative of Saint John the Baptist's relics, which begins in Chapter 22 and concludes in Chapter 23, is even more obviously an amalgam of diverse pericopes. The summary for Chapter 22 indicates that the narrative there was intended to vindicate Severin's authority against a rebellious priest, and the narrative in the 'Account', itself, apparently conflates two churches: one with a baptistery in Batavis (Passau) and a newly-built one at Severin's small monastery in

---

20 Indeed, Severin conforms so closely to Claudia Rapp's recent 'model' of the 'holy bishop', deriving authority from pragmatic and spiritual qualities actualized through asceticism, that this 'holy man' is – apparently – considered relevant evidence for her episcopal 'model' (*Holy Bishops in Late Antiquity; The Nature of Christian Leadership in an Age of Transition*, The Transformation of the Classical Heritage 37 (Berkeley, Los Angeles & London 2005), 232-33.

21 It is quite possible that Eugippius also intended the offer of episcopal office and its rejection to dissipate criticism that Severin was migratory and not under episcopal authority as required in 451 by the famous Canon 4 (and 5) of the Council of Chalcedon (in Denis the Short's Latin translation): '… Quoniam vero quidam utentes habitu monachi ecclesiastica negotia civiliaque conturbant circumeuntes indifferenter urbes nec non et monasteria sibi instituere temptantes, placuit nullum quidem usquam aedificare aut constituere monasterium vel oratorii domum praeter conscientiam civitatis episcopi, monachos vero per unamquamque civitatem aut regionem subiectos esse episcopo … ieiunio et orationi, in locis quibus renuntiaverunt saeculo, permanentes, nec ecclesiasticis vero nec saecularibus negotiis communicent …' (*Concilium Universale Chalcedonense 2/2*, ed. E Schwartz, Acta Conciliorum Oecumenicorum 2 (Berlin & Leipzig 1936), 55). See also the interesting comments on this passage by Dickerhof, 'De Instituto', 11; neither Dickerhof nor Wood, 'Monastic Frontiers', notes this highly-relevant canon.

Boiotro across the river Inn. The connection of this Chapter to the relics of Saint John in the next is an extremely tenuous literary bridge: the common site of the priest's impudence and his violent end in the baptistery at Batavis. In contrast, the liturgical intent of the narrative's ostensible continuation in Chapter 23 is quite pronounced. Although Eugippius uses almost identical language to describe Severin's disposition of the relics in Chapters 9 and 23 (App. 3), his vocabulary in Chapter 23 – explicitly the consecration of a monastic church to Saint John the Baptist – has caused trouble for commentators and translators who focus on his lack of episcopal authority.[22] But, as the episode of Gervasius and Protasius indicates, this was less evidently a concern to Eugippius, and contemporary evidence provides a meaningful context for Severin's unusual liturgical actions.

In 1930, Hippolyte Delehaye assembled from a variety of sources the earliest references to the consecration of churches by investing their altars with relics.[23] Apparently, this liturgical practice originated with Saint Ambrose's 'invention' of the relics of Saints Gervasius and Protasius.[24] His example was followed quickly in Italy and Gaul (App. 4).[25] As Delehaye remarked (p. 13), 'Toutes ces listes [of relics] offrent bien peu de variété.' Gervasius, Protasius and John the Baptist are precisely the saints whose relics we should expect to find at a fifth-century consecration; the only remarkable aspect is to encounter them in frontier Noricum. But the distribution of relics in the table, App. 4 provides a clue for their origin and – in support of Severin's method described in Chapter 9 (App. 1) – it provides a possible confirmation of their authenticity.

In 452, Attila led a devastating expedition across northern Italy.[26] It began

---

[22] Bieler's note to Chapter 23 (80, n. 24) is typical: 'Since Severin was no bishop, he could not have performed the liturgical consecration of the basilica. *Sacrare* here is not to be understood in this technical meaning.'

[23] H. Delehaye 'Loca Sanctorum' *Analecta Bollandiana* 48 (1930), 5-64, here 6-22.

[24] See E. Dassmann 'Ambrosius und die Märtyrer' *Jahrbuch für Antike und Christentum* 18 (1975), 49-68, here 52-57.

[25] For App. 4, see Delehaye, 'Loca Sanctorum', and the sources cited there; also Paulinus of Milan's 'Vita Ambrosii', in *Vita di Cipriano, Vita di Ambrogio, Vita di Agostino*, ed. A. Bastiaensen, Vite dei Santi 3 (Milan 1974), 51-125 (English translation: B. Ramsey, *Ambrose* (London & New York 1997), 195-218), c. 29 (Florence), c. 52 (Basilica Virginum, Milan).

[26] Good account in E.A. Thompson *The Huns* rev. edn (Oxford 1996), 157-60.

with a successful siege of Aquileia in the far northeast, which was plundered; it ended with the surrenders of Milan and Ticinum (Pavia) which, for some reason, were spared. According to Jordanes, writing in the following century, the other cities of Venetia, that is, suffragan churches of the patriarchate of Aquileia, were also despoiled by the Huns.[27] In the eighth century, Paul the Deacon provided a gloss on Jordanes' account naming Concordia, Altinum, Padua, Vicenza, Verona, Brescia and also Bergamo.[28] It is not clear whether Paul used another source or, more likely, was adding details from his own knowledge of the region. In either event, the route that Paul sketches follows the Roman road system precisely: from Aquileia the Via Annia led southwest directly to Julia Concordia, Altinum, and Padua from which a connecting road to the northwest would have brought the Huns to Vicenza on the Via Postumia which, in turn, led across northern Italy and through the balance of the cities enumerated by him. If we compare this very plausible itinerary with the cities of Exhibit 4, then it is evident that relics of Saints Gervasius and Protasius were not only available in Milan but also in Brescia at the Basilica Concilii Sanctorum consecrated by Bishop Gaudentius in 400/402. Relics of Saint John the Baptist were on offer – just possibly – in Milan and Aquileia (see below, 3b) and certainly in Brescia and Concordia. Thus, shortly before Severin's arrival in Noricum in the late 450s or early 460s, any of Attila's numerous barbarian allies could easily have plundered the very relics which subsequently turned up amongst the barbarians settled on the north bank of the Danube.

Although the original pericopes underlying these two accounts of relics may, thus, be historically credible, we must still ask why Eugippius chose to mention only these two explicitly when, by his own account in Chapter 9, Severin 'united the shrines of many martyrs' in his basilica.[29] Thus, we may

---

27 'Jordanis Getica', ed. T. Mommsen, MGH, AA 5 (Berlin 1882), 53-138, here: c. 42/222, 114: 'reliquas Venetum civitates Hunni bacchantur.'
28 'Pauli Historia Romana', ed. H. Droysen, MGH, AA 2 (Berlin 1889), 183-224, here: c. 14/11, p. 204: 'Concordiam, Altinum sive Patavium, vicinas Aquileiae civitates ... exinde per universas Venetiarum urbes, hoc est Vicetiam, Veronam, Brixiam Pergamum...' Brescia and Bergamo were likely in Milanese territory in the mid-fifth century. The ecclesiastical topography of Italy is discussed extensively in E. Park 'Italia I (landesgeschichtlich)', *Reallexikon für Antike und Christentum* 18 (1998), cols. 1049-1202, here: cols. 1166-73.
29 Chapter 9: 'Quo loco martyrum congregavit sanctuaria plurimorum...' This is consistent with the account in Chapter 22 where the search for 'martyrum reliquiae' at Boiotro is re-

reasonably suspect that Saints Gervasius and Protasius and Saint John the Baptist represented for Eugippius certain specific aspects of the 'message' that he was constructing around Severin. This possibility is already implicit in the passage from Maccabees cited by Paschasius where each of the Jewish patriarchs, prophets and commanders named by Mattathias is emblematic of loyalty, steadfastness and zeal for the Law. Paschasius then underscores this fundamental aspect of Mattathias' charge when he describes the Maccabees' very inheritance as 'the examples of the saints'.[30] What 'exempla' do Severin's saints embody?

'THE EXAMPLES OF THE SAINTS'

a. Saints Gervasius and Protasius

Gervasius and Protasius, because of their association with Bishop Ambrose of Milan, are exceptionally well documented saints.[31] We have three contemporary accounts of their famous 'invention': Ambrose's own letter to his sister Marcella, Augustine's recollections in his 'Confessions', and Paulinus of Milan's 'Life' of the Milanese bishop.[32] All of these sources would have been available to Eugippius. Their common theme is the efficacy of these saints against the Arian heresy. Thus, Paulinus concludes his account: 'Moreover, thanks to these martyrs' good works, the faith of the Catholic Church in-

---

garded as a common activity. Presumably, these relics were removed to Italy, ultimately to Lucullanum, along with Severin's body during Odoacer's enforced evacuation of Romans from Noricum in 488 (Chapter 44).

30 Paschasii Epistola: 'Mattathias morti gloriosissimae iam propinquans filiis suis hereditario iure sanctorum exempla distribuit…'

31 Besides Dassman, 'Ambrosius', see N. McLynn *Ambrose of Milan; Church and Court in a Christian Capital* (Berkeley, Los Angeles & London 1994), 181-85, 206-19. The Ambrosian connection is emphasized in Bóna 1973 (n. 14), 318-19.

32 *Sancti Ambrosi Opera*, Pars X, Epistulae et Acta, Tom. III, ed. M. Zelzer, Corpus Scriptorum Ecclesiasticorum Latinorum 82 (Vienna 1982), Book 10, no. 77, 126-40 (English translation: *Saint Ambrose, Letters*, ed. M. Beyenka, The Fathers of the Church 26 (New York 1954), no. 61, 377-84); Sancti Augustini Confessionum Libri XIII, ed. L. Verheijen, Corpus Christianorum, Series Latina 27 (Turnhout 1981), Book 9/7, 141-42; Paulinus of Milan, 'Vita Ambrosii', c. 14.

creased to the same extent as the perfidy of the Arians decreased.'

Ambrose's very public discovery of the two Milanese martyrs in 386 was hardly fortuitous. Just then he was engaged in a bitter theological struggle with Milanese church factions considered by him to be Homoian, that is, Arian heretics.[33] Moreover, they were supported by influential Homoian elements in the imperial court of Valentinian II then resident in Milan and of whom the emperor's mother, Justina, was a prominent exponent. Indeed, Justina's malevolent role is singled out in several passages by Paulinus, and Augustine, whose own mother, Monica, was an eyewitness to the miraculous event, identifies the empress dowager as Ambrose's chief opponent. Ambrose, himself, was more circumspect, but his letter to his sister leaves no doubt that he considered these two local saints, newly raised by his efforts, to be especially efficacious champions against the Arian heresy infecting Milan and the court (77/10):

> Thanks be to you, O Lord Jesus, for having aroused the spirit of the martyrs at this time when Your Church needs greater protection. Let everyone know the kind of defenders (*propugnatores*) I need, those who can fight back but are not wont to attack (*impugnare*). These I have secured for you, O holy people, so that they will bring help to all and harm to none. Such are the defenders I seek, such the soldiers I possess, that is, not soldiers of the world, but soldiers of Christ. With such as these, I fear no danger: the greater the number of them, the safer are my defenses. And I desire their protection for the very ones who grudge them to me. Let them come and see my bodyguards. I do not deny that I am surrounded with such arms: 'These are strong in chariots, these in horses, but we will be great in the name of the Lord our God'

These are strong words of defiance, and the Psalm (19:8) echoes the militant sentiments of Mattathias, but they are mixed with irenic sentiments reflecting the deference which Ambrose owed to the imperial house. They would have been well chosen to express Eugippius' own predicament under Theoderich.

---

33 For Ambrose's opposition to the Homoians see now, L. Ayres *Nicaea and its Legacy: An Approach to Fourth-Century Trinitarian Theology* (Oxford 2004), 260-67.

They also fit precisely the situation of Severin who was obliged to minister under other Arian rulers, the barbarian Rugians, who controlled the lands directly north of the Danube and who claimed tutelage over the Romans living south of the great river. Indeed, the analogy to Ambrose is very close. The consort of the Rugian ruler, Feletheus (also known by the hypocorism Feva) was Giso, possibly a member of the Gothic Amal dynasty, who was every bit as fierce an advocate of Arianism as Justina.[34] Eugippius leaves little doubt about his opinion of her: she was 'dangerous and intent on harm' and 'extremely cruel'.[35]

In Chapter 8 of the 'Account', immediately before the narrative of the Milanese saints, Eugippius records a very dramatic exchange between Severin and this harpy. Giso, 'amongst the other stains of her iniquity' had tried to rebaptize some Catholics but was restrained by her husband out of respect for Severin. Nevertheless, she proceeded to oppress the Roman population in other ways and even removed some of them to the Rugian side of the Danube where they labored as slaves. After rejecting Severin's warnings in the harshest terms, however, she suffered divine punishment. Her son, Frederic, was taken hostage by some of the Roman captives working for the Rugians as goldsmiths. Only after she had repented, sought Severin's pardon, and freed her captives was her son released. Thereupon, Giso, together with her husband, 'immediately hurried to the servant of God ... and promised never again to oppose his commands.'

The charge against Giso of attempted rebaptism is particularly significant. Ambrose, in a letter to the Emperor Valentinian II, son of Justina, where he disputes the Arian bishop, Auxentius of Durostorum, takes particular exception to Auxentius' assertion that the (Catholic) faithful, baptized in the name of the Trinity, required (Arian) rebaptism.[36] This rite appears, in fact, to be an authentic element of the Arian faith, the theology of which is, how-

---

34 For the Rugian royal house see stemma 46 of *The Prosopography of the Later Roman Empire* 2, ed. J. Martindale (Cambridge 1980), 1337, and the appropriate individual entries referenced there. Giso's possible relationship to Theoderich is not included in the *Prosopography* which largely eschews speculative connections but is noted in H. Wolfram *History of the Goths* (Berkeley, Los Angeles & London 1988), 278, with references in n. 159 on p. 496.

35 Chapter 8: 'coniux feralis et noxia'; Chapter 40: 'uxor crudelissima'.

36 Ambrose, *Ep.* 10/75a, 37, p. 107: 'Cur igitur rebaptizandos Auxentius fideles populos putat baptizatos in nomine trinitatis ...'

ever, difficult to recover and was hardly likely to be uniform. One witness, the so-called 'Opus Imperfectum in Mattheum', commenting on Matthew 3:11, seems to imply that the Catholic baptism was merely the baptism by water of John whereas the Arian rite was the baptism of Christ in the Spirit which completed John's baptism.[37] Thus, from an Arian perspective it was not an illegitimate rebaptism; rather, it was the fulfillment of a process begun by the Catholic rite. Eugippius' inclusion of this theological detail, of itself only incidental to the course of the narrative in Chapter 8 where captivity and servitude are the dominant motivating themes, shows quite clearly that he considered Giso a second Justina against whom the Milanese saints, through their (second) timely arrival, were an appropriate prophylactic.

b. St John the Baptist

John the Baptist was, therefore, a potentially-significant 'example' in the contest between Catholics and Arians, but it is exceptionally difficult to be precise about this significance because, as the Precursor, he was revered by both parties. This can be seen clearly from the mosaics depicting the Jordan baptism in the two baptisteries in Ravenna – one Catholic, finished under Bishop Neon around 450, the other Arian, largely completed under Theoderich – where the placement, composition and iconography of the older baptistery is largely repeated with some idiosyncratic variations in the less impressive Arian structure.[38] Eugippius' narrative shows that by this

---

37 Matthew 3.11: 'I [John] baptize you with water, for repentance; but the one who comes after me [Jesus] is mightier than I am, whose sandals I am not worthy to remove. He will baptize you with the Holy Spirit and with fire…' (*REB*). 'Opus Imperfectum', Migne, Patrologia Graeca 56 (Paris, 1862), cols. 611-946, here, col. 653: 'Ergo Christi baptismus non solvit Joannis baptismum, sed in se inclusit… Joannis autem baptismus non inclusit in se baptismum Christi… et ideo baptismum tuum [i.e. Catholic] etsi non esset rectum, tamen baptismum erat, id est, simile baptismo Joannis erat, id est, in aqua, non in spiritu…' On this difficult text, see the remarks in M. Wiles *Archetypal Heresy; Arianism through the Centuries* (Oxford 1996), 38-40.

38 Plates and commentary in F. Deichmann, *Ravenna, Hauptstadt des spätantiken Abendlandes*, 1: Geschichte und Monumente (Wiesbaden 1969) 133-36, 209-12; 2: Kommentar, 1. Teil (Wiesbaden 1974) 32-38, 254-55. For an Arian exposition of this scene and a sermon on the Baptist's feast see *Scripta Arriana Latina I*, ed. R. Gryson, Corpus Christianorum, Series Latina 87 (Turnhout 1982) 51-56, 72-74; I am not aware that the peculiarities of the

time a special place, the baptistery, might be closely associated with John even in a remote frontier province. But this obvious, biblical association did not necessarily imply patronage nor was it exclusive. Only a few years before the events narrated in Chapter 22, Pope Hilarius (461-468) established three oratories or chapels in the Lateran baptistery; one was, indeed, dedicated to John the Baptist, but the others, of equal precedence, honored his homonym, the Evangelist, and the Holy Cross. This triple dedication was then reprised in Eugippius' time by Pope Symmachus for the baptistery attached to St Peter's.[39] It is likewise, questionable whether Severin's monastic basilica at Favianis, with its unusual consecration to John, was intended to serve any baptismal function – unless we interpret this as another indication of Severin's episcopal status.[40]

Thus, although Eugippius clearly was attuned to John's baptismal significance, his intent was probably not limited to that 'example' alone. One additional meaning is implicit in his description of Severin's courageous opposition to Giso in Chapter 8, reprised in his dealings also with her consort, Feva, in Chapters 31 and 40, which echo Elijah's confrontations with Ahab and Jezebel.[41] John the Baptist was, of course, the new Elijah, and his own confrontation with Herod and Herodias proved fatal.[42] Eugippius, despite

---

Arian baptistery have ever been considered as an aspect of Arian theology.

39 H. Brandenburg, *Die frühchristlichen Kirchen Roms vom 4. bis zum 7. Jahrhundert. Der Beginn der abendländischen Kirchenbaukunst* (Milan & Regensburg 2004) 50; 106.

40 Baptism was originally an episcopal prerogative, and baptisteries were still normally associated with episcopal churches as was, apparently, the case at Batavis, or with important parochial churches such as the Roman *tituli*. The earliest Roman *church* dedicated to the Baptist may be the unusual S. Ioannis in Portam Latinam which appears to have been in existence by Theoderich's reign but does not seem to have had local parochial functions or a baptistery; the dedication, itself, may even be a later substitution for the Evangelist (Brandenburg 2004: 165, 220-22).

41 This implicit parallel is drawn by Berschin 1986 (n. 1) 175. If Giso's genealogical connection to Theoderich (see above) is correct, then Eugippius' portrait of Giso is not only indiscreet but even risky, particularly if her son, Frederic, had finally been reconciled with Theoderich; an explicit comparison with Jezebel, daughter of the king of Sidon who influenced Ahab to worship Baal, would clearly have stepped far over the line.

42 Matthew 11.7-14 (*REB*): 'Jesus began to speak to the crowds about John... "For until John all the prophets and the Law foretold things to come, and John is the destined Elijah, if you will but accept it"'.

his desire to 'socialize' Severin, surely meant the saint with his relentless asceticism – the 'fasts and vigils' that so wearied the priest and people of Batavis – to be seen in this austere and uncompromising prophetic tradition which, in contrast to Ambrose, showed no special deference to royal authority.

Despite John's prominence, his relics were very recent and exceptionally rare arrivals at the time of Severin's ministry. They comprise, as it were, two parts: his head and his body.[43] The story of John's head, for which Herodias' daughter danced before Herod, was mediated to the Latin West by a member of Eugippius' intellectual circle, the polymath, Denis the Short, who translated from Greek into Latin two successive accounts of its wondrous mid-fifth-century recovery.[44] However, this relic – now, according to Denis' account, at a new basilica in Emesa – is not immediately relevant to Eugippius' account.[45] Rather, the key text for the relics of John the Baptist is Rufinus of Aquileia's continuation of Eusebius' 'Ecclesiastical History'.[46] Rufinus, born in Concordia, undertook his Latin translation and continuation of Eusebius at the request of Bishop Chromatius of Aquileia in 402/3 while living there after his return from an extended stay in the Holy Land. We know from other witnesses – principally Rufinus' early associate and

---

[43] Matthew 14.9-12 (*REB*): 'At this time the king [Herod] was distressed, but because of his oath... [he] had John beheaded in prison. The head was brought on a dish and given to the girl; and she carried it to her mother [Herodias]. Then John's disciples came and took away the body, and buried it; and they went and told Jesus.'

[44] Dionysius Exiguus, 'De Inventione Capitis S. Joannis', Migne, Patrologia Latina 67, cols. 417-23, 423-32. For Denis see P. Courcelle, *Late Latin Writers and their Greek Sources* (Cambridge, MA, 1969), 331-34; and Moorhead, *Theoderic*, 207-9.

[45] In Sozomen's *Historia Ecclesiastica* (ed. G. Hansen, Fontes Christiani 73/3 (Turnhout 2004), Book 7/21, 912-15) there is another, contemporary (443-450) and quite different account of the head's removal in 391 to a shrine at Hebdomon outside Constantinople by Emperor Theodosius I; presumably, it is this discrepancy to which the so-called 'Decretum Gelasianum' refers when it questions the validity of Denis' popular work (*Das Decretum Gelasianum*, ed. E. von Dobschütz, Texte und Untersuchungen zur Geschichte der altchristlichen Literatur 38/4 (Leipzig 1912) 43-44: 'Item scriptura de inventione crucis et alia scriptura de inventione capitis beati Iohannis Baptistae novellae quidem relationes sunt et nonnulli eas catholici legunt; sed cum haec ad catholicorum manus advenerint, beati Pauli apostoli praecedat sententia: "omnia probate, quod bonum est tenete."').

[46] Published in *Eusebius Werke* 2.2: 'Die Kirchengeschichte', ed. E. Schwartz and T. Mommsen, 2nd ed., Die Griechischen Christlichen Schriftsteller der ersten Jahrhunderte, Neue Folge 6,2 (Berlin 1999), 951 ff, here: Book 11/28, 1033-34.

later opponent Jerome — that by the later fourth century, the relics of John the Baptist were still believed to be interred in Sebaste, the ancient Samaria, in Palestine where, presumably, they had been buried by the Baptist's disciples near the much older remains of Elisha and Obediah.[47] Rufinus, however, tells us that John's relics had been profaned, burned and scattered in 362/3 during the reign of Julian the Apostate. Fortunately, according to Rufinus, some remnants had been rescued by monks from Jerusalem and then sent to Bishop Athanasius of Alexandria where they had been preserved and subsequently installed in a former pagan temple there, the Serapeum. His account suggests a two-stage route for the relics to the West. Rufinus, himself, fresh from Aquileia, visited Alexandria in 373. Although it is unlikely that he met there with the aged Athanasius who died on 2 May in that same year, he may well have acquired the relics at that time.[48] Rufinus also tells us that the messenger who brought the precious relics of the Baptist from Jerusalem to Alexandria was the deacon, Julianus, who afterwards became bishop of Parenzo in Histria and, thus, a suffragan of Aquileia.

It is significant that the two earliest explicit references to the relics of John the Baptist both have connections to Aquileia (App. 4). Bishop Chromatius, the patron of Rufinus' continuation of Eusebius with its unique account of the relics, preached the consecration sermon at Rufinus' hometown, Concordia.[49] There he referred to a friendly competition between Concordia

---

[47] Jerome (transl.), *Eusebius: Das Onomastikon der biblischen Ortsnamen*, ed. E. Klostermann, Die Griechischen Christlichen Schriftsteller der ersten Jahrhunderte 11.1 (Leipzig, 1904), 155: '...Sebasten vocari oppidum Palaestinae, ubi sancti Ioannis baptistae reliquiae conditae sunt' (ed., p. xxxii: 'unzweifelhafte Zutaten des Hieronymus'). For the ancient Jewish graves see J. Jeremias, *Heiligengräber in Jesu Umwelt... Ein Untersuchung zur Volksreligion in der Zeit Jesu* (Göttingen, 1958), 30-31. Elisha's example is cited twice by Eugippius, in Chapters 28 and 43. The proximity of John's tomb to this disciple of Elijah may be understood as a proxy for Elijah who, of course, was buried nowhere; Obediah is most likely Ahab's official who protected 100 prophets against Jezebel (I Kings 18).

[48] For Rufinus see F. Murphy, *Rufinus of Aquileia (345-411); His Life and Works*, The Catholic University of America Studies in Mediaeval History, New Series 6 (Washington 1945).

[49] *Chromace d'Aquilée Sermons 2*, ed. J. Lemarié, Sources Chrétiennes 164 (Paris 1971), no. 26, 92-101; see Lemarié's commentary in part 1, Sources Chrétiennes 154 (Paris 1969), 103-8. The possible archaeological remains of the church in Concordia are discussed in J.-P. Caillet, *L'évergétisme monumental chrétien en Italie et à ses marges d'après l'épigraphie des pavements de mosaïque (IVe-VIIe s.)*, Collection de l'école française de Rome 175 (Rome, 1993), pp. 122-23.

and Aquileia to complete a suitable 'basilica in honor of the saints'. Concordia had begun later, but finished first and, 'for that reason, you have deserved to possess the relics of the saints earlier; we have received the relics of the saints from you.'[50] We do not know the precise identity of either the church or the local churchman in Concordia, but the shrine there may well have been patronized by Rufinus himself. Chromatius implies that a common group of relics supplied both places. It is possible that Aquileia's share was not deposited in Chromatius' large, new cathedral basilica – for which we seem to have a distinct record of relics (App. 4) – but rather in another newly-erected church in the southern suburbs, the 'Basilica del fondo Tullio'.[51] Bishop Gaudentius of Brescia, who consecrated his basilica at the same time, although he is often associated with Ambrose as the presence of the Milanese relics suggests, was, likewise, closely connected to Aquileia.[52] He spent several years in the East where he met Rufinus and there collected many relics as the unusually long list attached to his shrine indicates. It is this Rufinian connection that likely accounts for the presence of the Baptist at Brescia.[53]

In view of this history, does Eugippius' 'example' of John the Baptist have any further meaning? The transmission of his rescued relics to Bishop Athanasius certainly speaks well for the Baptist's orthodoxy! No churchman was a more zealous opponent of Arianism than Athanasius; Aquileia, with which he had established friendly relations during his western exile, was, likewise, noted for its staunch orthodoxy. This association with Athanasius clearly underscores the Baptist's 'example' in opposition to Arianism. But an additional aspect of John's significance may be jurisdictional. The close associa-

---

50 Sermon 26/1, p. 92: "tardius enim coepistis, sed prius consummastis, quia ante habere sanctorum reliquias meruistis. Nos a vobis reliquias sanctorum accepimus…".

51 J. Lemarié, 'La liturgie d'Aquilée et de Milan au temps de Chromace et d'Ambroise', in *Aquileia e Milano*, ed. S. Tavano, Antichità Altoadriatiche 4 (Udine 1973) 249-70, here 268-69; C. Jäggi, 'Aspekte der städtebaulichen Entwicklung Aquileias in frühchristlicher Zeit', *Jahrbuch für Antike und Christentum* 33 (1990) 158-96, here 177-78, 180-81; Caillet, *L'évergétisme monumental*, 145; 156.

52 Chromatius (*Chromace*, Sermon 26, p. 96), Gaudentius refers to John the Baptist as an 'angelus' (*S. Gaudentii Episcopi Brixiensis Tractatus*, ed. A. Glueck, Corpus Scriptorum Ecclesiasticorum Latinorum 68 (Vienna 1936), Tractatus 17, 141-51, here 142).

53 There is, to my knowledge, no certain evidence that relics of the Baptist were present in Milan at this time, but that possibility cannot be completely excluded.

tion of his relics with Aquileia may identify John the Baptist as a counterpart to Milan's Gervasius and Protasius. There was a long-standing rivalry between Milan and Aquileia for control of these frontier territories where Severin ministered.[54] Milan had a political claim to the province of *Raetia II* which pertained to *Italia Annonaria*; its authority there would have reached to Passau on the left bank of the river Inn where John's relics are first mentioned.[55] With the decline of Milan's political influence after the removal of the imperial court to Ravenna, Aquileia seems, finally, to have asserted its claims in part of Noricum although we know nothing about the precise status of the northern areas along the Danube. However, there may be a more contemporary aspect to this metropolitan rivalry. Eugippius had no reason to view the Milan of his own day favorably. In both 501 and 502 the metropolitan bishop there, another Laurentius, had come south with four, possibly five, suffragans to provide crucial support for Pope Symmachus at synods held in Rome.[56] In contrast, as Abbé Duchesne long ago remarked, 'les évêques de Vénétie brillèrent par leur absence', and the bishop of Aquileia clearly was of a different mind than his fellow patriarchs at Milan and Ravenna.[57] Perhaps, this was a consideration for Eugippius – albeit a

---

54 G. Menis, 'Le giurisdizioni metropolitiche di Aquileia e di Milano nell'Antichità', in *Aquileia e Milano* (n. 51) 271-94.

55 It is possible that the emphasis on the *bearer* (*portitor*) of the relics in the summary for Chapter 9 and the abrupt transition there to Severin's rejection of episcopal office, was intended by Eugippius to indicate that the unnamed intermediary was rather more, perhaps, a 'messenger' or 'envoy', which seems consistent with the use of the word 'portitor' also to designate the 'letter-carrier' (*baiulus*) who brings Eugippius' initial letter of request to Paschasius: 'fidelis portitor, filius vester, Deogratias'. This reading might imply that Severin, while accepting these implicit tokens of Milanese affinity, at the same time rejected any canonical claim by Milan to authority over him and Noricum Ripense.

56 The Milanese suffragans were the bishops of Aosta, Turin, Bergamo, Pavia and probably Cremona, located in the extreme southwest of the Venetia. See the attendance and signatory lists in the protocols of the synods, ed. T. Mommsen, *MGH*, AA 12 (Berlin 1894), 416-55; I here follow Wirbelauer (1993: 21-23)in his redating of the 6 November list to 501 and the 23 October list to 502.

57 L. Duchesne, *L'église au VIe siècle* (Paris 1925), 122. Bishop Marcellianus of Aquileia opposed Symmachus, and, when opponents of Symmachus compelled Theoderich to appoint a 'visitor' to investigate serious charges against the pope in early 501, Marcellianus' suffragan and neighbor, Bishop Peter of Altinum, was chosen for this potentially-hostile task (Wirbelauer 1993: 21; 29).

subsidiary one – in balancing a saint whose cult was closely associated with Aquileia against the prominent Milanese duo.[58]

CONCLUSION

I would hesitate to call 'the examples of the saints', as presented here, an 'underside'. They are tendentious – and clearly so by the author's design – but they lack any sinister connotations. Eugippius' great 'Example' was Severin, himself, who was intended to provide a model of exemplary behavior for Eugippius and his contemporaries. To that end, Eugippius showed the monk Severin exercising quasi-episcopal authority and confronting barbarian rulers with unflinching courage and integrity. Nevertheless, the saint's words and actions followed the prophetic types of Elijah and John the Baptist, not the warrior and rebel, Mattathias. Here, Eugippius parts company with the more aggressive 'example' advocated by Paschasius, and conforms more closely – though not exactly – to the 'example' offered by Bishop Ambrose. Moreover, although Arianism and barbarism may have been conjoined by the early sixth century, it was Arianism that was Eugippius' primary concern as the 'examples' of Gervasius and Protasius and John the Baptist indicate.

This appears to be the essence of Eugippius' ideology and it is deeply embedded in the portions of his 'Account' that we have examined closely. However – in my view – this does not vitiate its value as an historical source for Severin's Norican past as opposed to Eugippius' Italian present. To use the 'Account' profitably, however, we must first reduce the material to its constituent elements, its 'pericopes' (Lotter) or its 'exempla' (Berschin). Eugippius has taken these fundamental units related to him by his informants and combined them for his own purposes so that the resulting episodes – even in

---

[58] A final possibility may have more relevance to Severin's own interests. In his Prologue to the account of the 'invention' of John's head, dedicated to an Abbot Gaudentius, Denis the Short praised John as the 'institutorque monachorum' (col. 417). A century later Isidor of Seville in his 'Etymologies' provided a concise elaboration in his chapter 'Concerning Monks': 'Anchorites follow Elijah and John; coenobites the Apostles' (Migne, *Patrologia Latina* 82 (Paris, 1850), col. 293: 'sed anachoritae Eliam et Joannem, coenobitae apostolos imitantur'). But it is difficult to believe that Eugippius would have found this congenial.

an assemblage (Berschin: 'Reihe') as brief as most chapters – are suspect as authentic narratives of historical events. Nor are the pericopes themselves beyond suspicion; they are still highly-selective messages of how the members of Severin's monastic congregation (their primary source, with Eugippius first amongst them) wished his ministry to be seen. That is why we have only these two instances of relics; they were selected by Eugippius as particularly relevant to his overall objective. It is only when we have contextualized the individual pericopes and learned their intended 'examples' within Eugippius' narrative that we can evaluate their historical plausibility and, perhaps, in a few cases also draw inferences about what has been omitted. This procedure may allow us to penetrate even further beyond the literary text to the historical reality underlying it.

APPENDIX 1: EUGIPPIUS' ACCOUNT OF THE RELICS OF GERVASIUS AND PROTASIUS

Capitulum VIIII. De portitore reliquiarum sancti Gervasii et Protasii martyrum mira viro dei revelatione monstrato, vel qua responsione, dum rogaretur, episcopatus declinaverit honorem.

Commemoratorium VIIII. Magna quoque famulo dei prophetiae gratia praedito in redimendis erat captivis industria. Studiosus etenim insistebat barbarorum dicione vexatos genuinae restituere libertati. Interea cuidam cum coniuge liberisque redempto praecepit transvadare Danuvium, ut hominem ignotum in nundinis quaereret barbarorum, quem in tantum divina revelatione didcerat, ut etiam signa staturae capillorumque colorem vultus eius ac vestis habitum indicaret et in qua parte nundinarum reperturus eum foret ostenderet, addens, ut, quicquid ei reperta diceret persona, reversus sibi maturius intimaret. Profectus itaque cuncta, sicut vir dei praedixerat, miratus invenit. Is igitur ab eodem homine, quem repperisse se mirabatur, interrogatus adivit dicentem: 'Putasne possum invenire hominem, qui me ad virum dei, cuius ubique fama diffunditur, qua voluerit mercede perducat? Diu est enim, quod ipsos sanctos martyres, quorum reliquias fero, suppliciter interpello, ut a tali ministerio tandem aliquando solvar indignus, quod huc usque non temeraria praesumptione, sed religiosa necessitate sustinui.' Tunc nuntius hominis dei eius se aspectibus praesentavit.[59] Qui debito sanctorum Gervasii et Protasii martyrum reliquias honore suscipiens in basilica, quam in monasterio construxerat, collocavit officio sacerdotum. Quo loco martyrum congregavit sanctuaria plurimorum, quae tamen praeeunte semper revelatione promeruit, sciens adversarium saepe subrepere[60] sub nomine sanctitatis. Episcopatus quoque honorem ut susciperet postulatus praefinita responsione conclusit, sufficere sibi dicens, quod solitudine desiderata privatus ad illam divinitus venisset provinciam, ut turbis tribulantium frequentibus interesset. Daturus nihilominus monachis formam sollicitius admonebat beatorum patrum

---

59 One Class II manuscript (M) adds here as a transitional clarification: *reliquiasque sanctorum ab eo suscipiens viro dei detulit.*

60 'Subrepere' (sneak in) emended from manuscript 'subripere' (snatch away).

vestigiis inhaerere, quibus sanctae conversationis adquireretur instructio, adhibendamque operam, ne is, qui parentes reliquit et saeculum, pompae saecularis inlecebras retrorsum aspiciendo cuperet, quas vitaverat, et ad hoc uxoris Loth exemplum terribile proponebat…

Table of Chapter 9. Concerning the bearer of the relics of the martyrs St Gervasius and St Protasius who was made known by a miraculous revelation to the man of God, and what was his answer when he declined the honor of a bishop's office.

Account 9. The servant of God, possessing a great gift of prophecy, showed also much concern in the liberation of captives. He strove eagerly to restore those suffering under servitude to barbarians to the freedom into which they had been born. In the course of such work he gave orders to a man, whom with his wife and children he had ransomed, to cross the Danube and to search in the market of the barbarians for an unknown person whom, by divine revelation, he was able to describe so accurately that he could tell even details of his physique, the color of his hair, his features, the clothes he was wearing, and in what part of the marketplace he would find him. He added that the man should return to him at once and report what that person, having been found, would tell him. So the man went and, to his surprise, found everything just as the man of God had foretold him. As soon as he had so unexpectedly found that man, he heard himself being addressed by him and being asked: 'Do you think I can find somebody who for any sum of money he might name would lead me to the man of God whose fame is spreading everywhere? For a long time I have insistently been beseeching these holy martyrs here, whose relics I carry with me, to be released at last from this service of which I am unworthy and which, so far. I have undertaken, not in bold presumption, but by a pious necessity.' Then the man of God's messenger made himself known to him. Upon taking up the relics of the holy martyrs, Gervasius and Protasius, with due honor in the basilica which he had built within the monastery, he dedicated it for divine service. In that place he united the shrines of many martyrs. He was vouched safe always to know about them beforehand by revelation, for he knew that the Enemy often sneaks in under the name of holiness. He was also urged to accept the honorable office of bishop, but he settled the matter with a determined reply, saying that it was sufficient for him to have deprived himself of his beloved solitude and by a divine call to have come to this province in order to help the crowds of people who turned to him in their tribulations. Likewise, wishing to set an example for his monks, he warned them earnestly to follow the footsteps of the blessed fathers from whom one might acquire instruction in holy ways, and to be on their guard lest one who had left behind his family and the world, looking back on the temptations of worldly pomp, might wish for the things he should avoid. And, as a terrible example, he put before them the wife of Lot...

APPENDIX 2: EUGIPPIUS' ACCOUNT OF THE RELICS OF JOHN THE BAPTIST

Capitulum XXII. Quod, dum basilicae novae sanctuaria quaererentur, ultro sibi sancti Iohannis Baptistae benedictionem praenuntiaverit deferendam et illi oppido cladem se absente futuram, qua in baptisterio presbyter vaniloquax interfectus est.

Capitulum XXIII. Qualiter sanctuaria praedicta susceperit.

Commemoratorium XXII. Basilicae extra muros oppidi Batavini in loco nomine Boiotro trans Henum fluvium constitutae, ubi cellulam paucis monachis ipse construxerat, martyrum reliquiae quaerebantur. Ingerentibus ergo se presbyteris, ut mitterentur ad sanctuaria deferenda, haec beatus Severinus monita proferebat: 'Quamvis cuncta mortalium opere constructa praetereant, haec tamen aedificia prae ceteris celerrime relinquenda sunt.' Et ideo pro reliquiis sanctorum nullum laborem debere suscipere, quia et ultro eis sancti Iohannis benedictio deferretur... Quidam presbyter[61] haec diabolico spiritu repletus adiecit: 'Perge, quaeso, sancte, perge veolciter, ut tuo discessu parumper a ieiuniis et vigiliis quiescamus.' Quo dicto vir dei lacrimis urguebatur ingentibus, quod in ridiculam vanitatem cunctis audientibus sacerdos eruperit. *Aperta namque scurrilitas latentium est*

---

61 Translated below as 'priest', but possibly 'abbot' as Eugippius, himself.

testificatio delictorum.[62] Sanctus itaque vir cur ita fleret interrogatus a fratribus: 'Video', inquit, 'plagam gravissimam nobis absentibus huic loco protinus eventuram, et Christi sacraria, quod non sine gemitu cogor exprimere, humano sanguine redundabunt in tantum, ut etiam locus iste violandus sit.' Nam in baptisterio loquebatur. Ad antiquum itaque et omnibus maius monasterium suum iuxta muros oppidi Favianis, quod centum et ultra milibus aberat, Dannuvii navigatione descendit. Mox igitur eo descendente Hunumundus paucis barbaris comitatus oppidum, ut sanctus praedixerat, Batavis invasit … Presbyterum quoque illum, qui tam sacrilega contra famulum Christi in baptisterio fuerat elocutus, ad eundem locum confugientem insequentes barbarri peremerunt. Frustra enim illuc offenso deo veritatis inimicus accessit, ubi tam imprudenter excesserat.

Commemoratorium XXIII. Igitur sanctissimus Severinus, dum in monasterio Favianis evangelium legeret, oratione suppleta consurgens scafam sibi iubet ilico praeparari et mirantibus ait: 'Sit nomen domini benedictum. Sanctuariis beatorum martyrum nos oportet occurrere.' Nec mora, transmeato Danuvio inveniunt hominem considentem in ripa ulteriore fluminis ac multis eos precibus postulantem, ut ad servum dei, ad quem fama vulgante olim venire cuperet, duceretur. Mox itaque ei Christi famulo demonstrato suppliciter sancti Iohannis Baptistae reliquias optulit multis apud se servatas temporibus. Quas dei servus debita veneratione suscipiens, basilicam sancti Iohannis, sicut praedixerat, ultronea benedictione collata, sacravit officio sacerdotum.

Table of Chapters 22. That, when holy relics were being sought for a new basilica, he foretold that the blessing of St John the Baptist would be bestowed on him without asking, and that in that town during his absence, there would be a massacre in which a slanderous priest would be killed.

Table of Chapters 23. How he received the said holy relics.

Account 22. Relics of martyrs were sought for the basilica outside the walls of Batavis [Passau] in a place called Boiotro, across the river Inn, where he had bult a small abode for a few monks. Priests volunteered to be sent in

---

[62] Omitted in one Class II manuscript (M).

search of holy relics, but the blessed Severin uttered these words of warning: 'Although everything built by the hands of mortals will pass away, these buildings will have to be abandoned more quickly than others.' And, therefore, he said, that they should not take any trouble procuring the relics of saints because the blessed relics of St John would come to them by themselves... A priest, filled with the spirit of the devil added: 'Go saint, I beg you, go quickly, so that by your departure we may get a little rest from fasts and vigils.' At these words, the man of God was moved to floods of tears because a priest had given vent to his ridiculous vanity within the hearing of all. For open scurrility bears witness to hidden sins. When, therefore, the holy man was asked by his brethren why he thus lamented, he said: 'I see a great disaster coming over this place as soon as we have left, and the sanctuaries of Christ – to my grief I am compelled to say so – will be flooded with human blood. Even this place will be violated.' For he was speaking in the baptistery. He then sailed down the Danube to his oldest and biggest monastery outside the walls of the town of Favianis which was a hundred miles and more away. Soon afterwards, while he was still sailing down the river, Hunumund with a few barbarians in his retinue, invaded the town of Batavis, as the saint had foretold... The priest who had spoken such blasphemous words against the servant of Christ in the baptistery took refuge in that very same place, but the barbarians pursued him and killed him there. In vain did the enemy of truth, who had offended God, take refuge in the place which he had transgressed so shamelessly.

Account 23. One day St Severin, while reading the Gospel in his monastery at Favianis, after offering prayer arose and ordered a boat to be made ready for him. When they wondered, he said: 'Blessed be the name of the Lord. We must go to meet the relics of the blessed martyrs.' They crossed the Danube without delay and found a man sitting on the opposite bank of the river who asked them with many entreaties to be led to the servant of God, to whom, on account of his widespread fame, he had long wished to come. The servant of Christ was pointed out to him, and he humbly offered him relics of St John the Baptist which he had kept with him for a long time. The servant of God, taking them up with due veneration, consecrated the basilica of St John – which, just as he had predicted, had been blessed without asking – for divine service.

APPENDIX 3: TEXTS AND TRANSLATIONS OF THE CONSECRATION DOUBLETS IN CHAPTER 9 AND 23

Commemoratorium VIIII. Qui debito sanctorum Gervasii et Protasii matyrum reliquias honore suscipiens in basilica, quam in monasterio construxerat, collocavit officio sacerdotum.

Robinson:	Severinus received with due honor the relics of Saint Gervasius and Saint Protasius the martyrs, placed them in the church which he had built within the monastery, and committed them to the care of priests.
Noll:	Dieser [Severin] übernahm die Reliquien der heiligen Märtyrer Gervasius und Protasius mit der gebührenden Ehrfurcht und hinterlegte sie under Assistenz der Priester in der Basilika, die er im Kloster erbaut hatte.
Bieler:	St. Severin received with due honor the relics of the holy martyrs, Gervasius and Protasius, and placed them a the disposal of priests in the basilica which he had built in his monastery.
Régerat:	Ce dernier [Severin] reçut les reliques des saints martyrs Gervais et Protais avec la vénération qui leur était due et les déposa par le ministère des prêtres dans la basilique qu'il avait fait construire dans le monastère.
Author:	Upon taking up the relics of the holy martyrs, Gervasius and Protasius, with due honor in the basilica which he had built within the monastery, he dedicated it for divine service.

Commemoratorium XXIII. Quas dei servus debita veneratione suscipiens, basilicam sancti Iohannis, sicut praedixerat, ultronea benedictione collata, sacravit officio sacerdotum.

Robinson:	The servant of God received the relics with the veneration they deserved; and so the blessing of Saint John was bestowed unasked upon the church, as he had foretold, and Severinus consecrated the relics by the hands of priests.
Noll:	Der Knecht Gottes übernahm sie mit der gebührenden Ehrer-

	bietung und weihte unter Assistenz der Priester die Basilika ein nachdem sich so, wie er prophezeit hatte, der Segen des heiligen Johannes von selbst eingestellt hatte.
Bieler:	The servant of God received them with due reverence, and solemnly dedicated to the service of the priests the basilica of St John whose blessed relics, as he had prophesied, had come without their asking.
Régerat:	Le serviteur de Dieu les reçut avec les marques de vénération qui leur était dues et consacra la basilique par le ministère des prêtres, la bénédiction de saint Jean ayant été accordée par surcroît, comme il l'avait annoncé.
Author:	The servant of God, taking them up with due veneration, consecrated the basilica of St John – which, just as he had predicted, had been blessed without asking – for divine service.

APPENDIX 4: RELICS ASSOCIATED with EARLY
(City/Church/Date/Ecclesiastical Patron/Relics)

MILAN (1a/b)	MILAN (2)	FLORENCE	MILAN (3)	MILAN (4)	BRESCIA
a. BASILICA ad PORTAM ROMANAM/IN ROMANA b. *Ibidem?*	BASILICA AMBROSIANA	BASILICA JULIANAE	BASILICA APOSTOLORUM in ROMANA	BASILICA VIRGINUM	BASILICA CONCILII SANCTORUM
a. 9 MAY b. 27 NOVEMBER	386	393	395	397	400x02
a/b. AMBROSIUS?	AMBROSIUS	AMBROSIUS	AMBROSIUS	SIMPLICIANUS	GAUDENTIUS
a. IOHANNES APOSTOLUS	GERVASIUS	VITALIS	NAZARIUS	SISINNIUS	IOHANNES BAPTISTA
ANDREAS APOSTOLUS	PROTASIUS	AGRICOLA		MARTYRIUS	ANDREAS
THOMAS APOSTOLUS				ALEXANDER	THOMAS
b. LUCAS					LUCAS EVANGELISTA
ANDREAS					GERVASIUS
IOHANNES					PROTASIUS
SEVERUS					NAZARIUS
EUPHEMIA					SISINNIUS
					MARTYRIUS
					ALEXANDER

WESTERN CHURCH CONSECRATIONS

CONCORDIA	AQUILEIA	NOLA	FONDI	ROUEN	ROME
BASILICA in HONOREM SANCTORUM	CATHEDRAL?	BASILICA NOVA of St FELIX	CATHEDRAL BASILICA	CATHEDRAL	TITULUS VESTINAE
ca 400	3 SEPTEMBER	ca 403	ca 403	404x05?	401x17
RUFINUS?	CHROMATIUS?	PAULINUS	PAULINUS	VICTRICIUS	INNOCENTIUS I
IOHANNES BAPTISTA	ANDREAS APOSTOLUS	FELIX	ANDREAS	IOHANNES BAPTISTA	GERVASIUS
IOHANNES EVANGELISTA	LUCAS	ANDREAS	LUCAS	ANDREAS	PROTASIUS
ANDREAS	IOHANNES	IOHANNES BAPTISTA	NAZARIUS	THOMAS	
THOMAS	EUPHEMIA	THOMAS	PROTASIUS	LUCAS?	
LUCAS		LUCAS	GERVASIUS	GERVASIUS	
		VITALIS		PROTASIUS	
		AGRICOLA		AGRICOLA	
		PROCULUS		EUPHEMIA	
		EUPHEMIA			
		NAZARIUS			

TADPOLES!

By David Sansone

Summary: The Greek word for 'tadpole' is γυρῖνος.[1] Not everyone seems to have known this, or cared. The history of the use of this word is traced in reverse chronological order, from the Byzantine period to the time of its first attested use, in Plato. Later authors (Tzetzes, Psellus and Libanius) misused the word as a result of misreading what they found in earlier literary texts, seemingly their sole source of information regarding both the word and the creature to which it refers. Finally, an attempt will be made to enhance our appreciation of Plato's lone reference to tadpoles at *Theaetetus* 161d.

---

* For their advice, encouragement and inspiration I should like to thank Antonia Ruppel, Angeliki Tzanetou and Zina Giannopoulou.

1 This is the correct accentuation according to Herodian (1.183.11 Lentz); the word is proparoxytone at Hsch. Γ 1028, Phot. Γ 238 and *EM* 243.49 s.v. γύρινοι (but not at 243.52 s.v. Γυριννώ). The length of the iota is confirmed by the metre at Arat. 947. Also attested are the spellings γέρυνος (Nic. *Ther.* 620 and *Alex.* 563, both with short ypsilon, Hdn. Gr. 1.185.17 Lentz, St. Byz. 170.5 Meineke), γόρυνος (Hsch. Γ 861, Zonar. 448.16), γερῖνος (Paus. Gr. s.v. γυρῖνοι· Ἀττικοί, γερῖνοι Ἴωνες) and γόρινος (in the manuscripts of Ps.-Gal. Λέξεις βοτανῶν s.v., according to A. Delatte (ed.) *Anecdota Atheniensia*, vol. 2: *Textes grecs relatifs à l'histoire des sciences* (Liège and Paris 1939) 388.7). R. Strömberg *Studien zur Etymologie und Bildung der griechischen Fischnamen*, Göteborgs Högskolas Årsskrift 49.2 (Göteborg, 1943) 88, refers to yet another form, γαρῖνος, which he claims is attested at Marc. Sid. 37 and which he derives from γάρος = *garum*; but according to Ernst Heitsch's text of Marcellus (*Die griechischen Dichterfragmente der römischen Kaiserzeit*, vol. 2, Abh. der Akad. der Wiss. zu Göttingen, Phil.-hist. Kl. 58 (Göttingen 1964) 18) the ms. reading there is γερῖνοι. H. Frisk *Griechisches etymologisches Wörterbuch* (Heidelberg 1954-1972) and P. Chantraine *Dictionnaire étymologique de la langue grecque: Histoire des mots* (Paris 1968-1980) both ignore these variant spellings in deriving the word from γυρός (s.v.).

TZETZES' CONFUSION OF (AND ABOUT) ARATUS AND NICANDER

Let us begin with the twelfth-century polymath Joannes Tzetzes. Among the thousands of other curious bits of information with which he fills his *Histories*, Tzetzes includes the following, entitled 'Concerning the Inability of Seriphian Frogs to Vocalize':

Πᾶς μὲν χερσαῖος βάτραχος ἐστὶν ἐκ τῶν ἀφώνων·
οἱ δ' ἔνυδροι, οὓς Ἄρατος γερύνους ὀνομάζει
καὶ καναχούς, φωνητικοὶ πλὴν Σεριφίων μόνων.
Ἐκεῖ γὰρ καὶ οἱ ἔνυδροι τελοῦσι τῶν ἀφώνων,
ὅτι τὸ ὕδωρ τὸ ἐκεῖ τελεῖ τῶν ὑπερψύχρων.

Every frog that lives on land is mute. Aquatic frogs, however, which Aratus calls *gerynoi* and 'noisy,' are capable of vocalizing, excepting only those from Seriphos. For in that place even the aquatic frogs belong to the class of mute creatures, owing to the fact that the water there is exceptionally cold.[2]

The first of these verses, with its confident misstatement of the facts, reveals that Tzetzes does not rely upon observation in the wild. Neither do I, but at least I have at my disposal the resources of one of the world's great libraries, from which it emerges that terrestrial frogs are by no means silent and that, for example, the central European tree frog (*Hyla arborea*), widely distributed from France to Turkey, 'has the loudest voice of all the European anurans'.[3] The remaining lines confirm that, like me, Tzetzes derives his in-

---

2 Tz. *H.* 8.167. The text is that of P.A.M. Leone (ed.), *Ioannes Tzetzae Historiae* (Naples 1968); the translation is my own. The verse-form is the standard fifteen-syllable accentual metre known as the 'political verse' (πολιτικὸς στίχος); see H. Hunger *Die hochsprachliche profane Literatur der Byzantiner*, vol. 2 (Munich 1978) 95-97.

3 B. Grzimek *Grzimek's Animal Life Encyclopedia*, vol. 5 (New York 1974) 435. Tzetzes' commentary on Aristophanes' *Frogs* survives (see W.J.W. Koster (ed.) *Jo. Tzetzae commentarii in Aristophanem*, vol 3: *Commentarium in Ranas et in Aves, Argumentum Equitum* (Gron-

formation from books.[4] But Tzetzes tells us that, for financial reasons, it became necessary for him to sell off his personal library volume by volume.[5] As a result, he had to rely on his memory, which was impressive, but not infallible. What Tzetzes has remembered (imperfectly) is a line of Aratus, which he has conflated with what he has remembered (imperfectly) from Nicander, an author with whom he was at one time quite familiar.[6] Aratus does not in fact call aquatic frogs γέρυνοι (or καναχοί), nor does he use this anapaestic form of the word. Rather, in speaking of the signs of impending rain, Aratus gives as an example: 'The fathers of tadpoles cry out from the very waters' (αὐτόθεν ἐξ ὕδατος πατέρες βοόωσι γυρίνων, *Phaenomena* 947). Tzetzes seems to have assumed that πατέρες γυρίνων is merely an epic periphrasis, equivalent to γυρῖνοι, on the model of Homeric υἷες Ἀχαιῶν (= Ἀχαιοί), and that what can be said of the fathers of *gyrinoi* can be said of *gyrinoi* themselves. Therefore, in Tzetzes' mind Aratus was simply using a fancy, epic word for 'frog'. But, while the fathers of Achaeans are Achaeans, the fathers of tadpoles are not tadpoles, a fact of which Aratus was surely aware. Aratus was also aware of the fact that the croaking of frogs and toads is the mating call of the male (see Arist. *HA* 536a11-14), so that 'fathers' is not loosely used here in the *Phaenomena* merely as a synonym for 'parents'.[7] In-

   ingen 1962)), but I have found nothing in it about terrestrial frogs being mute. Of course, as Tzetzes knew, Aristophanes' frogs are aquatic, and quite musical. Nicander (*Alex*. 567-93) distinguishes between mute and vocal toads, referring to their habitat, but he does not suggest any correlation between where they live and how much noise they make.
4 For the alleged silence of frogs from Seriphos, see [Arist.] *Mir*. 835b3, Antig. 4.1, Plin. *Nat*. 8.227, Diogenian. 1.49, 3.44, Ael. *NA* 3.37, Theophyl. Sim. *Quaest. nat.* p. 10.8 and p. 36.1 Massa Positano, Suda B 190. Aelian cites Theophrastus (= frag. 186 Wimmer) for the coldness of the water as the cause; see R.W. Sharples *Theophrastus of Eresus: Sources for his Life, Writings, Thought and Influence, Commentary* vol. 5: *Sources on Biology* (Leiden 1995) 56-57.
5 N.G. Wilson, *Scholars of Byzantium* (London 1983) 190-91.
6 For Tzetzes' commentary on Nicander, see C. Wendel, *RE* VIIA (1948) 1982. At *H*. 1.11.303-7 Tzetzes quotes (accurately) Nic. *Ther*. 902-6 and at 1.15.363-66 he quotes (again accurately) *Alex*. 301-4. He also quotes Nicander half a dozen times in the scholia to Lycophron and three more times in the *Exegesis in Homeri Iliadem* (for details, see O. Schneider (ed.) *Nicandrea* (Leipzig 1856) 136-56), but only in Book 1 of the *Histories*. Did he sell his text of Nicander between the time of composition of Books 1 and 8?
7 So J. Martin (ed.) *Aratos: Phénomènes*, 2 vols. (Paris 1998) *ad loc*. This is surely more pertinent than Douglas Kidd's suggestion (D. Kidd (ed.) *Aratus: Phaenomena* (Cambridge 1997) *ad loc.*), 'The quaint periphrasis perhaps recalls Ar. *Ran*. 211 λιμναῖα κρηνῶν

deed, Aratus is here playing with the notion that the notoriously noisy frog is the adult version of an aquatic creature, which creatures are notoriously silent.[8] We will encounter this notion again.

Nicander for his part refers to tadpoles on two occasions. At *Theriaca* 620–22 he gives the following remedy for snakebite:

ἀλλ' ἤτοι γερύνων καναχοὶ περίαλλα τοκῆες
βάτραχοι ἐν χύτρῃσι καθεψηθέντες ἄριστοι
βάμματι.

But of a truth the tadpoles' all too noisy parents, frogs, are excellent when boiled with vinegar in a pot.[9]

This, in fact, is the source of Tzetzes' καναχούς, a word not found elsewhere before Tzetzes, and of the anapaestic form of the word for tadpole. Gow and Scholfield are undoubtedly correct to suggest that Nicander had Aratus' line in mind; unlike the reference in the *Phaenomena*, there is here no particular point to the specification of the frogs' vocalizing and Nicander has replaced 'fathers' with the less precise 'parents'. Nicander repeats this formulation in his *Alexipharmaca*, where he recommends that 'you should bend to your service the tadpoles' impudent parents' (γερύνων λαιδροὺς δαμάσαιο τοκῆας, 563). 'Impudent' presumably refers to the obstreperousness of the tadpoles'

τέκνα.' The mating times and, hence, the mating calls of frogs are independent of the weather, for which reason Martin translates, 'crient plus fort que de coutume'; cf. Thphr. *Sign.* 1.15, Plin. *Nat.* 18.361, Plut. *Mor.* 982e (reading μᾶλλον δὲ λαμπρύνουσι?).

8 Thus Aeschylus can refer to fishes with the kenning, 'the voiceless children of the undefiled' (*Pers.* 577-78, ἀναύδων ... παίδων τᾶς ἀμιάντου); cf. Soph. frag. 762 Radt, Eub. frag. 28 K-A, Pherecr. frag. 117 K-A, Call. frag. 533 Pf., Nic. frag. 16 Gow-Scholfield, Lucr. 2.342-43, 1082-83, Hor. *Carm.* 4.3.19, Plut. *Mor.* 728e, Lucian. *Pisc.* 51, *Gall.* 1, Ath. 308b, Σ Opp. *Hal.* 2.658, Tzetzes *ad* Lyc. 796 (p. 250.15-16 Scheer) ἔλλοψ πᾶς ἰχθὺς παρὰ τὸ ἐλλείπεσθαι ὀπὸς καὶ φωνῆς. A sophist who dreams of catching fish will fail to make his pupils eloquent (Artem. 2.14) and a woman who dreams of giving birth to a fish will deliver a mute child (2.18). The astrological sign Pisces is mute (Vett. Val. 1.2.78, Firm. Mat. 2.10.5) and those born under it are likely to have speech impediments (Vett. Val. 2.36.19).

9 Text and translation here and below are those of A.S.F. Gow and A.F. Scholfield (eds.) *Nicander: The Poems and Poetical Fragments* (Cambridge 1953). J.-M. Jacques, in his recent Budé edition (Paris 2002) prints the same text as Gow and Scholfield at *Ther.* 620–22.

parents.[10] There appears to be a thematic significance in the allusion here to the raucous parents of silent offspring, although the significance is fairly obscure. The line just quoted follows immediately upon Nicander's praise of the curative value of pork boiled together with the limbs of 'the mountain tortoise that feeds on tree-medick, the creature that Hermes the Gracious endowed with a voice though voiceless' (οὐρείης κυτισηνόμου ἥν τ' ἀκάκητα / αὐδήεσσαν ἔθηκεν ἀναυδητόν περ ἐοῦσαν / Ἑρμείης, 559-61).[11] The poet is here, for whatever reason, alluding to the oracle given to Croesus, quoted by Herodotus at 1.47.3, in which the Pythia claims to 'understand the mute and hear the voiceless' (κωφοῦ συνίημι καὶ οὐ φωνεῦντος ἀκούω) and then goes on to reveal that Croesus had boiled together the meat of lambs, who may go quietly to slaughter but whose silence is otherwise the stuff of novels and film, and the more genuinely taciturn tortoise. Immediately after his reference to the tadpoles' impudent parents, Nicander launches into his discussion (567-93) of mute and vocal toads, which was mentioned in note 3 above.

PSELLUS' (OR AFRICANUS'?) CONFUSION ABOUT TADPOLES

It is clear, then, that Tzetzes was merely confused when he claimed that the word he read in Aratus (and Nicander) referred to frogs. He was not the only Byzantine scholar to make this mistake. Michael Psellus, who lived almost exactly one hundred years before Tzetzes, wrote a treatise[12] similar to the Aristotelian *Mirabilium auscultationes*, entitled Περὶ παραδόξων ἀκουσ-

---

10 So the scholiast: λαιδρούς· τοὺς ἀναιδεῖς, διὰ τὸ βοᾶν ἀεὶ τῇ φωνῇ τραχυτέρᾳ.
11 For the text of *Alex.* 554-57, with a defense of the authenticity of line 556a, where the pork is mentioned, see S. Ihm 'Einige textkritische Anmerkungen zu Nikanders Alexipharmaka' *Hermes* 124 (1996) 243-47. Hermes (the god) created the lyre out of the shell of the tortoise: *h.Merc.* 24-51.
12 For the text, see J.M. Duffy (ed.) *Michael Psellus: Philosophica minora*, vol. 1 (Stuttgart & Leipzig 1992) 109-13. The quotation below can be found on p. 110, lines 29-34; the translation is my own.

μάτων. It contains a summary of a portion of Sextus Julius Africanus' charming *Cesti*.[13] Included is the following:

> καί τινα ἔλεγχον ποιεῖται κλεπτῶν ἀφανῶν, γυρίνων βατράχων τὰς γλώσσας ἀποτέμνων καὶ ταριχεύων, εἶτα ἐπὶ τῆς χρείας ἀλφίτοις ἀναμιγνὺς καὶ τοῖς ἐν ὑπονοίᾳ τῆς ἀφαιρέσεως τοῦ ζητουμένου προδιδούς· καὶ ὁ ἀφελόμενος, φησί, τὸ φώριον ἐν ἐκστάσει ὥσπερ γενόμενος ἑαυτὸν ἀριδήλως δημοσιεύει· ὀνομάζει δὲ τὸ βρῶμα κλεπτέλεγχον.

> He [Africanus] supplies a means of discovering undetected thieves, by cutting out the tongues of *gyrinos* frogs and salting them down; then, as needed, mixing them with barley flour and serving them up to those suspected of having made off with the object one is looking for. According to him, the man who took the stolen property turns himself in without further ado, as though in a trance. He calls this confection *kleptelenchos*.

Despite Vieillefond's translation, 'têtards de grenouilles',[14] what is at issue here are obviously frogs, not tadpoles. For one thing, it is hard to imagine anyone seriously contemplating amputating tadpoles' tongues. For another, frogs' tongues conspicuously possess a potency that tadpoles' tongues conspicuously lack, namely a capacity for unremitting vociferation, and it is this potency on which Africanus' magical device relies in order to make public the identity of the thief.[15] Frogs are creatures who are notorious for not be-

---

13 So rightly J.-R. Vieillefond *Les 'Cestes' de Julius Africanus: Etude sur l'ensemble des fragments avec édition, traduction et commentaires* (Florence & Paris 1970) 311.
14 Vieillefond (previous note) 316. Likewise, R. Volk *Der medizinische Inhalt der Schriften des Michael Psellos*, Miscellanea Byzantina Monacensia 32 (Munich 1990) 213, translates 'Kaulquappen'. Volk goes on to note, however, 'Für die Verwendung von Kaulquappenzungen scheint es keine Parallele zu geben, wohl aber von Froschenzungen' (213 n. 50). F.C.R. Thee *Julius Africanus and the Early Christian View of Magic* (Tübingen 1984) 233-34, suggests that, 'while tadpole tongues are not quite in the same class as "hen's teeth",' it was the difficulty of obtaining them that made them desirable, according to Africanus, as a magical ingredient.
15 This is the widely attested 'persuasive analogy' or '*similia similibus* formula,' for which see C.A. Faraone 'The Agonistic Context of Early Greek Binding Spells' in C.A. Faraone and

ing able to hold their tongues. So, for example, the reason Athena gives for her unwillingness to lend support to the frogs' war effort in their epic battle against the mice (*Batrachomyomachia* 187-92) is that they would not let her sleep when she was herself worn out from combat. Nor did the chorus of frogs allow Perseus to rest when he tried to recover on Seriphos from his exertions after confronting the Gorgon (Aelian, *De natura animalium* 3.37).

Indeed, according to Ovid (*Metamorphoses* 6.317-81), the frogs owe their origin as a species to their transformation from raucous Lycian farmers who threatened and insulted the hard-pressed, pregnant Latona. For this reason, frogs' tongues are commonly used in sympathetic magic 'pour déceler les pensées de quelqu'un'.[16] Pliny (*Naturalis historia* 32.49) quotes 'Democritus' to the effect that, if one removes the tongue from a living frog and places it over the beating heart of a sleeping woman, she will give truthful replies to all one's questions. This is particularly useful in revealing adultery on the part of the woman, and so two recipes, very similar to the one quoted by Pliny and involving the use of frogs' tongues, are given in a Greek manuscript under the heading, 'On Finding Out if a Woman has been Faithful or Not.'[17] The *Cyranides* goes even farther, saying that if one inscribes χουοχ οδαμενοφ on the severed frog's tongue before placing it on the breast of the sleeping woman, she will tell of 'everything she has done in her life' (p. 123.3-6 Kaimakis). Finally, a fourth-century magical papyrus in the British Museum, Papyrus graecus XLVI, records a recipe for identifying a thief that includes a frog's tongue among its ingredients; if it is offered to someone who refuses it, that person is revealed as the thief (*PMG* V 200-12).

Both Tzetzes and Psellus, then, mistakenly think the word γυρῖνος (or γέρυνος) refers to a frog. But questions remain. In the case of Psellus, for instance, is the expression γυρίνων βατράχων Psellus' own, or does it originate with Africanus?[18] And, further, what was the expression thought (either

---

D. Obbink (eds.) *Magika Hiera: Ancient Greek Magic and Religion* (New York and Oxford 1991) 3-32, at 6-9.

16 Vieillefond (above, n. 13) 362, from whom the first two examples in the text are derived.

17 The manuscript is Parisinus graecus 2286 and the recipes, from fol. 61 v, are edited by J.-F. Boissonade *Notices et extraits des manuscrits de la Bibliothèque du Roi* 11 (1827) 240.

18 As we will see in the following section, a misunderstanding of a passage in Plato is responsible for Libanius' mistaken belief that the word γυρῖνος means 'frog.' Given the primacy of Plato's influence on the style of Psellus (for which see E. Renauld, *Étude de la*

by Psellus or by Africanus) to mean? Was a '*gyrinos* frog' considered to be a particular type of (vocal and therefore adult) frog?[19] Or were the words *gyrinos* and *batrachos* regarded as more or less synonymous, with the second appearing in explanatory apposition to the first? Unfortunately, I do not think these questions can be adequately answered, for reasons that are themselves potentially interesting. For it is clear that the word for 'tadpole' was not part of the active vocabulary of either Tzetzes or Psellus. It is a rare word, at least in the surviving texts from antiquity, and the overwhelming majority of its occurrences are in the works of the grammarians, lexicographers and scholiasts, where there is little agreement even over the form of the word (see n. 1). A quick survey of the evidence will show that only in rare instances do these scholars evince a secure understanding of the word's meaning. Occasionally, indeed, γυρῖνος is simply defined as a frog.[20] Somewhat more helpful is the definition τὸ ἐκ τοῦ βατράχου παιδίον.[21] Less helpful is the common gloss μικρὸς βάτραχος,[22] which is ambiguous. Does it refer to a young frog or to a small variety of frogs, say *Hyla arborea* as opposed to *Rana ridibunda*?[23] The only truly satisfactory definition is given by the scholia to Aratus,

---

langue et du style de Michel Psellos (Paris 1920) 436-38), it is perhaps more likely that he, rather than Africanus, is responsible for introducing the word into a context that plainly refers to frogs, as a result of a misunderstanding similar to, or even derived from, that of Libanius.

19 For the compound designation, compare English 'jaybird,' H. *Od.* 19.548 αἰετὸς ὄρνις, Cratin. frag. 241 K–A παρεῖαι ὄφεις, Ar. *Av.* 515 αἰετὸν ὄρνιν, 568 ὀρχίλος ὄρνις, Eur. *Hel.* 19 κύκνου ... ὄρνιθος; although, as E.R. Dodds points out (*ad* Eur. *Bacch.* 1024-26), 'usually the general name is put first', giving further examples, to which may be added H. *Il.* 7.59 ὄρνισιν ... αἰγυπιοῖσι, 17.21 συὸς κάπρου, *Od.* 13.86-87 ἴρηξ κίρκος, Epimenid. 3 B 2.2 D-K θῆρα λέοντα, Pi. *I.* 3.64 θηρῶν λεόντων, Hdt. 3.112 τῶν αἰγῶν τῶν τράγων, and perhaps the 4th-century magical papyrus *P.Osl.* I 235 βάθρακον φροῦνον, i.e. βάτραχον φροῦνον.

20 Orion 44.8 *s.v.* γυρῖνοι, *Et. Gud.* 327.2 *s.v.* γυρῖνοι, *EM* 243.52 *s.v.* Γυρινvώ.

21 Hsch. Γ 1028 *s.v.* γύρινον, Σ Pl. *Tht.* 161c.

22 Hdn. Gr. 1.183.11 and 1.185.17 Lentz, Ps.-Gal. Λέξεις βοτανῶν 2.388.7 Delatte (above, n. 1), Arcadius 74.20 Schmidt, St. Byz. 170.5 Meineke, Σ Nic. *Alex.* 563, Hsch. Γ 861 *s.v.* γόρυνος, Zonar. 448.16 *s.v.* γόρυνος and 458.15 *s.v.* γυρῖνοι, *Et. Gud.* 327.17 *s.v.* γυρίν καὶ γυρῖνος, *EM* 243.49 *s.v.* γύρινοι.

23 See E.N. Arnold and D.W. Ovenden *Reptiles and Amphibians of Europe*, 2nd ed. (Princeton and Oxford 2002) 77 (*Hyla arborea*: 'Adults up to 5cm but usually smaller') and 89 (*Rana ridibunda*: 'Adults up to 15cm (rarely 18cm)').

Phaenomena 947 and 953, where *gyrinoi* are said to be 'not fully formed (ἀδιάπλαστοι) frogs'[24] and 'lacking feet' (ἄποδες).[25]

This should not be entirely surprising. Tadpoles are creatures one rarely comes in contact with and even more rarely talks about. Some languages even manage to subsist without feeling the need for a word corresponding to English 'tadpole.' One can infer from two passages in the elder Pliny that Latin, for example, was one of those languages. At *Naturalis historia* 9.159, after describing the mating practices of frogs, Pliny tells us that 'they give birth to tiny bits of black flesh, distinguished only by having eyes and a tail, called *gyrini*', that is, using the Greek word.[26] And at 32.122, when giving a recipe for stanching blood-flow, he uses a periphrasis to refer to tadpoles, mentioning 'the ashes of frogs that are just developing in the water, still having tails'. One expects Pliny to be conversant with the life-cycle of, and the vocabulary for, frogs and other amphibians. And the same is true of only a handful of ancient writers.[27] That handful does not include Tzetzes or Psellus. Nor does it include the fourth-century orator Libanius, to whom we turn next.

LIBANIUS' CONFUSION ABOUT PLATO AND TADPOLES

Libanius' *Declamation* 26 purports to be an address by a classic grouch begging to be allowed to die, as death is his only means of finding peace and quiet, especially given his wife's unrelenting talkativeness. In section 36 the

---

24 Cf. Σ Nic. *Ther.* 620 (οἱ μικροὶ καὶ ἀδιάπλαστοι βάτραχοι). Remarkably, the Suda has an entry (Φ 768) φρῦνος· ὁ ἀδιάπλαστος βάτραχος.

25 Cf. Paus. Gr. *s.v.* γυρῖνοι (p. 171.7-8 Erbse): βάτραχοι γυροὶ τὸ σχῆμα, τοὺς πόδας οὔπω ἔχοντες, Phot. Γ 238, Theognost. 2.19.16 Cramer.

26 Nor can the compilers of the *TLL*, s.v., find a suitable Latin word with which to gloss *gyrinus*. Of the passages cited in the lexica for the diminutives *ranula* and *ranunculus*, all certainly refer to frogs or toads, with one exception (Gell. 14.1.31), and that too may well do so. Likewise, Horace's *ranae pulli* (S. 2.3.314; cf. Babr. 28.1 γέννημα φρύνου) are manifestly toads, not tadpoles, since they are trampled under foot by a calf.

27 Aristotle can be counted among them. At *HA* 568a1 he speaks of fishes newly hatched from their eggs as being 'like tadpoles in shape' (γυρινώδεις), having conspicuously large, spherical eyes.

speaker complains that there is nowhere he can go to escape noise. Can he go to the *agora*? But the people there are shouting and hawking their goods. Then to the countryside? The frogs are croaking, the asses braying, the sheep bleating. 'Well, then, to the lawcourts? The pleaders are worse than the frogs.' (ἀλλ' ἐν τοῖς δικαστηρίοις; χείρους τῶν γυρίνων οἱ ῥήτορες.) The context makes it abundantly clear that this is what the words mean.[28] The article with γυρίνων can only be taken as anaphoric, referring to the croaking of frogs (βοὴ βατράχων) that has just been mentioned. In other words, to Libanius γυρῖνος and βάτραχος are synonyms. That is not, however, how the (generally reliable) *Diccionario Griego-Español* sees it. Under 'γυρῖνος' this passage is cited to illustrate the use of the word 'de individuos ... poco eficaces.' The explanation for this lapse is not far to seek (although the failure to consult the context is reprehensible). The immediately preceding citation in the *DGE* is from Plato (*Tht.* 161d1), οὐδὲν βελτίων βατράχου γυρίνου, accurately glossed 'de individuos poco sensatos.' What has happened is that Libanius has misunderstood Plato's expression and the *DGE*, by failing to recognize Libanius' misunderstanding, has in turn misunderstood Libanius.[29] At this point in Plato's dialogue Socrates is criticizing Protagoras' claim that man is the measure of all things. According to Socrates, it would have made as much sense for him to have said that pig or baboon or some even more ridiculous creature, so long as it possessed powers of perception, was the measure of all things; in that way it would have been made clear that, when it came to discernment, any given human being 'is no better than a tadpole, let alone any other human being.' Tadpoles are the perfect specimen for Socrates to use in this *reductio*. They have conspicuously large eyes with which they can perceive the world, but they have little else. And, unlike the noisy gnat, for example, they are dumb, in every sense of the word.

Why, then, did Libanius suppose that Plato was referring here to frogs? For one thing, the expression βατράχου γυρίνου, if one were unaware of the meaning of the latter word, might appear to designate some sort of frog (see

---

28 So D.A. Russell, *Greek Declamation* (Cambridge 1983) 91-96, who has an excellent discussion of *Decl.* 26 and who translates (p. 95) 'the rhetors are worse than the frogs.'
29 The new *Revised Supplement* (1996) to *LSJ*, on the other hand, perhaps reflecting a more accurate understanding of the passage from Libanius, amends the entry *s.v.* γυρῖνος in the ninth edition as follows: 'after "*tadpole*" insert "or *frog*"'.

n. 19). For another, later in the dialogue, there is what appears to be a reference back to this passage, when Socrates, adopting the persona of Protagoras, rejects the notion that a frog is a suitable analogue (*Tht.* 167b5, πολλοῦ δέω βατράχους λέγειν), seemingly reinforcing the notion that frogs had been mentioned earlier. Some editors, to be sure, have felt that βατράχου at 161d1 is an intrusive gloss, perhaps prompted by the appearance of βατράχους at 167b5. Cobet, for example, recorded and approved the deletion of βατράχου proposed in Valckenaer's unpublished 'Schedae criticae'.[30] And, independently, Heindorf noted that he suspected the word of being a gloss, although he left it in his text.[31] But regardless of whether Plato wrote βατράχου γυρίνου or γυρίνου *tout court*, he surely intended the later passage to refer to the earlier. For the transformation from tadpole to frog has a thematic significance that Plato wishes to exploit. In the earlier passage, the reference was merely to sensation, and to the uniqueness of each individual's perception of the environment. A tadpole, being an aquatic creature, lives in a fluid environment. This is of relevance since Socrates attributes to Protagoras (152c-e) a version of the Heraclitean flux-doctrine according to which nothing is in a stable state and everything is in a constant process of change and movement. Further, since everything is perpetually changing, that means that the perceiving 'self' is also unstable (158e-59b), so that even if the environment were stable, perceptions of that environment would differ from one moment to the next as the perceiving subject underwent the inevitable and constant process of transformation. The tadpole conveniently exemplifies this feature of the doctrine, being, in effect, nothing other than a creature in the process of becoming something else.

---

30 C.G. Cobet 'Platonica' *Mnem.* 9 (1860) 337-89, at 352.
31 L.F. Heindorf (ed.) *Platonis Dialogi selecti*, vol. 2, 2nd ed. (Berlin 1829) 325. On the other hand, Lewis Campbell *The Theaetetus of Plato, With a Revised Text and English Notes*, 2nd ed. (Oxford 1883) 77, defends the ms. reading by saying, 'The introduction of γυρίνου alone would be too abrupt, and the reference in infr. 167 B would not be clear'. In any event, the appearance of γυρίνων βατράχων in Psellus/Africanus, whatever it means there and despite the reversed word order, shows that βατρ. γυρ. is in and of itself beyond suspicion.

PLATO ON FROGS AND TADPOLES

Socrates' suggestion, then, that Protagoras ought to have espoused a *gyrinus-mensura* doctrine well serves the purpose of this part of the argument, being at once compatible with Protagoras' thinking and introducing an element of gentle ridicule. By 167b, however, the situation has changed and the tadpole has been transformed into a frog. Here we are dealing with the 'Defense of Protagoras' that Socrates mounts on behalf of the sophist, aimed especially at the objection that, if everyone's perceptions and judgments are equally valid, no one individual can be considered more wise than another. 'Protagoras' is in the position of having to defend his own claim to wisdom, a claim that Socrates had implicitly referred to when he introduced the expression of the *homo-mensura* doctrine as the words of a wise man (σοφὸν ἄνδρα, 152b1). By way of reminding his imagined audience of the terms with which Socrates had begun his criticism, 'Protagoras' dismisses as absurd the talk about pigs and baboons (166c7-8, referring to 161c5) and then says that, so far from identifying the wise with frogs (167b5), he identifies them with recognized experts like physicians, agronomists and sophists. 'Protagoras' disdains referring to so trivial a creature as a tadpole, but his mention of frogs is sufficient to recall the earlier reference by Socrates, who is, after all, notorious for introducing the most mundane elements into his discussions.[32] But the frog is still sufficiently contemptible to make a striking contrast with the human experts that 'Protagoras' rates so highly.[33] There is, however, one respect in which they resemble the frog, and it is this resemblance – which is not shared with the tadpole – that makes the frog relevant here, namely its vocal skills. For wisdom, according to Protagoras, consists in the ability to induce others to replace degraded perceptions with sound ones, which is done most effectively through persuasion.[34] The difference, then, between the expert and the majority of human beings is that, while the latter are, like frogs, capable of expressing themselves, the former can do so effectively.

32 See, e.g., Pl. *Gorg.* 490c-91a, 494e, *Hipp. mai.* 288d, *Symp.* 221e, X. *Mem.* 1.2.37, 4.4.5-6.
33 Frogs are mentioned elsewhere in Plato only at *Phd.* 109b2, where they serve as a metaphor for human insignificance.
34 Even the physician is ineffective unless the patient can be persuaded to undergo the necessary treatment, and Plato's Gorgias claims that he is more productive in accomplishing this aim than many physicians, including his own brother (*Gorg.* 456b).

But, as is so often the case with Plato, there are multiple levels of meaning. For the ancients, frogs (and toads, from which they were rarely distinguished) were characterized not only by their noisy voices, but also by their habit of puffing themselves up, both of which characteristics contributed to their being thought of as insignificant creatures whose sound and appearance make them seem more imposing than they are in fact. The evidence for this comes mostly from the time after Plato, but the behavior of Aristophanes' chorus of frogs indicates that already in Plato's lifetime they were regarded as the type of contentious and conceited creatures who cannot substantiate their grandiose self-image.[35] They are quite proud of the beauty of their song (*Ranae* 213), they claim to be beloved of the Muses, Pan and Apollo (229-34), and they contend that they will not be defeated by Dionysus (262). But the voice of the frog is generally considered to be annoyingly coarse and, in the end, they are appropriately defeated by the god of tragedy, comedy and dithyramb.[36] They are, as Dionysus puts it, 'nothing but *koax*' (οὐδὲν γάρ ἐστ' ἀλλ' ἢ κοάξ, 227). These, then, are the creatures to whom 'Protagoras' denies the title of 'wise', reserving that designation instead for sophists like himself, creatures whom Plato considers the type of contentious and conceited creatures who cannot substantiate their grandiose self-image. Thus, by putting this reference to frogs in the mouth of 'Protagoras', Plato allows the sophist to express himself disdainfully but, at the same time, he very subtly undercuts what Protagoras has to say, thereby expressing his own disdain for the sophist's profession.

Plato and Libanius were not alone in making a connection between frogs and public speakers. According to a saying attributed variously to Gorgias, Glycon (i.e. the Peripatetic Lycon) and the fabulist Aesop, 'Orators are like frogs; the latter make a racket in the water while the former do so against the water-clock' (τοὺς ῥήτορας ἔφη ὁμοίους εἶναι τοῖς βατράχοις· τοὺς μὲν

---

35 Aesop. 44, 90, 141, 289 Perry, Petr. 74.13, Babr. 28, [Arist.] *Phgn.* 810b14-16. In Phaedr. 1.24 a frog attempts to compete with an ox in size, inflating herself until she bursts. Aristophanes' Dionysus seems to allude to the source of this fable when he says that the exertions of his contest with the frogs are such that he is in danger of bursting (*Ran.* 255, διαρραγήσομαι).

36 The nature of the contest is itself contested, the most satisfying proposal being that of G. Wills 'Why are the Frogs in *The Frogs?*' *Hermes* 97 (1969) 306-17, namely that they are overpowered by Dionysus' crepitation, the implication being that whatever surpassing excellence the frogs' song is supposed to possess, a divine fart possesses more of it.

γὰρ ἐν ὕδατι κελαδεῖν, τοὺς δὲ πρὸς κλεψύδραν).[37] If this saying was already current in Plato's day it will have enhanced the irony of putting into the mouth of the sophist Protagoras a denial that frogs and the wise are to be identified. In any event, Plato makes much in the *Theaetetus* of the constraints imposed on the orator by the clepsydra – constraints from which the philosopher is free – which prevent the orator from attaining the truth.[38]

Clearly the distinction between frogs and tadpoles was not lost on Plato; indeed, he exploited that distinction to good literary effect in his *Theaetetus*. Apart from Plato, however, only a few ancient sources provide evidence of knowing (or caring) what tadpoles are or of knowing the meaning of the word γυρῖνος.[39] Other writers, being familiar with Plato's text but not appreciating the subtlety with which he introduces his lone reference to the creature, appear to have misunderstood him and taken the word γυρῖνος to refer to some kind of frog.

---

37 Gorgias 82 B 30 D–K, Aesop. *Sent.* 22a Perry, where the alternative attribution to Glycon is found.
38 See 172e1 κατεπείγει γὰρ ὕδωρ ῥέον, 201a10–b3 ἢ σὺ οἴει...δύνασθαι πρὸς ὕδωρ σμικρὸν διδάξαι ἱκανῶς τῶν γενομένων τὴν ἀλήθειαν;
39 Namely Aristotle, Aratus, Nicander (with the scholia to these last two) and a few of the lexicographers (see notes 24, 25, and 27). Ael. *NA* 1.58 records a means that bee-keepers use to kill τοὺς γυρίνους (because frogs are thought to be a threat to the bee population), but it is not clear whether he is referring to the killing of frogs or to the pre-emptive extermination of tadpoles.

THE DATE OF WALTER OF CHÂTILLON'S *ALEXANDREIS* ONCE AGAIN

By Neil Adkin

Summary: This article endeavours to rebut the objections raised by Orlandi to the present writer's attempt to date the publication of Walter of Châtillon's *Alexandreis* between autumn 1179 and autumn 1180. It also adduces arguments which would seem to allow a more exact dating to the spring of 1180. Examination of the political situation during these months would appear to provide corroboration for this new date.

If Walter of Châtillon's *Alexandreis* is agreed to have been the most admired epic of the Latin Middle Ages,[1] there is no agreement about the great work's date. At the beginning of the last century Christensen argued that the *Alexandreis* was completed in 1182 and published 'einige Jahre später'.[2] As late as 1986 Pritchard maintained that this view 'seems as good as any'.[3] Such complacency is no longer *de mise*. Most recently Traill has argued for publication in 1178,[4] while 1177-1179 and 1176 have been proposed respectively by Orlandi[5] and Dionisotti.[6] On the other hand, a datal *non liquet* is recorded by

---

1 It rapidly outstripped even the classics in the favor of the schools; cf. M.L. Colker *Galteri de Castellione Alexandreis* (Padua 1978) XIX-XX.
2 H. Christensen *Das Alexanderlied Walters von Châtillon* (Halle 1905) 1-13.
3 R.T. Pritchard *Walter of Châtillon: The Alexandreis* (Toronto 1986) 4-5.
4 D.A. Traill 'Walter of Châtillon's Prosimetron *In Domino Confido* (W. 3): Where and When was it Performed?' in J.M. Díaz y Díaz & J.M. Díaz de Bustamante (eds.) *Poesía Latina Medieval (Siglos V-XV)* (Florence 2005) 851-62: 859-61.
5 G. Orlandi 'San Brendano, Gualtiero di Châtillon e Bernhard Bischoff' *RIL* 128 (1994) 425-40: 434-39.

Lafferty's monograph[7] and Townsend's translation.[8] The present writer has already adduced evidence in support of a date between autumn 1179 and autumn 1180.[9] The aim of the present article is to be more precise: in the light of Traill's recent contribution it would seem possible to argue for a specific date of spring 1180.

Traill has carefully examined the circumstances in which Walter produced his prosimetron *In Domino confido*,[10] which contains the following list of poets:

Stephanus flos scilicet   *Aurelianensium*
et Petrus, qui dicitur   *de castro Blesensium.*

Istis non inmerito   *Berterus adicitur,*
set nec inter alios   *quartus pretermittitur*

ille, quem Castellio   *latere non patitur,*
in cuius opusculis   *Alexander legitur.*[11]

Traill argues that this catalogue is one of several later additions to the poem: the resultant revision is likely to have been performed on March 30th, 1180. Here it is noteworthy that Walter is the only one of the four authors to be associated with a particular work. Such an allusion to the *Alexandreis* is not necessary in order to identify the writer, as this function has already been clearly served by the antecedent line's mention of Châtillon: *ille, quem Castellio latere non patitur*. Since a mere item of bibliographic information is

---

6 A.C. Dionisotti 'Walter of Châtillon and the Greeks' in Godman, P., O. Murray (eds.) *Latin Poetry and the Classical Tradition* (Oxford 1990) 73-96: 90-96.
7 M.K. Lafferty *Walter of Châtillon's Alexandreis: Epic and the Problem of Historical Understanding* (Turnhout 1998) 183-89.
8 D. Townsend *The Alexandreis of Walter of Châtillon* (Philadelphia 1997) XIV-XV.
9 'The Proem of Walter of Châtillon's *Alexandreis*: *si...nostros vixisset in annos*' MAev 60 (1991) 207-21: 214-15.
10 Ed. K. Strecker *Moralisch-satirische Gedichte Walters von Châtillon* (Heidelberg 1929) 33-57.
11 3.7.6-3.8.4 ('Namely Stephen, the flower of Orléans, and Peter, who gets his name from the town of Blois. To these Berter is rightly added, but neither is a fourth overlooked among the rest, he whom Châtillon does not allow to be concealed, in whose humble works Alexander is read of').

pointless, there must accordingly have been a very good reason for introducing such a specific reference to the *Alexandreis*. The explanation is evidently the poem's topicality: in this recitation of the revised *In Domino confido* on March 30th 1180 Walter is advertising a poem that came out at the same period.[12]

The present writer's earlier endeavor to set the parameters for the *Alexandreis*' date of publication between autumn 1179 and autumn 1180 was based on an examination of lines 5-6 of the work's proem: *qui* (sc. Alexander) *si senio non fractus inermi / pollice fatorum nostros vixisset in annos*.[13] It was argued that the key to this astonishing suggestion that Alexander could have lived for over 1,500 years to the present is to be found in the foregoing *senio ... fractus inermi*, which by the rhetorical figure of *signification/emphasis*[14] is an allusion to Louis VII, who was totally incapacitated by a devastating stroke from September 1179 until his death in September 1180; hence the next line's 'Alexander who lives to the present' is Louis' son, Philip Augustus. This interpretation has been attacked in Orlandi's afore-mentioned discussion of the poem's date. It would therefore seem appropriate to attempt a detailed refutation of his arguments.

Orlandi begins by taking exception to the present writer's 'equilibrismi ermeneutici in chiave retorica'. Such an objection would seem to be unwarranted. In the above-cited prosimetron *In Domino confido* Walter classes his *Alexandreis* under the heading of the trivium (3.7.1), in which rhetoric played a cardinal role.[15] Since moreover one of the medieval *Vitae* says that Walter himself taught rhetoric,[16] he may be supposed to have been inti-

---

12 The immediately preceding diminutive (*opusculis*) tempers the ostentation; cf. *Thes. Ling. Lat.* s.v. IX.2 (1968-81) 862.21-2 (*saepius modestiae causa apud scriptores de suis scriptis loquentes*).
13 'If, unbroken by unarmed senility, by the thumb of the Fates he had lived on to our own day'.
14 Cf. Quint. *Inst.* 9.2.64: *est emphasis...cum ex aliquo dicto latens aliquid eruitur* (cf. ibid. 9.2.65: *per quandam suspicionem quod non dicimus accipi volumus, non utique contrarium, ut in εἰρωνείᾳ, sed aliud latens et auditori quasi inveniendum*). *Significatio* is the *Rhetorica ad Herennium*'s term for the figure (4.53.67).
15 Cf. (e.g.) the present writer 'Christianity and Language in the Middle Ages' in *Enc. Lang. Ling.* II (2006) 386-89: 387. Shortly after mentioning the *Alexandreis* the prosimetron goes on to deal specifically with rhetoric, which it describes as *domum Sapientie poliens mirifice* (3.10.2).
16 Cf. Colker 1978: xii (*Vita* 2, l. 7).

mately acquainted with all the prescriptions of the subject.[17] Orlandi concludes his sally against 'canoni retorici' with the dictum: 'alla fine deve prevalere il buon senso'. Since, however, the poem as well as the poet is deeply imbued with rhetorical theory, it would seem to be methodologically 'good sense' to apply the same theoretical considerations in endeavoring to understand both. The rhetorical principles in question are conveniently expounded in the *Artes Poetriae*, which laid down the rules for poetic composition in Walter's day: they regularly assign an important place to *significatio*.[18]

Orlandi then makes various attempts of his own to extract an acceptable meaning from the afore-cited lines 5-6 of Walter's proem. He turns first to the gloss in what seems to be the oldest extant manuscript of the work: '*nostros vixisset in annos*': *id est quantum nostrates vivere solent*.[19] According to Orlandi the gloss assumes that Alexander died naturally because life expectancy was lower in the 4th century BC than in the glossator's own day. It would seem however that this scholium is simply referring to a 'normal' lifespan: *nostrates* just means 'ordinary people' like us, as opposed to the great Alexander.[20] In his rebuttal of the scholiast, Orlandi is accordingly wrong to invoke the autopsic data of Alexander's death as well as the relative rates of life-expectancy in 4th century BC Greece and in 12th century AD France. A more plausible refutation of the glossator's view is supplied by Walter himself, who points out that by the time of Alexander's early death he had already conquered the whole world (5.502-3). Hence a life as long as 'ordinary people's' would have made no difference: there was nothing left for Alexander to conquer.[21]

Orlandi next proceeds to offer his own paraphrase of *si senio non fractus inermi / pollice fatorum nostros vixisset in annos* (1.5-6). It runs as follows:

---

[17] It is the rhetorical finesse of the *Alexandreis* that was largely responsible for its eclipse of the classics themselves in the schools of the next century.
[18] Cf. the conspectus in Adkin 1991: 219 n. 55.
[19] Geneva, Bibliothèque publique et universitaire, MS lat. 98 (s. XII); cf. Colker 1978: 277.
[20] Cf. (e.g.) Cic. *Fam.* 2.11.1: *nostratia* (our 'ordinary ... speech as opposed to ... grand oratory'; so Shackleton Bailey ad loc.).
[21] Orlandi appends to his 'rebuttal' a rejection of the idea that *nostros* denotes Walter's own time of life. In this connection he fails to notice that on his own view of the poem's date of composition Walter may not have been any older than Alexander; cf. Lafferty 1998: 4.

> Se per qualche miracolo del fato Alessandro avesse conservato l'età giovanile che aveva al tempo dell'impresa di Persia, giungendo in quelle condizioni fino a noi.

Here it may be observed that Walter makes no mention of a 'miracolo'. Nor does he refer to an 'età giovanile':[22] instead of youth, what Walter does talk about is old age (*senio*). Orlandi then observes: 'Iperbole talmente bizzarra da rasentare la balordaggine'. Here it might have been more pertinent to note that *Rhetorica ad Herennium* identifies hyperbole as a means of alerting the reader to *significatio*.[23] Orlandi concludes that the hyperbole is 'confermata, parrebbe' by 5.510 ff., which he paraphrases as follows: 'ci vorrebbe un condottiero giovane e valoroso come Alessandro per sconfiggere gl'infedeli'. Again, the paraphrase is unacceptable. In these closing lines of book 5 Walter is not speaking of a 'condottiere', but of a French king: *talem Francorum regem*. The same is evidently the case in the proem.

Orlandi's tendentious paraphrase of lines 5-6 fails even to satisfy himself. He therefore ends up opting for the conjecture made nearly a century and a half ago by Mueldener, who altered *nostros* to *iustos*.[24] The emendation is paleographically improbable. It also fails to give an acceptable meaning, since it is open to the same objections as the afore-mentioned gloss *nostrates*. Because Alexander conquered the entire world by the amazingly young age of 33, it would be pointless to wish for such an 'età matura', which instead of enhancing his achievement would actually diminish it. A further stipulation about *senium* ('ma non alla vecchiaia') has even less point. Again Orlandi himself is unconvinced: he rounds off with the remark that this passage of the proem 'tuttora appare enigmatico'.

Walter's use of *senium* calls for closer examination.[25] Orlandi complains that the present writer fails to provide any 'reale dimostrazione' that *senium* must refer to Louis VII. In this connection it is helpful to quote the defini-

---

[22] In significant contrast to 5.501 (*tenero sub flore iuventae*) the entire proem says nothing whatsoever about 'youth'. Naturally there is also nothing in the language of 1.5-6 corresponding to Orlandi's 'in quelle condizioni'.

[23] 4.53.67 (*cum plus est dictum, quam patitur veritas, augendae suspicionis causa*).

[24] F.A.W. Mueldener *M. Philippi Gualtheri ab Insulis dicti de Castellione Alexandreis* (Leipzig 1863) 5.

[25] The points to be made in this and the following paragraphs are not to be found in the present writer's previous treatments of Walter's proem.

tion of *significatio/emphasis* given by the rhetorician Tiberius: ἔμφασις ... ἐστιν ὅταν μὴ αὐτό τις λέγῃ τὸ πρᾶγμα, ἀλλὰ δι' ἑτέρον ἐμφαίνῃ.²⁶ It is therefore of the very nature of this rhetorical figure that the poet should deliberately avoid providing concrete evidence for the sort of 'reale dimostrazione' that Orlandi desiderates. There was no reason whatsoever for Walter to mention *senium*: had he merely wished to express the hypothesis that Alexander had lived to the present, line 5 would simply have run something like *Musa refer, qui si nunc usque adviveret acer*. Walter's *senium* is very conspicuous: the word opens the poem's second sentence and occupies the same line as the invocation itself. Moreover it is used in connection with a king; it also stands in the same clause as an explicit mention of 'our own time' (*nostros ... annos*), which occupies the same sedes in the immediately succeeding line. Such a salient combination of regal and contemporary reference in the use of *senium* cannot have failed to put the audience in mind of old King Louis. Orlandi, Dionisotti and Traill place the publication of the *Alexandreis* between 1176 and the summer of 1179. Though ailing, at this period Louis was still active.²⁷ During these years an allusion to royal *senium* would accordingly have been inadmissibly offensive. After Louis' devastating stroke in autumn 1179 on the other hand, it was clear that he was on his death-bed. Hence an allusion *per significationem* to the *senium* of the king could now be ventured.²⁸ The same *significatio* also makes possible the identification of the ensuing reference to the 'Alexander who lives to our time' as an encomiastic allusion to Louis' newly crowned son, Philip Augustus.

Senium is a very strong word: it certainly connotes more than Orlandi's mere 'vecchiaia'. Forcellini defines the term as follows: *est ... plus aliquid, quam senectus*.²⁹ Reference might also be made to the glossaries: *senium: senectus extrema* (IV 390.43; V 539.26). Here it may be noted that both *senectus* and *senecta* were perfectly at home in epic, since they are used eight and nine

---

26 *Fig.* 14 ('Emphasis is when one does not speak of the thing itself, but hints at it by other means').
27 Even as late as August 1179 he was able to make a pilgrimage all the way to Canterbury.
28 Orlandi states that such a reference to Louis' total incapacitation 'sarebbe stato indelicato, credo'. Here it is pertinent to cite the treatment of *significatio* in Quintilian, who defines its use as follows: *si non decet* (*Inst.* 9.2.66). It is therefore precisely the indirectness of this figure that enables the poet to avoid the 'indecorousness' with which Orlandi taxes him.
29 A. Forcellini and V. de Vit *Totius latinitatis lexicon* V (Prato 1871) 445. Articles on *senium* in *Thesaurus linguae latinae* and *Mittellateinisches Wörterbuch* have not yet appeared.

THE DATE OF THE ALEXANDREIS ONCE AGAIN   207

times respectively in the *Aeneid*; *senium* on the other hand occurs nowhere in Virgil. Walter has also heightened the effect by the addition of *fractus*. In this connection a remark of Seneca may be adduced: *senectus lassae aetatis, non fractae nomen est* (*Epist.* 26.1). This Senecan text further defines *fractus* with the phrase *decrepitos ... et extrema tangentis*. The epithet *fractus* is also the *mot juste* for a stroke-victim.[30] Such very strong language is quite inappropriate to Alexander. On the other hand it is eminently applicable to the bed-ridden Louis after his crippling stroke.

The proem of the *Alexandreis* is closely linked to the end of book 5, where Walter expresses the wish for *talem Francorum regem*.[31] The two texts are clearly contemporaneous: their topicality indicates that both were composed immediately before the poem's publication. Walter puts his wish for 'such a king' in the following terms:

> *Si gemitu commota pio votisque suorum*
> *flebilibus divina daret clementia talem*
> *Francorum regem, toto radiaret in orbe*
> *haut mora vera fides.*[32]

Here Orlandi comments:

> I congiuntivi imperfetti (*daret, radiaret*) implicavano chiaramente che nulla di ciò che si auspicava stesse avverandosi; il che nei confronti del giovane re non poteva non suonare come un'offesa gratuita.

---

30 Cf. (e.g.) Firm. *Math.* 6.31.69: *paralyticos...fractis...viribus*.
31 The parallels between the two passages may be briefly enumerated: 1.1 (*gesta ... Macedum*) = 5.502 (*quanta ... Macedo*); 1.1 (*totum ... orbem*) = 5.503 (*totus ... orbis*); 1.2-3 (series of indirect questions: *quam ... quo ... quo*) = 5.500-2 (series of indirect questions: *quam ... quanta ... quam*); 1.2 (*milite*) = 5.500 (*milite*); 1.5 (*qui*) = 5.511 (*talem*); 1.5 (*si* introducing unreal condition) = 5.510 (*si* introducing unreal condition); 1.5 (*fractus inermi*) = 5.513 (*fracta sub armis*); 1.6 (*fatorum*) = 5.511 (*divina ... clementia*); 1.6 (*nostros*) = 5.512 (*Francorum*); 1.7-8 (*Cesareos ... Romuleae*) = 5.508 (*Cesareum ... Romae*); 1.9 (*preradiaret*) = 5.512 (*radiaret*); 1.15 (*Tarpeiam Brennius arcem*) = 5.497 (*Tarpeiam Iulius arcem*); 1.17 (*Remensis*) = 5.520 (*Remorum*); 1.25 (*sacros fontes*) = 5.520 (*sacrum ... fontem*).
32 5.510-13 ('If, moved by the pious groan and tearful wishes of his own people, God's mercy would grant such a king of France, without delay the true faith would shine in all the world').

Orlandi fails to perceive that such an oblique form of expression is simply an encomiastic convention.[33] Walter himself is merely voicing a conventionally flattering wish for something that has already happened. The subjunctives at issue in fact constitute a further case of *significatio*. Handy corroboration is supplied by a near-contemporary *Ars Poetriae*, whose treatment of the figure explicitly associates it with encomium: the rubric of the section in question reads *Significatio cum qu[a]dam [ratione] dignitatis et laudis*.[34] This laudatory *significatio* is then illustrated by a poem addressed to King Henry III of England, who is told: *in Domino confide! tuos tibi cedere cernes / hostes* (ll. 252-3). On Orlandi's logic the reader would have to conclude that the eminently devout Henry did not 'trust in the Lord'.[35] Far, however, from being a 'gratuitous insult' to the king's godliness, this exhortation is merely an encomiastic *significatio* commending the trust which Henry does in fact have in the Lord. It is noteworthy that in both Walter and John of Garland the referent is a king, who is assured of victory over his enemies: on each occasion the fulfillment of a condition is represented as the prerequisite for this victory.[36] It may accordingly be concluded that Orlandi is quite wrong to maintain that 'nei confronti del giovane re' the subjunctives *daret* and *radiaret* are an insult: on the contrary they are only suitable in the context of Philip Augustus' coronation.[37]

The present article began by arguing that the *Alexandreis* was published in the spring of 1180. It will be appropriate to end by adducing a number of reasons why at this time Walter had particular occasion to resort to the figure of *significatio* at both the start of book 1 and the close of book 5. In his

---

[33] He goes on to mention the particular case of poets who issue 'advice', which he takes at face value. In this connection reference may be made to the very recent observation by F. Cairns *Sextus Propertius: The Augustan Elegist* (Cambridge 2006) 23: 'It is now recognized that, rather than proffer unsought and unwelcome advice to his patrons, Horace's injunctions in his *Odes* flatter the already established traits, interests and attitudes of his addressees'.

[34] Ed. E. Habel 'Die *Exempla honestae vitae* des Johannes de Garlandia, eine lateinische Poetik des 13. Jahrhunderts' *RomForsch* 29 (1911) 131-54: 151 (l. 249).

[35] On this monarch's well-known piety cf. (e.g.) D.A. Carpenter *The Reign of Henry III* (London 1996) 437-38.

[36] At the same time John's imperatival form of expression (*confide!*) is noticeably more peremptory than Walter's subjunctives.

[37] Similarly *gemitu* and *flebilibus* fit Louis' total incapacitation: before his stroke such strong language would have been unacceptably offensive.

discussion of this figure Quintilian observes: *eius triplex usus est: unus, si dicere palam parum tutum est, alter, si non decet, tertius, qui venustatis modo gratia adhibetur et ipsa novitate ac varietate magis, quam si relatio sit recta, delectat.*[38] Besides the issue of 'decorum'[39] it would seem that the poet has also been strongly influenced by the first of these considerations: *si dicere palam parum tutum est*. On November 1st 1179 Philip Augustus had been crowned King by Walter's patron, William of the White Hands, Archbishop of Reims and scion of the great house of Blois-Champagne. However, the spring of 1180 witnessed a decline in William's influence to the advantage of his rival, Count Philip of Flanders. In March the young king was betrothed to the Count's niece by Guy of Sens: William's exclusion caused him deep resentment.[40] In April the couple was married: again William was not involved. In May Philip Augustus and his bride were crowned by Guy of Sens:[41] the date and place of the coronation had to be changed for fear that the house of Champagne would resort to force in order to prevent it. Sens had been William's see before his move to Reims. Dionisotti is puzzled by the disproportionately large space that Walter's proem allots to the former city.[42] The poet's intention is evidently to suggest that William had been a better archbishop of Sens than the present incumbent.[43]

Two final points may be made which would seem to supply further evidence that the *Alexandreis* was published in spring 1180. Firstly it may be noted that the historical Alexander was already 18 when he received his first experience of war (Iust. 9.1.8). The reader is therefore surprised to find that at the start of the *Alexandreis* Walter places such stress on his own Alexander

---

38 *Inst.* 9.2.66 ('Its use is threefold: first, if it is not safe enough to speak openly, second, if it is indecorous, third, when it is used just to charm, and through mere novelty and variety it delights more than if the statement were straightforward').

39 Cf. n. 28 above. Quintilian's last reason (*venustatis...*) will also have appealed to someone of Walter's rhetorical virtuosity.

40 Cf. *Frg. hist. vit. Ludov. VII* (ap. *Recueil des historiens des Gaules et de la France* XII (Paris 1877) 287a): *maxime contra voluntatem domini Remensis Willelmi*.

41 For William's dudgeon cf. Benedict of Peterborough *Gesta Regis Henr. II* (ed. W. Stubbs *Rolls Series* XLIX (London 1867) 246): *doluit vehementer*; Roger of Hoveden *Chron.* (ed. W. Stubbs *Rolls Series* LI.2 (London 1869) 197): *indignatus est vehementer*.

42 Dionisotti (n. 6) 90-91.

43 Cf. in particular Walter's stress on the honour conferred by William on Sens: *quo presule non minor urbi / nupsit honos quam cum Romam ... / fregit ... Brennius* (1.13-5).

as a mere *puer* impatient for *arma*.⁴⁴ Walter's remarkable emphasis does however become intelligible when it is recalled that Philip Augustus would seem to have become a knight on Whitsunday 1180.⁴⁵ The second point concerns the apodosis of Walter's conditional sentence about 'such a king of France' at the end of book 5: *toto radiaret in orbe | haut mora vera fides*. These words were understood by Giesebrecht⁴⁶ and Toischer⁴⁷ as a reference to Philip Augustus' persecution of the Jews early in 1180: according to Rigord the measures in question came into effect on the 16th of February.⁴⁸ Christensen⁴⁹ then maintained that Walter's statement could not postdate these anti-Jewish measures, since in that case the subjunctive (*radiaret*) would constitute a 'Vorwurf' against the king: like Orlandi, Christensen fails to recognize the encomiastic convention whereby a hypothetical form of expression is employed to describe what has actually happened already. The likelihood of a reference to these steps against the Jews can in fact be supported by a number of novel arguments. In the first place the syntagm *vera fides* is appropriate to anti-Jewish polemic.⁵⁰ Secondly, Philip Augustus' measures against the Jews are described by both Giesebrecht and Toischer as 'Bekehrungen': it is therefore noteworthy that exactly the same idea of 'conversion' should be accorded a surprising prominence in the poem's immediately succeeding panorama of conquest.⁵¹ Thirdly, these forced 'conversions'

---

44 Cf. 1.30; 1.33; 1.37; 1.40; 1.42; 1.56.
45 Cf. A. Cartellieri *Philipp II. August, König von Frankreich* I (Leipzig 1899-1900) 88.
46 W. Giesebrecht 'Die Vaganten oder Goliarden und ihre Lieder' *Allgem. Monatsschr. f. Wiss. u. Lit.* (1853) 344-81: 367.
47 W. Toischer 'Ueber die *Alexandreis* Ulrichs von Eschenbach' *SAWW* 97 (1880) 311-408: 313.
48 *Gesta Phil. Aug.* 6 (ed. H.F. Delaborde *Oeuvres de Rigord et de Guillaume le Breton* I (Paris 1882) 16 with n. 1). Ralph de Diceto on the other hand gives the date as the 18th of January; cf. *Imag. hist.* (ed. W. Stubbs *Rolls Series* LXVIII.2 (London 1876) 4).
49 Christensen (n. 2) 9-10.
50 For a contemporary instance cf. (e.g.) Hildegard of Bingen *Sciv.* 3.10.30 (ed. A. Führkötter *CCCM* XLIIIA (Turnhout 1978) 570): *Iudaei...veram fidem abnegantes*.
51 Christensen (1905: 9) notes that here an emphasis on martial rather than missionary accomplishments is to be expected. In this connection particular reference may be made to 5.514 (*baptismo*; in the same sedes as *vera fides* in the immediately antecedent line) and 5.520 (*fontem*; cf. the gloss in Colker 1978: 439: *id est exspectaret baptizari*); since *fontem* is the last word of the book, the idea accordingly frames the whole tableau.

of the Jews were 'die erste, klar hervortretende Tat des jungen Fürsten';[52] they accordingly fit Walter's *haut mora* (5.513). They are also admirably suited to a publication date for the *Alexandreis* shortly afterwards, in spring 1180.

---

52 Cartellieri (n. 45) 58.

GREEKS AND LATINS IN MEDIAEVAL HUNGARY

By Elöd Nemerkényi

Summary: The terms Greeks and Latins had at least three different and specific meanings in mediaeval Hungary: first, they denoted ancient Greeks and Romans; second, Eastern and Western Christians; and third, Byzantines and Westerners. The following three Latin sources are discussed: the *Admonitions* of King Saint Stephen of Hungary, the *Legenda maior*, as well as the *Deliberatio* of Bishop Saint Gerard of Csanád.

The purpose of the following discussion is to demonstrate that the terms Greeks and Latins had at least three different and specific meanings in mediaeval Hungary: first, they denoted ancient Greeks and Romans; second, Eastern and Western Christians; and third, Byzantines and Westerners. As a point of departure, however, an approximate definition is needed for the sake of clarity regarding the relevant terminology used in the mediaeval West. Overall, the labels 'Greeks' and 'Latins' designate the advocates of Greek and Latin cultures and their diverse manifestations in language, culture, and religion. The eleventh-century author, Ekkehard IV of Saint Gall reported on a student in his monastic school who produced a hexameter after being exposed to training in both the Greek and the Latin languages: *Esse uelim Graecus, cum uix sum, domna, Latinus*.[1] The chronicles of Hungary in the thirteenth and fourteenth centuries provide relatively convenient

---

1 P. Stotz 'Esse velim Graecus…: Griechischer Glanz und griechische Irrlichter im mittelalterlichen Latein' in, Engels, O. and P. Schreiner (ed.) *Die Begegnung des Westens mit dem Osten* (Sigmaringen 1993) 433-51.
2 G. Kristó 'Latini, italiani e veneziani nella cronaca ungherese' in Graciotti, S. and C. Vasoli (ed.) *Spiritualità e lettere nella cultura italiana e ungherese del basso medioevo* (Florence 1995) 345-54.

material to illustrate the local development of this terminology.² However, the sources pertaining to the period of state formation and also to the formation of Latin literacy in mediaeval Hungary are fairly limited. They indicate, nonetheless, that the eleventh century witnessed the influence of Byzantium and Rome not only as simple antecedents but also as linguistic, cultural, religious, and political models in Hungary during the long process of converting not only to Latin but to Greek Christianity as well. These sources do not offer the full scale of the various types of Western insight into Greek and Latin continuities in terms of the languages,³ the schools,⁴ or the study of Graeco-Roman mythology, for example.⁵ They have nevertheless invited valuable scholarly endeavours in Hungary and beyond. Two Hungarian scholars of classical philology and Byzantine studies deserve special recognition in this regard: Gyula Moravcsik and István Kapitánffy.⁶ It is in the spirit of their inspiration that the following three Latin sources will be subject to discussion in order to trace the different meanings of the terms Greeks and Latins in medieval Hungary: the *Admonitions* of King Saint Stephen of Hungary, the *Legenda maior*, as well as the *Deliberatio* of Bishop Saint Gerard of Csanád.

---

3 B.M. Kaczynski 'Medieval Translations: Latin and Greek' in Mantello, F.A.C. and A.G. Rigg (ed.) *Medieval Latin: An Introduction and Bibliographical Guide* (Washington, DC 1996) 718-22.
4 B. Bischoff 'Das griechische Element in der abendländischen Bildung des Mittelalters' *Byzantinische Zeitschrift* 44.1-2 (1951) 27-55; P. Riché 'Le grec dans les centres de culture d'Occident' in M.W. Herren & S.A. Brown (ed.) *The Sacred Nectar of the Greeks: The Study of Greek in the West in the Early Middle Ages* (London 1988) 143-68; Walter Berschin 'La cultura greca' in *Lo spazio letterario del Medioevo: Il Medioevo latino*, vol. 1.1, *La produzione del testo*, ed. G. Cavallo, C. Leonardi, and E. Menestò (Rome 1992) 183-97.
5 M.W. Herren 'The Earliest European Study of Graeco-Roman Mythology (600-900 AD)' *Acta Classica Universitatis Scientiarum Debreceniensis* 34-35 (1998-1999) 25-49.
6 G. Moravcsik (ed.) *Fontes Byzantini historiae Hungaricae aevo ducum et regum ex stirpe Árpád descendentium* (Budapest 1988). See G. Moravcsik *Die byzantinische Kultur und das mittelalterliche Ungarn* (Berlin 1956); I. Kapitánffy *Hungarobyzantina: Bizánc és a görögség középkori magyarországi forrásokban* (Hungarobyzantina: Byzantium and the Greeks in the sources of medieval Hungary) (Budapest 2003). See also T. Olajos 'A magyarországi bizantinológia a XX. században' (Byzantine studies in Hungary in the twentieth century) in L. Koszta (ed.) *Kelet és nyugat között: Történeti tanulmányok Kristó Gyula tiszteletére* (Between East and West: historical studies in honor of Gyula Kristó), (Szeged 1995) 381-99.

The first source, the *Admonitions* is an anonymous mirror of princes attributed to King Saint Stephen of Hungary. At about the time of its composition, Stephen founded the Greek nunnery in Veszprémvölgy and issued its foundation charter in the Greek language around 1018. This foundation charter is lost but the transcription of its Greek text survives along with its royal confirmation in the Latin language in a charter by King Coloman from 1109.[7] In Chapter Eight of Stephen's *Admonitions*, entitled *De executione filiorum*, the king addresses his son, Prince Emeric: *Graue enim tibi est huius climatis tenere regnum, nisi imitator consuetudinis ante regnantium extiteris regum. Quis Grecus regeret Latinos Grecis moribus, aut quis Latinus regeret Grecos Latinis moribus? Nullus.*[8] Regarding the terms *Grecus* and *Latinus* of the *Admonitions*, three observations are in order. First, the Classical Latin antecedents of the work suggest that these terms denote ancient Greeks and Romans. Second, as István Kapitánffy already proposed, the terms Greeks and Latins denote Eastern and Western Christians and do not necessarily imply national or linguistic categories – the monks of the Greek monasteries in medieval Hungary adopted the liturgy and the doctrine of the Byzantine church but they were usually of Hungarian and Slavic origin, and the language of their liturgy was probably Slavic as well.[9] The third observation is that the terms Greeks and Latins simply denote contemporary Byzantines and Westerners. The Byzantine and Roman policy of the Ottonian emperors supports this interpretation: Emperor Otto II married the

---

7   G. Györffy (ed.) *Árpád-kori oklevelek* (Charters from the Árpád age) (Budapest 1997) 35-37. See M. Komjáthy 'Quelques problèmes relatifs à la charte de fondation du couvent des religieuses de Veszprémvölgy' in P. Brière (ed.) *Mélanges offerts à Szabolcs de Vajay* (Braga 1971) 369-80; G. Érszegi 'Szent István görög nyelvü okleveléről' (On the Greek charter of Saint Stephen) *Levéltári Szemle* 38.3 (1988) 3-13; S. Vajay 'Vesz-prémvölgy és alapítói' (Veszprémvölgy and its founders) *Levéltári Szemle* 38.4 (1988) 20-24.

8   'It is indeed difficult for you to keep the kingdom in this region unless you start to imitate the custom of previous kings. Which Greek would rule the Latins by Greek customs or which Latin would rule the Greeks by Latin customs? None.' 'Libellus de institutione morum' in *Scriptores rerum Hungaricarum tempore ducum regumque stirpis Arpadianae gestarum*, ed. J. Balogh, vol. 2 (Budapest 1938) 626. See G. Érszegi 'Exsecutio maiorum – exsecutio filiorum' in *Kelet és nyugat közöt:* (note 6), 161-68.

9   See I. Kapitánffy (2003) 17-37. See also K. Szovák 'Egy kódex két tanulsága' (Two readings of a codex) in L. Horváth, K. Laczkó, G. Mayer & L. Takács (ed.) *Genesia: Tanulmányok Bollók János emlékére* (Genesia: studies in memory of János Bollók) (Budapest 2004) 145-67.

niece of the Byzantine Emperor John I Tzimisces, Theophano, in Rome in 972. Gerbert of Aurillac raised the following question about their son, Otto III in 984: *Forte quia Grecus est, ut dicitis, more Grecorum conregnantem instituere uultis?*[10] During the Ottonian period, the monastery of Sant'Alessio on the Aventine hill in Rome cultivated the traditions of Greek monasticism in Italy, and the celebrated bishop, missionary, and martyr of Central Europe, Saint Adalbert, once belonged to this monastic community as well. Archbishop Anastasius of Esztergom, on the other hand, was allegedly Adalbert's 'Graecophile' disciple which would partly explain the coexistence of Greek and Latin spirituality in Hungary.[11] The statement about the different customs of Greeks and Latins in the *Admonitions* can also be interpreted in the light of the preface to the first law code of King Stephen: *Et quoniam unaqueque gens propriis utitur legibus, idcirco nos quoque dei nutu nostram gubernantes monarchiam, antiquos ac modernos imitantes augustos…*[12] The *Admonitions* and the law code both reflect the Carolingian literary tradition of *antiqui* and *moderni* where the expression *antiqui* equally refers to classical and patristic authors – Greeks as well as Latins.[13] Art historical evidence

10 F.R. Erkens '… *more Grecorum conregnantem instituere vultis?* Zur Legitimation der Regentschaft Heinrichs des Zänkers im Thronstreit von 984' *Frühmittelalterliche Studien* 27 (1993) 283.

11 See B. Hamilton 'The Monastery of S. Alessio and the Religious and Intellectual Renaissance of Tenth-Century Rome' in *Monastic Reform, Catharism and the Crusades (900-1300)* (London 1979) III 265-310; B. Hamilton and P.A. McNulty '*Orientale lumen et magistra Latinitas*: Greek Influences on Western Monasticism (900-1100)' in *Monastic Reform, Catharism and the Crusades (900-1300)* (London 1979) V 181-216; W. Berschin *Griechisch-lateinisches Mittelalter: Von Hieronymus zu Nikolaus von Kues* (Bern and Munich 1980) 222-26; E. Nemerkényi 'The Medieval Rome Idea in the *Institutio* of King Stephen of Hungary' *Acta Classica Universitatis Scientiarum Debreceniensis* 36 (2000) 187-201; L. Havas 'La Hongrie de Saint Étienne entre l'Occident et l'Orient' *Acta Antiqua Academiae Scientiarum Hungaricae* 41.1-2 (2001) 175-92; L. Havas 'La naissance de la littérature hongroise en latin (Entre la civilisation byzantine et la culture latine occidentale)' *Camoenae Hungaricae* 1 (2004) 7-50.

12 G. Györffy & E. Bartoniek (eds.) *Szent István törvényeinek XII. századi kézirata az Admonti kódexben (Hasonmás kiadás)* (The twelfth-century manuscript of the laws of Saint Stephen in the Admont codex: facsimile edition) (Budapest 1988), 49. See J. Szücs 'König Stephan in der Sicht der modernen ungarischen Geschichtsforschung' *Südost-Forschungen* 31 (1972) 17-40.

13 W. Hartmann '"Modernus" und "antiquus": Zur Verbreitung und Bedeutung dieser Bezeichnungen in der wissenschaftlichen Literatur vom 9. bis zum 12. Jahrhundert' in A.

also provides a spectacular display of the significant mixture of Greek and Roman influence: it is possible that King Saint Stephen's sarcophagus at Székesfehérvár was originally a Roman sarcophagus, reworked in the Middle Ages with Byzantine motifs.[14]

The second source, the *Legenda maior* of Bishop Saint Gerard of Csanád, is the longer of the two Gerard legends whose datings are problematic – the compact *Legenda minor* was probably composed in the twelfth century and the extensive *Legenda maior* in the fourteenth century.[15] The *Legenda maior* provides colourful stories where the term 'Greeks' denotes Eastern Christians. It reports on the Greek baptism of the Hungarian leader Ajtony at Vidin, Bulgaria, around 1002 and on the subsequent foundation of the Greek monastery of Saint John the Baptist in Marosvár: *In diebus illis erat quidam princeps in urbe Morisena, nomine Acthum, potens ualde, qui secundum ritum Grecorum in ciuitate Budin fuerat baptizatus... Accepit autem potestatem a Grecis et construxit in prefata urbe Morisena monasterium in honore beati Iohannis Baptiste, constituens in eodem abbatem cum monachis Grecis, iuxta ordinem et ritum ipsorum.*[16] Another Hungarian leader and an ally of

---

Zimmermann (ed.) *Antiqui und Moderni: Traditionsbewusstsein und Fortschrittsbewusstsein im späten Mittelalter* (Berlin & New York 1974) 21-39.

14 T. von Bogyay 'Über den Stuhlweissenburger Sarkophag des hl. Stephan' *Ungarn-Jahrbuch* 4 (1972) 9-26; Á. Nagy 'Origine et iconographie du sarcophage de Székesfehérvár' *Alba Regia* 13 (1972) 167-84; S. Tóth 'A székesfehérvári szarkofág és köre' (The sarcophagus of Székesfehérvár and its circle) in Á. Mikó & I. Takács (ed.) *Pannonia regia: Müvészet a Dunántúlon 1000-1541* (Pannonia regia: art in Transdanubia 1000-1541) (Budapest 1994) 82-86.

15 G. Klaniczay and E. Madas 'La Hongrie' in G. Philippart (ed.) *Hagiographies: Histoire internationale de la littérature hagiographique latine et vernaculaire en Occident des origins à 1550*, vol. 2 (Turnhout 1996) 113-14; 138-40. See also S. Tramontin 'Problemi agiografici e profili di santi' in F. Tonon (ed.) *La chiesa di Venezia nei secoli XI-XIII* (Venice 1988) 160-66.

16 'In those days, there was a certain prince in the town of Marosvár, called Ajtony, very powerful, who was baptized according to the rite of the Greeks in the city of Vidin... Moreover, he received his power from the Greeks and constructed a monastery in honor of Saint John the Baptist in the aforementioned town of Marosvár where he introduced an abbot with Greek monks according to the manner and the rite of the Greeks themselves.' 'Legenda sancti Gerhardi episcopi' in *Scriptores rerum Hungaricarum tempore ducum regumque stirpis Arpadianae gestarum*, ed. I. Madzsar, vol. 2 (Budapest 1938) 489-90 (henceforth *SRH* 2). See G. Silagi 'Gerhardslegenden' in T. von Bogyay (ed.) *Ungarns Geschichtsschreiber* vol. 1, *Die heiligen Könige*, (Graz, Vienna & Cologne 1976) 180.

King Stephen, Csanád, later defeated Ajtony in a battle. The *Legenda maior* records that those killed in the battle were buried at the Greek monastery of Saint John the Baptist of Marosvár because that was the only monastery in the region at the time: *Corpora uero Christianorum, qui ceciderant in prelio, tollentes duxerunt in Moroswar et sepelierunt in cimiterio Sancti Iohannis Baptiste in monasterio Grecorum, quia in eadem prouincia aliud monasterium illis temporibus non erat.*[17] After his victory over Ajtony, Csanád founded the monastery of Saint George of Oroszlámos: *Post hec ueniens Chanadinus ad locum, ubi leonem in sompnis uiderat, in honore beati Georgii martiris monasterium edificauit introducens illuc memoratos Grecos monachos de monasterio beati Iohannis Baptiste una cum abbate.*[18]

The arrival of the newly appointed Bishop Gerard started a series of events as a chain reaction: the leader Csanád evacuated the Greek monks from the monastery of Saint John the Baptist of Marosvár and transferred them to the recently established monastery of Saint George of Oroszlámos in order to make room for the bishop and his Latin monks who moved into the Greek monastery of Saint John the Baptist of Marosvár. As the *Legenda maior* reports: *Inde proficiscentes uenerunt in urbem Morisenam, ubi erant monachi Greci, qui diuina secundum ritum et consuetudinem suam celebrabant. Episcopus autem, inito consilio cum comite Chanadino, eundem Grecum abbatem cum monachis suis transtulit in Orozlanos, monasterium uero ipsorum episcopo cum fratribus suis assignauit, qui in eodem habitauerunt, donec monasterium beati Georgii martiris perficeretur.*[19] Marosvár thus became the first

---

[17] 'Indeed, they carried the bodies of the Christians who died in the battle to Marosvár and buried them in the cemetery of St. John the Baptist in the monastery of the Greeks, because there was no other monastery in that region in those times.' *SRH* 2, 491-92.

[18] 'After these, Csanád came to the place where he saw the lion in his dreams and built a monastery in honor of St. George the Martyr, introducing there the aforementioned Greek monks from the monastery of St. John the Baptist along with the abbot.' *SRH* 2, 492.

[19] 'Thereupon, they left and arrived at the town of Marosvár where the Greek monks were staying who celebrated the liturgy according to their own rite and custom. Then the bishop, having consulted with the leader Csanád, transferred the same Greek abbot with his own monks to Oroszlámos and designated their monastery to the bishop and his brothers who stayed there until the monastery of St. George the Martyr was completed.' *SRH* 2, 493. See B.F. Romhányi *Kolostorok és társaskáptalanok a középkori Magyarországon: Katalógus* (Monasteries and collegiate chapters in mediaeval Hungary: catalog) (Budapest 2000) 18; 48.

residence of Bishop Gerard upon the establishment of the bishopric in 1030. Eventually, Gerard also dedicated the new cathedral to Saint George. This choice of patron saint reflects Byzantine models as well as Venetian ones because Gerard's original home was the monastery on the Isola di San Giorgio Maggiore in Venice.[20]

The third source, the *Deliberatio* of Bishop Saint Gerard of Csanád, is a peculiar exegetical treatise on a passage of the Prophet Daniel, written in Hungary in the first half of the eleventh century. Gerard's treatise is strongly dependent on the Biblical, the patristic, and the classical traditions.[21] Its references to the Greeks reveal traces of the Byzantine influence in and around

20 See C. Juhász *Das Tschanad-Temesvarer Bistum im frühen Mittelalter 1030-1307: Einfügung des Banats in die westeuropäische germanisch-christliche Kulturgemeinschaft* (Münster 1930) 63-76; E. von Ivánka 'Griechische Kirche und griechisches Mönchtum im mittelalterlichen Ungarn' *Orientalia Christiana Periodica* 8.1-2 (1942) 183-94; M. Gyóni 'L'Église orientale dans la Hongrie du XIe siècle' *Revue d'Histoire Comparée* 25.3 (1947) 42-49; G. Moravcsik 'The Role of the Byzantine Church in Medieval Hungary' in *Studia Byzantina* (Budapest 1967) 326-40; G. Székely 'La Hongrie et Byzance au Xe-XIIe siècles' *Acta Historica Academiae Scientiarum Hungaricae* 13.3-4 (1967) 291-311; J. Leclercq 'Saint Gerard de Csanád et le monachisme' *Studia Monastica* 13.1 (1971) 13-30; J.P. Ripoche 'La Hongrie entre Byzance et Rome: Problème du choix religieux' *Ungarn-Jahrbuch* 6 (1974-1975) 9-23; G. Kristó 'Ajtony and Vidin' *Studia Turco-Hungarica* 5 (1981) 129-35; F. Makk 'Les relations hungaro-byzantines aux Xe-XIIe siècles' in F. Glatz (ed.) *European Intellectual Trends and Hungary* (Budapest 1990), 11-25; I. Pirigyi *A magyarországi görög katolikusok története* (History of the Greek Catholics in Hungary), vol. 1 (Nyíregyháza 1990), 36-41; Z. Magyar 'Szent György középkori kultusza Magyarországon' (The mediaeval cult of Saint George in Hungary) *Századok* 132.1 (1998) 161-82; P. Püspöki Nagy *Szent Gellért csanádi püspökvértanú élete és műve* (The life and work of the bishop and martyr Saint Gerard) (Budapest 2002), 49-52.
21 See G. Silagi *Untersuchungen zur 'Deliberatio supra hymnum trium puerorum' des Gerhard von Csanád* (Munich 1967); Z.J. Kosztolnyik 'The Importance of Gerard of Csanád as the First Author in Hungary' *Traditio* 25 (1969) 376-86; L. Szegfű 'La missione politica ed ideologica di San Gerardo in Ungheria' in V. Branca (ed.) *Venezia e Ungheria nel Rinascimento* (Florence 1973) 23-36; J. Török 'Gherardus de Venetis auctor et monachus? (Un clerc medieval et la Bible)' in S. Graciotti and C. Vasoli (ed.) *Spiritualità e lettere nella cultura italiana e ungherese del basso medioevo* (Florence 1995) 203-9; B. Déri 'Ambrosius-idézetek Gellértnél' (Quotations from Ambrose in Gerard) in T. Almási, I. Draskóczy and& É. Jancsó (ed.) *Studia professoris – professor studiorum: Tanulmányok Érszegi Géza hatvanadik születésnapjára* (studies dedicated to the sixtieth birthday of Géza Érszegi) (Budapest 2005) 75-81.

Gerard's home cloister in Venice.²² In Gerard's *Deliberatio*, the term 'Greeks' denotes ancient Greeks and Eastern Christians, as well as Byzantines. When reviewing the seven liberal arts, Gerard often refers to ancient Greeks – usually through the mediation of the *Etymologiae* of Isidore of Seville. The Isidorian description of the ancient Greek origins of the art of rhetoric is the following (*Etymologiae* 2.2.1): *Haec autem disciplina a Graecis inuenta est, a Gorgia, Aristotele, Hermagora, et translata in Latinum a Tullio uidelicet et Quintiliano, sed ita copiose, ita uarie, ut eam lectori admirari in promptu sit, conprehendere inpossibile.*

Gerard breaks this Isidorian description into two parts and consequently provides their paraphrases in two separate sections regarding ancient Greek and Latin rhetoric, respectively: *Gorgia, Aristotiles, Ermachora Greci rethorice artis inuentores benedicendi? – Ciceronem, qui totam argumentose rethoricam e Greco in Latinum transtulit, ut magis amirari quam compraehendi possit a lectoribus.*²³ The Isidorian description of the ancient Greek origins of physics (*Etymologiae* 2.24.4: *Physicam apud Graecos primus perscrutatus est Thales Milesius*) also appears in the *Deliberatio* (*Tales Milisius, qui apud Grecos fisice primus perscrutator perhibetur*).²⁴

As opposed to Gerard's approach to the seven liberal arts, when discussing various schools of heretics, his use of the term Greeks denotes Eastern Christians of Byzantium where heresies had never been absent: *Gretia infelix, sine quibus numquam uiuere uoluit.*²⁵ The Greek and Latin terminology of chiliastic or millenarian heretics is almost literally adapted from Isidore's *Etymologiae* 8.5.8 – *mille annos post resurrectionem in uoluptate carnis futuros praedicant. Unde et Graece Chiliastae, Latine Miliasti sunt appellati –*; Gerard introduces only slight changes of word order into the second part of the relevant Isidorian passage (*mille annos post resurrectionem in uoluptate carnis fu-*

---

22 See D.M. Nicol *Byzantium and Venice: A Study in Diplomatic and Cultural Relations* (Cambridge 1988) 35-49.
23 Gerard of Csanád 'Deliberatio supra hymnum trium puerorum' in *Corpus Christianorum: Continuatio mediaeualis*, ed. G. Silagi, vol. 49 (Turnhout 1978) 40; 83 (henceforth *CCCM* 49).
24 *CCCM* 49, 40. See E. Nemerkényi 'The Seven Liberal Arts in the *Deliberatio* of Bishop Gerard of Csanád' *Studi Veneziani* 42 (2001) 215-23; E. Nemerkényi 'Ancient Rhetoric and the *Deliberatio* of Bishop Gerard of Csanád' *Journal of Medieval Latin* 14 (2004) 118-27.
25 *CCCM* 49, 51.

turos praedicant, unde et Ciliaste atque Miliasti Grece et Latine appellantur).²⁶

Isidore of Seville's Greek and Latin etymology of the noun angel (*Etymologiae* 7.5.1: *Angeli Graece uocantur... Latine uero nuntii interpretantur, ab eo quod Domini uoluntatem populis nuntiant*) is also the immediate source of Gerard's corresponding terminology (*Omnes namque cognoscimus, quod angeli Grece Latine nuntii dicantur, propter quod Domini uoluntatem populis nunciant*).²⁷ He later aggressively denounces what he considers a heretic view of angels held by Greeks, that is, Eastern Christians of Byzantium: *Errauerunt isti, quemadmodum et illi, qui simili errore latrauerunt angelos desiderasse corpora, nimirum filias hominum. Proiecti autem sunt licet Grecorum multi illos sequantur*.²⁸ Finally, the Isidorian etymology of the name of the archangel Uriel (*Etymologiae* 7.5.15: *Uriel interpretatur ignis Dei*) appears in Gerard's assertion about Greek heretics who venerate this archangel (*Greci autem hec et unum, utique Uriel, qui ignis Dei dicitur, quem specialius heretici inuocare dicuntur*).²⁹ His use of the term Greeks, denoting ancient Greeks, Eastern Christians, as well as Byzantines, is complemented with his adaptations of artificial Latin technical terms from John Scottus Eriugena's Latin translation of Pseudo-Dionysius Areopagita. In fact, the Hungarian paleographer and codicologist László Mezey proposed that the mid-eleventh century codex fragment of John Scottus Eriugena's Latin translation of the

---

26 *CCCM* 49, 9. See I. da Milano 'Le eresie popolari del secolo XI nell'Europa occidentale' *Studi Gregoriani* 2 (1947) 43-89; G. Rónay 'Bogumilizmus Magyarországon a XI. század elején, Gellért püspök 'Deliberatio'-jának tükrében' (Bogumilism in Hungary at the beginning of the eleventh century, as reflected in the 'Deliberatio' of Bishop Gerard), *Irodalomtörténeti Közlemények* 60.4 (1956) 471-74; K. Redl 'Probleme in der Deliberatio des Bischofs Gerhard' in *Neue Beiträge zur Geschichte der alten Welt*, vol. 2, *Römisches Reich*, ed. E.C. Welskopf (Berlin 1965), 249-66; L. Szegfü 'Eretnekség és tirannizmus' (Heresy and tyranny) *Irodalomtörténeti Közlemények* 72.5 (1968) 501-16; B. Stock *The Implications of Literacy: Written Language and Models of Interpretation in the Eleventh and Twelfth Centuries* (Princeton 1983) 146-47.

27 *CCCM* 49, 14.

28 'They have been mistaken, just like those who by similar error roared that the angels wished for the bodies, that is, the daughters of men. They have been thrown away, although many Greeks follow them.' *CCCM* 49, 133.

29 *CCCM* 49, 137. See E. von Ivánka 'Gerardus Moresanus, der Erzengel Uriel und die Bogomilen' *Orientalia Christiana Periodica* 21.1-2 (1955) 143-46; D. Keck *Angels & Angelology in the Middle Ages* (New York & Oxford 1998) 47-58; G. Peers *Subtle Bodies: Representing Angels in Byzantium* (Berkeley, Los Angeles, & London 2001), 90-95.

Pseudo-Dionysian *De coelesti hierarchia* and its marginal glosses (Budapest University Library, U.Fr.l.m. 9) might have been known to Bishop Gerard of Csanád himself or at least to a master of the cathedral school of Esztergom in the eleventh century. However, the Byzantinist István Kapitánffy later rejected Mezey's proposal about this codex fragment and its provenance.[30] Gerard's alleged knowledge of the Greek language has also been a contested matter in philological studies.[31] The apparently random instances of Greek vocabulary is indeed a peculiar feature of Gerard's *Deliberatio* but it is more of an indirect stylistic device, so typical in Medieval Latin, than it is an indication of the level of the author's knowledge of Greek.[32]

In conclusion, the preceding discussion of these three Latin sources, the *Admonitions* of King Saint Stephen of Hungary, the *Legenda maior*, as well as the *Deliberatio* of Bishop Saint Gerard of Csanád, reveals the range of different meanings of the terms 'Greeks' and 'Latins' in medieval Hungary. Further pieces of evidence can obviously expand this modest list of sources. One example is the book list of the Benedictine monastery of Pannonhalma, surviving in a charter issued by King Ladislas around 1093-1095. It records the following entry of interest: *Psalterium gallicanum, ebraycum, grecum*. The *Psalterium Gallicanum* contains the textual variant once popular in Gaul; the *Psalterium Hebraicum* contains the Latin translation from the Hebrew; the

---

30 L. Mezey (ed.) *Fragmenta Latina codicum in Bibliotheca Universitatis Budapestinensis* (Budapest 1983) 36-37. See P. Lehmann 'Zur Kenntnis der Schriften des Dionysius Areopagita im Mittelalter' *Revue Bénédictine* 35.1-4 (1923) 81-97; M. Grabmann 'Die mittelalterlichen lateinischen Übersetzungen der Schriften des Pseudo-Dionysius Areopagita' in *Mittelalterliches Geistesleben: Abhandlungen zur Geschichte der Scholastik und Mystik* vol. 1 (Munich 1926), 449-68; E. von Ivánka 'Das "Corpus Areopagiticum" bei Gerhard von Csanád (†1046)' *Traditio* 15 (1959) 205-22; I. Kapitánffy 'Pseudo-Dionysios Areopagita latin fordításának töredéke a budapesti Egyetemi Könyvtárban' (The fragment of the Latin translation of Pseudo-Dionysios Areopagita in the Budapest University Library) *Magyar Könyvszemle* 101.2 (1985) 133-37.

31 See L. Szegfü 'Adalékok Szent Gellért görög müveltségének kutatásához' (On the research of the Greek culture of Saint Gerard) *Acta Academiae Pedagogicae Szegediensis* 3 (1985) 43-49.

32 See E. Mészáros 'A magyarországi közép-latinság föbb szabályai, 3.' (The major rules of Medieval Latin in Hungary, 3) *Mühely* 2.3-4 (1938) 98. See also O. Prinz 'Zum Einfluss des Griechischen auf den Wortschatz des Mittellateins' in J. Autenrieth and F. Brunhölzl (ed.) *Festschrift Bernhard Bischoff zu seinem 65. Geburtstag*, (Stuttgart 1971), 1-15; D. Sheerin 'Christian and Biblical Latin' in *Medieval Latin* (note 3) 137-56.

Psalterium Graecum might be a variant of the *Psalterium Romanum*, which in turn contains the Latin translation from the Septuagint. If the Greek text itself or a Latin transliteration of the Greek original of the Septuagint is also added, the book is called a *psalterium quadruplex*. Without the Greek text, the book is called a *psalterium triplex* – and this is what the Pannonhalma book list records: one single codex, probably a complete copy of the Psalter with its three Latin translations maybe in three parallel columns.[33]

Another example is Cerbanus' Latin translation of passages from Maximus Confessor. Like Gerard of Csanád, Cerbanus may also have arrived from Venice to Hungary a century later. In the first half of the twelfth century, he discovered a Greek manuscript of Maximus Confessor's *De caritate* in the Benedictine monastery of Pásztó which he translated into Latin and dedicated his Latin translation to Abbot David of Pannonhalma.[34]

These two examples still do not do any justice to the Byzantine Greek sources that are altogether excluded from the scope of the present discussion. This is therefore only one side of a twofold story: all about Greeks as portrayed by Latins. The opposite side will be the other way around: about Latins as portrayed by Greeks.[35] The outcome for now, however, is clear enough from the Mediaeval Latin perspective – the terms Greeks and Latins

---

33 G. Györffy (ed.) *Árpád-kori oklevelek* (Charters from the Árpád age) (Budapest 1997), 32-34. See A. Siegmund *Die Überlieferung der grieschischen christlichen Literatur in der lateinischen Kirche bis zum zwölften Jahrhundert* (Munich and Pasing 1949) 24; C. Csapodi 'Le catalogue de Pannonhalma, reflet de la vie intellectuelle des Bénédictins du XIe siècle en Hongrie' in P. Cockshaw, M.-C. Garand & P. Jodogne (ed.) *Miscellanea codicologica F. Masai dedicata*, vol. 1 (Ghent 1979) 165-73; P. Stotz 'Le sorti del latino nel Medioevo' in G. Cavallo, C. Leonardi & E. Menestò (ed.) *Lo spazio letterario del Medioevo: Il Medioevo latino*, vol. 1.2, *La circolazione del testo*, (Rome 1994) 159-60; L. Veszprémy 'La biblioteca nell'inventario della fine del secolo undicesimo (1093-1095)' in J. Pál and Á. Somorjai (ed.) *Mille anni di storia dell'Arciabbazia di Pannonhalma*, (Rome 1997) 83-99; E. Nemerkényi 'Latin Classics in Pannonhalma in the Eleventh Century' *Philobiblon* 8-9 (2003-2004) 512-24.

34 See I. Kapitánffy 'Cerbanus e la sua traduzione di San Massimo' in *Mille anni di storia dell'Arciabbazia di Pannonhalma* (note 33) 101-20.

35 See D.M. Nicol 'The Byzantine View of Western Europe' in *Byzantium: Its Ecclesiastical History and Relations with the Western World* (London 1972), I 315-39.

had indeed at least three different and specific meanings in mediaeval Hungary: first, they denoted ancient Greeks and Romans; second, Eastern and Western Christians; and third, Byzantines and Westerners.[36]

---

[36] This paper is part of a postdoctoral research project on *The Formation of Latin Literacy in Medieval Hungary* – see E. Nemerkényi *Latin Classics in Medieval Hungary: Eleventh Century* (Debrecen & Budapest 2004). The paper was presented in the session on *Eastern Europe and Hungary* at the interdisciplinary conference on *Religion and State Formation: Comparative Perspectives from Late Antiquity and the Middle Ages* in the Department of Medieval Studies at Central European University in Budapest 2006 (co-organized by the Religious Studies Program at Central European University and the Centre for Mediaeval Studies at the University of Bergen). The author wishes to acknowledge the support of Eötvös Collegium at the University of Budapest and the Hungarian Scientific Research Fund Postdoctoral Fellowship.

KIERKEGAARD AND THE EUTHYPHRO DILEMMA

By David Bloch

Summary: This article examines a passage from Plato's *Euthyphro* (9c-11b) which puts forward the argument that has become known as the Euthyphro Dilemma. The content of this argument is described and analysed, and, on the basis of a passage in his edifying discourse 'Every Good and Every Perfect Gift is from Above' (1843) and passages from his other writings, it is argued that Søren Kierkegaard has been able to bypass the dilemma. Thus, as some philosophers have already suspected, 'dilemma' is not really a fitting description of the problem.

INTRODUCTION: THE EUTHYPHRO DILEMMA[1]

In the *Euthyphro*, Plato presents a discussion between Socrates and the unfortunate Euthyphron who has felt forced to bring his own father to trial. Euthyphro claims that his action is pious, and this, of course, gives rise to a number of questions by Socrates concerning the nature of piety. That is: 'How does one define 'pious' (τὸ ὅσιον)?'. The result of the conversation, as most often in the aporetic dialogues, is tantamount to a humiliation of Euthyphro, who ends the dialogue by practically running away from the Socratic questioning.[2]

The *Euthyphro* is interesting for a number of reasons. Historically it is perhaps better known than most of the other aporetic dialogues, because it describes the preliminaries of the trial against Socrates, and philosophically

---

1 This article is a revised version of an article ('Kierkegaard og Euthyphrons Dilemma') published in Danish in the electronic journal *AIGIS* 7.1 (2007) 1-8.
2 But see M.J. Edwards 'In Defense of Euthyphro' *American Journal of Philology* 121 (2000) 213-24 for a defense of the character Euthyphro.

it is interesting, among other reasons, for containing some of the presumably earliest uses of εἶδος and ἰδέα in the *Corpus Platonicum*, which makes it an important source for identifying the progress of Plato's thought on the topic of 'forms'.[3] However, in my opinion, and in this I agree with several scholars, the most interesting part of the dialogue (9c-11b) belongs to the philosophy of religion and treats the relationship between pious actions or things and the gods. The problem that is discussed in this passage arose very often in the centuries that followed, and is still a valid subject for philosophical discussion today. In modern discussions it is known simply as the Euthyphro dilemma.

Socrates presents the classic formulation of this dilemma when in the *Euthyphro* he asks the following question:

> The point which I should first wish to understand is (i) whether the pious or holy is beloved by the gods because it is holy, (ii) or holy because it is beloved of the gods.[4]

As was to be expected, Euthyphro is baffled by the question, but, as Socrates proceeds to show, it is really very simple, at least on the surface. The question is: 'What is it exactly that makes an action or a thing pious or the opposite?' Either (i) it is because the action/thing has something in and by itself that makes it pious, and *therefore* it is loved by the gods, or (ii) it is precisely *because* the gods love the action/thing that we may call it pious.

As soon as Euthyphro has understood the question, he answers that the first solution must be the right one, and Socrates seems to agree that this is the correct answer: an action/thing is *not* pious simply by being loved by the gods; there must be something about it itself that makes it pious and that makes the gods love it. Euthyphro having answered the question in this way, immediately involves himself in different kinds of contradictions, and he never manages to disentangle himself again.

---

3 See R.E. Allen *Plato's Euthyphro and the Earlier Theory of Forms* (London 1970).

4 Plat., *Euthyphro* 10a, in: *The Dialogues of Plato*, Translated into English with Analyses and Introductions by B. Jowett, vol. I (Oxford 1953; 1st ed. 1871), p. 318. Greek text in Platonis Opera, vol. I, Oxford Classical Texts, edd. E.A. Duke et al. (Oxford 1995): τάχ', ὠγαθέ, βέλτιον εἰσόμεθα. ἐννόησον γὰρ τὸ τοιόνδε· ἆρα τὸ ὅσιον ὅτι ὅσιόν ἐστιν φιλεῖται ὑπὸ τῶν θεῶν, ἢ ὅτι φιλεῖται ὅσιόν ἐστιν;

Thus was created a philosophical problem that is still very much relevant to modern philosophy of religion. With a slight rephrasing of the original formulation to suit modern thoughts on the issue, it is often stated as a problem concerned with the moral content of God's commands, and thus it focuses in particular on the good and bad actions of human beings: (i) Does God command good and moral actions, because they are in themselves good and moral (that is, because there is something about them that makes them good *per se*), (ii) or are the actions only good and moral *because* God commands them?

The importance of this question, not least in contemporary monotheistic religions, is generally considered quite obvious and rightly so, I would argue. The Euthyphro dilemma questions the very foundation of divine commands in all religions and poses severe problems no matter which horn of the dilemma one takes.

First horn of the dilemma: If God commands something, because this 'something' is good in itself, that is, no matter whether God commands it or not, then God is apparently reduced to a kind of beneficial messenger of the good. The good would still be good, even if there were no God to command it.

Second horn of the dilemma: If the good is only good *because* God has chosen this particular piece of reality as the good, then one must face, among others, such difficulties as the arbitrariness problem and the problem of abhorrent commands. For a philosopher (or anyone else busying him- or herself with the dilemma) might well want to know more about the foundation of the divine decision; that is, why does God command, e.g., benevolence towards one's neighbor rather than violence? Or why does he generally prefer love over hate? However, it is rather difficult to see what kind of foundation that would provide. It might even be claimed to be a non-moral foundation, since morality requires the prior decision of God. If, then, the good is not really based on morality, it would have been equally possible for God to make abhorrent commands the good ones. Or at least, the reason why these are not the good ones is not the same as the one we would normally give when asked why rape, murder and similar acts are bad. They are not bad, because they are in themselves bad and evil; they are only bad and immoral, because God decided to make them so.

Some adherents of present-day monotheistic religions are troubled by this dilemma, some are not, and of course much more could be said on the subject.⁵ If believers give any thought to the dilemma at all, the second horn of it is usually preferred with the admission that we cannot expect to know and understand the foundation of God's decisions. They should just be accepted. However, the fact that acts such as murder, rape, genocide etc. are not in any sense bad in themselves, since God's explicit judgment is needed, is often regarded as somewhat disturbing, and there is still no generally accepted solution to the Euthyphro dilemma. Plato's presentation in the *Euthyphro* of the dilemma and of some of its major problems is still very much current.⁶

KIERKEGAARD ON THE EUTHYPHRO DILEMMA

In an article from 1987 in *Philosophy*, David Wisdo tried to 'illuminate one of Søren Kierkegaard's edifying discourses' by using the Euthyphro dilemma.⁷ However, it seems to me that Wisdo's initial insight in using the edifying discourse 'Every Good and Every Perfect Gift is from Above' (1843) in connection with the Euthyphro dilemma can be carried somewhat further than he actually does. In fact, it seems to me that Kierkegaard in this discourse presents a view that bypasses both horns of the dilemma, and thus might be claimed to invalidate the Euthyphro dilemma in its traditional form. That is, Kierkegaard seems to show that there are more than two pos-

---

5   For just a few informative works from the enormous literature, see, e.g., P. Brown 'Religious Morality' *Mind* 72 (1963) 235-44; P. Helm (ed.) *Divine Commands and Morality* (Oxford 1982); E. Stump & M.J. Murray (ed.) *Philosophy of Religion: The Big Questions* (Malden, MA. 1999).

6   For studies which take their point of departure from Plato's version of the Euthyphro dilemma, see J.H. Brown 'The Logic of the *Euthyphro* 10a-11b' *Philosophical Quarterly* 14 (1964) 1-14; L.E. Rose 'A Note on the *Euthyphro*, 10-11' *Phronesis* 10 (1965) 149-50; J.C. Hall 'Plato: *Euthyphro* 10a1-11a10' *Philosophical Quarterly* 18 (1968) 1-11; S.M. Cohen 'Socrates on the Definition of Piety: *Euthyphro* 10a-11b' *Journal of the History of Philosophy* 9 (1971) 1-13; R. Sharvy '*Euthyphro* 9d-11: Analysis and Definition in Plato and Others' *Nous* 6 (1972) 119-37; J.H. Lesher 'Theistic Ethics and the *Euthyphro*' *Apeiron* 9 (1975) 24-30; M. Macbeath 'The Euthyphro Dilemma' *Mind* 91 (1982) 565-71; G.W. Harris 'Religion, Morality, and the Euthyphro Dilemma' *International Journal for Philosophy of Religion* 15 (1984) 31-5; W.E. Mann 'Piety: Lending a Hand to Euthyphro' *Philosophy and Phenomenological Research* 58 (1998) 123-42; R. Joyce 'Theistic Ethics and the Euthyphro Dilemma' *Journal of Religious Ethics* 30 (2002) 49-75; L. Judson 'Carried Away in the *Euthyphro*' in D. Charles (ed.) *Definition and Essence in Ancient Philosophy* (Oxford, forthcoming).

7   D. Wisdo 'Kierkegaard and Euthyphro' *Philosophy* 62 (1987) 221-26.

sible answers to the question. Whether or not his answer is satisfactory from a rationalistic point of view is another question.

Kierkegaard would not have been very troubled by the Euthyphro dilemma. First of all, he might claim that speculations of this kind have no business in the area of religion. And if forced to take a stand, one might simply subscribe to a view that is similar to the one Wittgenstein puts forward in his remarks on Schlick's view, as quoted by Waismann.[8] Schlick had called the first horn of the Euthyphro dilemma 'die tiefere Deutung', but Wittgenstein objects that the rationalistic argument is really the superficial interpretation, because it poses as if it could explain what cannot be rationally explained. The beauty of the other interpretation ('the good is good, *because* God commands it') is, Wittgenstein claims, that nothing more can be said; it 'schneidet den Weg einer jeden Erklärung, "warum" es gut ist, ab'. And, of course, this would also be a valid and correct explanation, according to Kierkegaard.

However, Kierkegaard would also have a 'real' argument: the divine gifts (or commands) are not themselves of a particular character. That is, they are not good or bad in either of the senses described in the Euthyphro dilemma.

In 'Every Good and Every Perfect Gift is from Above' from 1843 (another with the same title published in 1844), Kierkegaard treats the statement made by James the apostle (Jam. 1.17-22), and asks: 'What does James mean by the word "every"?' He then continues:

> Does the apostle mean by this that the firmament of heaven is a great store-room, and that all the things which heaven contains are good gifts? Does he mean that God brings things out from this rich store, and sends them, according to time and opportunity now and then, sometimes to one, sometimes to another, to the one many, to another fewer, to a particular individual nothing at all, but that what He sends is good and perfect?[9]

Of course, this is not at all what Kierkegaard wants to answer, which is clear

---

8 F. Waismann 'Wittgenstein's Lecture on Ethics. II: Notes on Talks with Wittgenstein' *Philosophical Review* 74 (1965) 12-16.
9 *Edifying Discourses by Søren Kierkegaard, Volume I*, translated from the Danish by D.F. Swenson & L.M. Swenson (Minneapolis, Minnesota 1943) 44; the Danish text is found in *Søren Kierkegaards Skrifter*, edited by N.J. Cappelørn et al., vol. 5 (Copenhagen 1998) 48.

already from the tone of the passage. God is *not* simply the bringer of good and perfect gifts that he has previously found in his 'store-room' in heaven, and has now decided to give to some human being. James is not talking about the character of the individual gifts, says Kierkegaard (p. 44-45), but rather about 'God's eternal relation to the believer'.

> That which he emphasizes is that as God's all-powerful hand made everything good, so He, the Father of lights, still constant, makes everything good in every moment, everything into a good and perfect gift for everyone who has the heart to humble himself, heart enough to be confident.[10]

This states Kierkegaard's position very clearly, I think. God makes every action and event good for the believer; nothing in this life has absolute goodness in itself, but it achieves its status as good through the relationship between God and the acting or experiencing subject.

The result, then, regarding the Euthyphro dilemma is this: Kierkegaard would never accept that the objects themselves were good independently of God's judgment on them. Thus, like Wittgenstein and many others he seems on the surface to accept the second horn of the dilemma: acts, events and objects are good (or bad), simply because God has declared that they are so. Nevertheless, Kierkegaard does not fit comfortably into this category either. For even those who accept the second horn of the dilemma accept that the acts, events and objects do have *definite* values assigned to them, and even though these values have been assigned by God, the individual acts, events or objects are still objectively good or bad when the subject performs, experiences or receives them. But the real difference between good and bad, and thus the constitutive element of both, was not found at this stage but rather in the relationship between the human subject and God. Thus, faith is the deciding factor in determining whether something is good or bad, and only the believer can have a true relationship with such concepts. The non-believer, on the other hand, has severed his bonds with the provider of goods, and therefore he has also lost the possibility of obtaining them.

---

10 *Edifying Discourses by Søren Kierkegaard, Volume I,* Translated from the Danish by D.F. Swenson & L.M. Swenson (Minneapolis 1943) 45; the Danish text is found in *Søren Kierkegaards Skrifter,* edited by N.J. Cappelørn et al., vol. 5 (Copenhagen 1998) 49.

The view found in 'Every Good and Every Perfect Gift' is confirmed by a number of Kierkegaard's other works. In particular, *Fear and Trembling*, also published in 1843, illustrates the point. The story of Abraham and Isaac is the theme of the entire work,[11] and already at the beginning of the work, in four fascinating variations of the journey to Mount Moria, Kierkegaard (or rather: Johannes de Silentio) shows how the importance of the whole story from beginning to end lies in the respective reactions and states of mind found in Abraham and Isaac: Isaac may lose his faith (variation IV), Abraham may lose his faith (variation II), Isaac may be confused about the relationship between human ethics and divine commands (variation I), and Abraham may be confused about the relationship between human ethics and divine commands (variation III). On this interpretation of the four variations, nos. II and IV are true disasters; for the essential point of the whole story, from the Christian perspective, is that the actions are approved because of the importance of faith. If faith is lost, then it remains only to judge Abraham's actions on the basis of human ethics, and on this foundation they are decidedly wrong. Variations I and III, on the other hand, are both acceptable; for even though it is, of course, not entirely beneficial for human beings to be brought into confusion concerning human ethics and divine commands, it is certainly preferable to the loss of faith. A father who sets out to sacrifice his son is not commendable on ethical grounds. But, as shown in the four variations on the Abraham-Isaac story, the moral value of actions performed by the believer is not decided by clear-cut human ethics but by – faith. That is, there is no longer any true moral value in the action itself; for, to the believer, this value is found only in faith, which means in the relationship with God. This Kierkegaardian view is supported not only by the preliminary variations that I have now examined but also by the rest of *Fear and Trembling*, and so it seems to me that the solution to the Euthy-

---

[11] For this story in relation to the Euthyphro Dilemma, see also N. Kretzmann 'Abraham, Isaac, and Euthyphro: God and the Basis of Morality' in D.V. Stump et al. (ed.) *Hamartia: The Concept of Error in the Western Tradition. Essays in Honor of John M. Crossett* (New York 1983) 27-50; repr. in E. Stump & M.J. Murray (ed.) *Philosophy of Religion: The Big Questions* (Malden, MA 1999) 417-27.

phro dilemma that I have attributed to Kierkegaard on the basis of the edifying discourse is in accordance with his other writings as well.

Of course, all this does not say anything about the quality of Kierkegaard's solution; in particular, I think it is fair to say that most non-believers will not be very impressed. But the very fact that a *third* kind of answer is possible, is potentially very important both for our understanding of the Platonic dialogue – which, by the way, does not necessarily represent Plato's complete view on the issue – and for our understanding of the modern form of the Euthyphro dilemma.

LIST OF AUTHORS

Neil Adkin
University of North Carolina,
204A Spring Lane,
Chapel Hill, NC
27514, USA

Catalin Anghelina
Department of Greek and Latin,
The Ohio State University,
Columbus, OH 43210, USA

David Bloch
Saxo-instituttet/Afdeling for Græsk og Latin,
University of Copenhagen,
Njalsgade 80,
DK-2300 Copenhagen S, Denmark

Carl Hammer
527 Hastings Street,
Pittsburgh, PA 15206-4507, USA

Patrick Kragelund
Danmarks Kunstbibliotek,
Kongens Nytorv 1,
P.O. Box 1053,
DK-1007 Copenhagen K, Denmark

Marcel Lysgaard Lech
Rentemestervej 11c, st.tv.,
DK-2400 Copenhagen NV, Denmark

Elöd Nemerkenyi
Department of Medieval Studies,
Central European University,
9 Nador,
HU-1051 Budapest, Hungary

Erik Nis Ostenfeld
Munkebakkevej 15,
DK-8250 Egå, Denmark

Sebastian Persson
Ågade 106, 4. tv.,
DK-2200 Copenhagen N, Denmark

David Sansone
Department of the Classics,
University of Illinois, 4046 Foreign Languages Building,
707 South Mathews Avenue,
Urbana, IL 61801, USA

Elias Sverkos
Department of History,
Ionian University,
GR-49 100 Kerkyra, Greece

Ichiro Taida
Department of Applied Japanese,
I-Shou University,
Ni 1, Sect. 1, Syuecheng Road, Dashu Township,
Kaohsiung Country,
TW-840 Taiwan ROC

Spyridon Tzounakas
Department of Classics and Philosophy,
Faculty of Letters, University of Cyprus,
P.O. Box 20537,
CY-1678 Nicosia, Cyprus.

FORTHCOMING TITLE

Plotting with Eros
Essays on the Poetics of Love and the Erotics of Reading

Edited by Ingela Nilsson

The intricate relationship between the erotic and the literary is a recurring theme in Western literature, with a starting-point in Plato's dialogues. Our need to talk, write, and read about love has resulted in a rich tradition, ranging from theoretical and philosophical discussions of Eros to love romance and poetry, clearly marked by the classical heritage but continuously unfolding and rewriting itself.

The essays in the present volume aim at providing both students and scholars with a series of discussions of this long tradition of reading and writing the erotic, seen from a number of different perspectives. A certain emphasis is placed on Classical philology, and in particular Greek and Roman love poetry from Antiquity to the Byzantine period. Some of the texts under examination include those of Plato, Catullus, Sulpicia, Meleager and Niketas Choniates; but the anthology also offers more general treatments of Byzantine Studies, Iranian Languages, History of Ideas, and Comparative Literature with a view to understanding how Eros has been appropriated in a variety of ways for purposes of producing narratives of love.

Ingela Nilsson is Assistant Professor of Byzantine Studies at Uppsala University.

Exp. August 2009 · c 304 pp. · Hardback · 16 × 24 cm · ISBN 978 87 635 0790 5
c DKK 335 · € 45

MUSEUM TUSCULANUM PRESS
UNIVERSITY OF COPENHAGEN
Njalsgade 126 · DK–2300 Copenhagen S
tel. +45 3532 9109 · fax +45 3532 9113 · www.mtp.dk · order@mtp.dk

FORTHCOMING TITLE

From Artemis to Diana
The Goddess of Man and Beast

Edited by Tobias Fischer-Hansen & Birte Poulsen

The book contains 19 articles dealing with various aspects of the Greek goddess Artemis and the Roman goddess Diana.

The themes presented in the volume deal with the Near Eastern equivalents of Artemis, the Bronze Age Linear B testimonies, and Artemis in Homer and in the Greek tragedies.

Sanctuaries and cult as well as regional aspects are also dealt with – encompassing Cyprus, the Black Sea region, Greece and Italy. Pedimental sculpture, mosaics and sculpture form the basis of investigations of the iconography of the Roman Diana; the role of the cult of Diana in a dynastic setting is also examined. A single section deals with the reception of the iconography of the Ephesian Artemis during the Renaissance and later periods.

Exp. 2009 · c 550 pp. · 16,5 × 24,5 cm · c 10 colour and 167 b/w illustrations
ISBN 978 87 635 0788 2 · Series: Acta Hyperborea, vol. 12 · ISSN 0904 2067
c DKK 500 · € 67

MUSEUM TUSCULANUM PRESS
UNIVERSITY OF COPENHAGEN
Njalsgade 126 · DK–2300 Copenhagen S
tel. +45 3532 9109 · fax +45 3532 9113 · www.mtp.dk · order@mtp.dk

IN PREPARATION

Urban Development and Regional Identity in the Eastern Roman Provinces 50 BC–AD 250
Aphrodisias, Ephesos, Athens, Gerasa

By Rubina Raja

This book presents a comparative treatment of four East Roman provinces in the period 50 BC-AD 250: Aphrodisias and Ephesos i Turkey, Athens in Greece and Gerasa in Jordan. With carefully researched scholarship, Raja examines the instrumental factors behind regional and local urban developments and what these can tell us about identity in these areas. She argues that local communities were responsible for the organisation and development of public space and buildings, lending itself to an understanding of self-knowledge in these communities within the Roman Empire. In this way, the urban landscape can provide useful information about many aspects of regional identity of a particular society.

She furthermore discusses the influence which the wealth of liberated imperial slaves had on the development of their native towns once they had returned to their homes (in this case Aphrodisias). This phenomenon, which is considerably more characteristic of the early imperial period, is more widespread than previously assumed.

Through an examination of the interaction between architectural developments and historical and regional factors, this compelling study provides important insight into the processes nurturing the interaction between the built environment and the social and political culture and urban identity of individual towns in the eastern Roman Empire.

Ph.D. Rubina Raja is Research Fellow at the Department of Classical Archaeology, University of Aarhus.

c 350 pp. · Hardback · 17 × 24 cm · c 45 colour illustrations · ISBN 978 87 635 2606 7
c DKK 400 · € 54

MUSEUM TUSCULANUM PRESS
UNIVERSITY OF COPENHAGEN
Njalsgade 126 · DK–2300 Copenhagen S
tel. +45 3532 9109 · fax +45 3532 9113 · www.mtp.dk · order@mtp.dk

IN PREPARATION

Christian Conceptions of Jewish Books
The Pfefferkorn Affair

By Avner Shamir

This book explores how Christians understood the meaning and significance of Jewish books at the beginning of the sixteenth century. The book tells the story of the so-called Pfefferkorn Affair, the attempt to confiscate and burn all Jewish post-biblical literature in the Holy Roman Empire in the years 1509-10.

The author follows the fate of the confiscated books and their examination by a commission of experts and explores how Christians – a convert, an emperor, the members of city councils, an inquisitor, many theologians, and a hebraist – perceived Jewish scholarship and knowledge.

Avner Shamir is a Ph.D. Researcher at the Department of Culture and Identity at Roskilde University.

c 130 pp. · 15 × 21 cm · ISBN 978 87 635 0772 1
DKK 125 · € 17

FORTHCOMING TITLE

Lay Belief in Norse Society 1000-1350

By Arnved Nedkvitne

Did medieval lay people let their ideas about the supernatural world determine or influence their actions in this world? How strongly did religion influence the actions of laymen? What kind of actions did religion influence? What were the social consequences of religion in Norse society? These are some of the major questions that will be addressed and discussed in this book

Most sagas are dominated by secular values, and traditionally this has determined historians' understanding of Norse society. However, in recent years more attention has been paid to religious ideas, which Norse society had in common with the rest of Europe. Bourdieu's concept of "social fields" is used to analyse the relationship between religious and secular mentalities.

Karl Jaspers and Arnold Angenendt have discussed the relationship between rituals and ethics in pre-modern religion, and the idea of miracles and supernatural interventions have been added as a third main element. Taking its point of departure in these three elements, the author discusses how important religion was for lay people.

Dr. Arnved Nedkvitne is Professor of Medieval History at University of Oslo.

Exp. June 2009 · c 400 pp. · Hardback · 16 × 24 cm
24 colour and 30 b/w illustrations · ISBN 978 87 635 0786 8
c DKK 375 · € 50

MUSEUM TUSCULANUM PRESS
UNIVERSITY OF COPENHAGEN
Njalsgade 126 · DK–2300 Copenhagen S
tel. +45 3532 9109 · fax +45 3532 9113 · www.mtp.dk · order@mtp.dk

IN PREPARATION

From Viking Stronghold to Christian Kingdom

By Sverre Bagge

Taking the formation of the Norwegian state in the Middle Ages as his starting point Sverre Bagge widens his perspective to include a discussion of the emergence of the medieval state and state formation in the Middle Ages in general.

The book examines the emergence of religion, written culture, bureaucracy, etc. in medieval Europe and the spread of these to the eastern and northern fringes that were integrated into the sphere of western Christianity from around 900 and onwards.

Dr. Sverre Bagge is Professor of Medieval History at the Centre for Medieval Studies, University of Bergen.

c 500 pp. · Hardback · 17 × 24 cm · ISBN 978 87 635 0791 2
c DKK 550 · € 74

MUSEUM TUSCULANUM PRESS
UNIVERSITY OF COPENHAGEN
Njalsgade 126 · DK–2300 Copenhagen S
tel. +45 3532 9109 · fax +45 3532 9113 · www.mtp.dk · order@mtp.dk